DAMANHUR

the community they tried to brand a cult

damanhur

*the community they
tried to brand a cult*

Jeff Merrifield

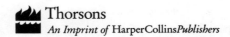
Thorsons
An Imprint of HarperCollins*Publishers*

Thorsons
An Imprint of HarperCollins*Publishers*
77–85 Fulham Palace Road
Hammersmith, London W6 8JB

First published in hardback by Thorsons 1998
This paperback edition published by Thorsons 1998

10 9 8 7 6 5 4 3 2 1

A catalogue record for this book
is available from the British Library

ISBN 0 7225 3700 X

Printed and bound in Great Britain by
Creative Print and Design (Wales), Ebbw Vale

For Dawn

contents

ACKNOWLEDGEMENTS

In researching and preparing the material for this book I am gratefully indebted to a number of people for their invaluable assistance.

Elaine Baxendale accompanied me on my second visit and translated as many interviews as could be crammed into five weeks. This material formed the basis for a large part of the book.

At Damanhur I was afforded splendid hospitality by the family groups of Rama, Magilla and Ogni Dove, and to them I am thankful for a unique insight into the daily social life of the communities. Usignolo Mirica spent many patient and unselfish hours helping me understand something of Damanhurian philosophy.

I am grateful to Oberto Airaudi and Sirena Ninfea, to the guides and leaders of the communities, and to all those who spared the time to answer my questions about some of the most important aspects and purposes of Damanhur. But most of all I am enormously indebted to Esperide Ananas for her constant support, advice, and for refining, polishing and elucidating my thinking.

At HarperCollins I am most grateful to Michelle Pilley for her initial confidence in the project, to my excellent editor, Elizabeth Hutchins, and to Eileen Campbell, Paul Redhead, Louise McNamara, Jo Ridgeway, Liz Hallam and Simon Weller.

Thanks also to Jan Turvey, Richard Beaumont, David Pearl, Duncan Walker, John Maynard, Irving Rappaport, Ken Campbell, John Joyce and other members of the McKee group for their support.

prologue – perchance to dream

---

*Damanhur is a dream come true… We have been able to create
a society which is very close to what we all desire.*

Esperide Ananas

A Rude Awakening

OCTOBER 1991

Cormorano rolls over, his sleep-heavy eyes glancing at the
clock lit by a shaft of early morning light. Six o'clock. Something
woke him, he's not sure what. Too early to be getting up just yet. His
arm naturally glides round the warm slumbering body of his wife
as he gives her a loving cuddle.

Suddenly the door bursts open and three uniformed men
charge into the room, armed with pistols and machine guns. Cormorano rubs his eyes in disbelief. He becomes aware of a loud
roaring sound somewhere overhead.

'What's the matter? What's all this about?' he manages to ask.

'Get out!' barks one of the intruders. They all seem tense, on
edge. 'And take it easy! Over here!' He waves his gun at the far wall.

Cormorano's wife, Ramarra, is shocked. She grabs the cover off the bed to hide her modesty and then gets out as instructed. 'What about the children?' she says, aware of crying coming from the next room.

'All in good time,' the man with the machine gun shouts, 'all in good time.'

The couple are shepherded out of the room and into the hall-way, where Ramarra meets her children and manages to give them a hug. Ordered outside, they are pushed into groups with their friends from adjoining houses and apartments. They stare at each other, wondering what all this is about. Five military helicopters fly overhead, their roaring rotors breaking the morning calm.

As Cormorano and his family look round they realize they are surrounded by armed officers – some police, some *carabinieri*, some military, some in uniforms they do not recognize. There seem to be hundreds of them. There are cars everywhere – police cars, lights flashing; troop carriers, doors open. Men in uniforms are rushing about, shouting orders, moving groups of people around. But no one is telling them what is happening, or why.

The square is now filling. People are milling about hopelessly. Children are crying, a sound not often heard at Damanhur. People are gradually being assembled into groups, each group guarded as if made up of dangerous and hardened criminals. A few individuals are being taken away towards the office block. Everyone is anxious, fearful, amazed.

Cormorano sees his friend Condor being led away by an armed officer. He shouts across and Condor gives him a wan smile before he is taken into the offices. Cormorano's mind swirls with thoughts. Have they found out about the temple? Is this the end of their secret plans? He thinks back to how it all began, almost 20 years before…

The Green Light

Since 1975 a young man called Oberto Airaudi had been teaching on spiritual matters and giving practical demonstrations. He had gathered a group of 15 to 20 people around him and they had established a centre, the Horus Centre, in Turin to run courses. Condor Girasole had been given the task of arranging conferences and healing courses there. The group then started meeting more often and getting into the study of meditation and philosophy. They experienced special events and little synchronicities, strange occurrences that helped bind them together. Oberto consolidated the work and began teaching a particular philosophy under the overall title of 'meditation'; the group considered organizing study programmes and publishing books on these teachings.

Out of this early work came the three criteria that would be most important in relation to the group's future development and the amazing task they were destined to undertake. First of all, the group itself. The main thrust of the spiritual progress was not on an individual basis, but was a group endeavour. This brought about a particular form of group process leading to the development of an abundance of energy – enough energy, in fact, to allow them to undertake seemingly impossible tasks. The second aspect was the realization that spiritual development came directly through action. It was not merely a question of meditating, but of *applying* meditation, of bringing about spiritual transformation through practical action in a material world. However, the third aspect defined an Enemy of Mankind – an absolute anti-life principle, not a dual force like yin and yang, but an active potential for destruction.

'With the group growing stronger,' Condor recalled, 'we wondered whether we could perhaps find a place where we could spend more time together. It was an idea that was discussed a lot. Oberto showed us a map...'

On the map was a series of strange lines, the result of years of dedicated research undertaken by Oberto and his close friends, travelling with groups of people all over the planet. He referred to them as 'synchronic lines', not like ley lines, but lines of energy that skirted around the Earth, a sort of telluric nervous system. There were only a couple of places where four synchronic lines converged. One of these was in Tibet, the other in Italy, just to the north of Turin, in the Piedmont valley of Valchiusella, near the Canavese village of Baldissero. When the group investigated further, they found that the surrounding area was rich in minerals of all kinds and had a freak gravitational quality. As Oberto said, it was the sort of place 'where satellites gave a little jump as they passed over it'.

They found a piece of property there, quite a large copse surrounded by untended ground, overgrown with weeds, dense thickets of shrubbery and wildly intertwined thorny creepers. 'So, here it was, in 1977, that we began to build Damanhur.'

As well as the dishevelled territory, the group bought a house up the hill above Vidracco. This is now known as *Porta del Sole*, Gateway to the Sun. Condor recalls:

We were camping out at Porta del Sole and that was where the first work was done. Down below, in the place where the Damanhur Centre now is, at Damjl, the land had been left to grow wild for many years. It was full of bushes and weeds, things that needed a lot of clearing away. We began building some apartments there, places for our families to live. We cleared a space that we dedicated as an Open Temple for meditation rituals and we left most of the copse in its original state, to be a special place where we could commune with nature.

Whilst we were living at Porta del Sole, we said that maybe we should think about building something there, a symbol of our spiritual intent. And Oberto said, if we were shown the right sign, maybe we should. Then, in the August of 1978, when we were having all manner of philosophical discussions about the path, the journey that we were on, the sign arrived.

It was time to start digging into the mountain.

A Glimpse of the Dream

MARCH 1996

The air is cool and balmy. There is a feeling of tranquillity here. It is a mild wintry day and I am being led across a farmyard, high on an Alpine mountainside, towards a somewhat nondescript door. Yet what I am to find beyond this door could be easily thought of as the eighth wonder of the world.

I am here with two theatrical mates, Ken Campbell and John Joyce. We came to the Alps to check out a weird news report of spontaneous combustions in the small village of Moirans on the French side. We had also noted that on the Swiss side of the Alps, in the village of Salvan, some of the Solar Temple followers had burned themselves to death. However, I recalled seeing something on TV about someone building a temple inside a mountain in the Italian Alps. The first two visits yielded nothing of significant interest, but then further Internet investigations of Damanhur brought us through the Monte Blanc tunnel to the 'closed valley' of Valchiusella, less than 48 km (30 miles) from Turin.

Our guides here are both Italians: Esperide Ananas, a most attractive young woman who has studied in America and speaks excellent English, and a mild-mannered man who turns out to be Oberto Airaudi himself. They lead me through the door and deep into the mountainside.

Here, underneath the Italian Alps, we are being led into a magnificent temple with fine mural paintings, intricate mosaic floors, superb stained glass windows and domed cupola ceilings. It is made up of seven large caverns linked by a labyrinth of passageways. These are not adapted caves – they were actually excavated by the builders themselves, by hand, without the use of any form of explosives. Though not a place of religious worship, nor aligned to any particular religious group, this remarkable construction is known as *il Tempio dell'Uomo*, the Temple of Mankind.

The first chamber encountered is Egyptian in style and gives the impression that this is as far as one can go. However, this is actually a fake, hiding and protecting the real temple. The Egyptian style is an indication that there is something hidden, beyond, literally deeper.

A remote control activates a huge slab of stone, which moves into the wall to reveal a passage leading into a long winding corridor and thence into a chamber. The beautiful mosaic floor in this chamber also conceals a secret. Again via remote control, part of it sinks downwards, in sections, to form a stairway into a chamber below. And so on, through the various halls and passages – the

Earth Hall, the Water Hall, the Hall of the Spheres, the Hall of Mirrors, the unfinished Labyrinth.

What is this place? Who created it? Who possesses the talent and the energy for such a superb architectural and artistic achievement? What could be its purpose?

It was questions such as these that were aired at meetings of Vidracco town council and the other ruling authorities in the Valchiusella region in 1992 when word of this amazing construction first reached the outside world. They knew those responsible for it called themselves the Nation of Damanhur and had been running all sorts of weird courses for some 16 years, yet they claimed to be innocent of any unscrupulous intent in building the remarkable temple. However, there had been no application for planning permission and the local councillors were embarrassed to admit that this enormous subterranean construction had been built without their knowledge or approval – especially when the television crews of the world began to arrive. They felt they were surely within their rights to seize the temple and to have it destroyed.

Strong objections to the temple also came from the Catholic Church and questions as to its purpose implied there could be links with religious cults. Much of the media was only too ready to leap on such accusations in the wake of the recent Solar Temple burnings in Salvan and the sinister goings on with nerve gas in the Japanese underground railway. Journalists came looking for the deranged fanatics behind the hair-brained scheme. *Asahi Shimbun* of Japan sent their Brussels correspondent, looking for a story to fit in with their series outlining a world map of new movements, cults who might be the new threat to the world following the mellowing of the Cold War. But he was not able to find a story at Valchiusella to fit into this pattern. Damanhur was not a bunch of crazies. In the end the *Asahi Shimbun* reporter decided not to write anything at all. He was quite high up in the newspaper's hierarchy, so was able to not file a story, even though they had spent money on it. With a lesser-ranking journalist, this would not have been the case. Another journalist who came looking for a story was Philip Short, from BBC Television's *Newsnight*. He tried to link Damanhur into a piece about the Solar Temple burnings, the Oklahoma City bombing and the Japanese nerve gas attack. Yet the footage of Damanhur and the

Tempio dell'Uomo just did not fit into this context and shone out like a beacon from the other material in the report. In fact, it was this television footage that first attracted me to the phenomenon of Damanhur.

Now I found myself being given a tour of the temple by the man originally responsible for putting it all together. Apparently Oberto started out in the insurance business and was very successful at it, but at the age of 23 he dived wholeheartedly into the Damanhur project. He explained that during its early years, the ethos was to create the basis of a spiritual community and differentiate it from the many other communities existing at that time. Esperide added confidently that Damanhur was born of the dream of a society able to nourish and mirror the spiritual achievements of its citizens. Their strong communal belief is that individual spiritual evolution can only be achieved in a group of people sharing the same commitment to self-improvement. This in turn will help the evolution of all humanity. As Esperide said:

> Damanhur is a dream come true. It is a place in which all the differences of the persons who live here have been exalted. Through this mixture of differences and qualities we have been able to create a society which is very close to all we desire.

From small beginnings, the number of residents increased and the community grew in quality and complexity. Bodies were elected to encourage ways of living based on the sharing of resources, space and management. All this was encapsulated in a formal constitution, though, like everything at Damanhur, this was not set in stone and over the years has been changed many times, developing as the community itself has developed. Damanhur today has over 700 inhabitants and over 25,000 supporters throughout the world. Its land and buildings, scattered all over the Valchiusella valley, include 120 hectares (300 acres) of woodland, 5 hectares (12 acres) of urban development, 60 hectares (150 acres) of farmland and around 60 buildings – private houses, productive plants, laboratories and farms. Oberto Airaudi has initiated not only the construction of a phenomenal temple, but also a unique social constituency and a way of life that many have chosen happily to follow.

On my very first visit to Damanhur I was impressed with what I saw there. Now, having spent much time in these Italian mountains and spoken at length with the people who live and work in the community, I am even more impressed with all that they have accomplished. This is a special place, a rare example of Mankind and nature working in tandem, of artistic endeavour and centred spirituality coming together in an enlightened way.

part one

a journey within: il tempio dell'uomo

We did all this in great secrecy. It was as if we were going inside ourselves, looking inside ourselves, and for this reason it was important that everything was carried out in secret.

Condor Girasole

The first pickaxe hit the rock on a warm August night in 1978. Some two decades later, well over two million buckets of rock, earth and clay have been taken out of the mountain, and *il Tempio dell'Uomo*, the Temple of Mankind, stands as a testament to the heroic struggle of those who built it.

The building of the temple is a legend in itself. Late one Saturday evening, Oberto Airaudi and a dozen of his close friends were sitting around a fire in an open space behind Porta del Sole, sheltered by the hill of Vidracco. Legend has it that a star fell through the sky, a star much larger than you would normally see, falling bright and slow, and leaving behind it a trail of gold dust that fell on the Earth.

Oberto took a couple of the others on one side and told them this was the sign that it was the right moment to start digging into the mountain. They were to dig towards the heart of the Earth in order to create a 'synchronic contact' and build a temple such as had not been seen for thousands of years. It was to be made by hand and by will, and in secret.

Oberto's unexpected words were warm and meaningful. As soon as the meeting ended, the two began to dig at the chosen point. All they had was a hammer and a pickaxe, but still they went on eagerly for the whole night; by the next morning, when others went to take over, they had already dug a metre into the mountain.

Orango Riso was one of those who first struck holes in the mountain.

Oberto took us behind the others and said, 'Look, here we are going to excavate a little chapel.' And after his first instructions, he said, 'Please excavate it!'

We went on, and on, the whole night, achieving almost nothing, excavating only by hand. Then we felt a real aggression towards the mountain. For a couple of days a small group of us dug hard, but managed to conquer only a couple of metres. Then we showed the others.

At first we were digging 24 hours a day. Then, after the first three or four days, shifts began, day and night. It is an experience I don't think I can adequately describe, taking shifts, and attacking the earth, and believing that this gallery we were digging could stay up. It was an act of faith because it was only our thoughts that did keep it up. There were no other supports. But the whole thing felt very positive. Everybody found that they could do things that should have been impossible.

The ground began to get harder as we reached the rock. So we began using heavy hammers and then the excavations slowed down somewhat. Later, we got electric hammers. But for about a month we were digging by hand only.

This 'chapel' we were building has been through many transformations since that time, but it was completed by 31 December and we celebrated the first marriage there…

That was the marriage of Lama and Sparviero, who have now been together for almost 20 years and are soon due their traditional porcelain or their modern platinum commemoratives.

Condor Girasole is another of those who has lived with this project from the beginning. He admits to not being so familiar with the technical aspects and to having few construction skills, but remembers with some degree of affection the warmth and sense of well-being that the building work engendered in those taking part:

> The digging was fun. It was enjoyable because of the secrecy and because of the pioneering nature of the activity. There was a great feeling of enthusiasm. It was a game. The great explorers, digging deep into the mountain – we felt great!
>
> The problem was, what to do with the material we were taking out? The soil and rock we took out were used in different places on our own territories. It had to be done very quietly, secretly. We could not shout to each other in the night, we had to work quietly and everything had to be covered over so that nobody could see what we were doing. The fact that it had to be done with some secrecy gave the situation a degree of tension, but a tension that leads to awareness.
>
> We were deeply engrossed in this first stage, elated and exceptionally pleased with our achievements so far. The act of building the temple became the focal point of our inner spiritual research. We became one with it, one with the Earth, one with the group of people we had been digging alongside.

The group was indeed working very closely together – each bucket of earth being passed along a human chain that reached right down the corridor to the truck outside. As the work progressed, there were chains of 20, 25, 30 people. But there was a real atmosphere of fun. 'The sound of the laughter,' remembers Oberto, 'was often louder than the sound of the hammers.'

At first Oberto's plan was largely in his head, but he did write down some measurements and drew little diagrams to help the builders. His idea was that the work had to be done in phases, that certain stages had to be completed when they were due to be completed. Orango takes up the story again:

Then came the day when Oberto showed us a plan. He unfolded it and said, 'More or less, it will be like this!' It was a schema for an elaborate series of temple chambers linked by passageways and corridors. These were the full plans for the proposed Temple of Mankind, with its many levels and chambers and its labyrinth of corridors.

There was a look of amazement on our faces. There were to be more stages in this building programme than we had ever imagined. What we had already done was astounding, but what we were required to do next was nothing short of miraculous. We all said, 'Yeah, yeah, yeah... Right!' We were incredulous.

Work carried on, constantly and intensely, with everyone excited by the fulfilling pleasure of group activity and by sweet thoughts of this phenomenal secret. Pick and paddle, buckets, pick and paddle, chisel and hammer, buckets... The earth fell in small clumps of mud. First clay, then rock. Elemental earth, untouched by humans. Working in the underground chamber seemed to give the diggers an energy of inexhaustible quality, of superhuman force. Everyone wanted to continue, to make progress and conquer new spaces. And the mountain, motherly and welcoming, allowed them to penetrate it.

The diggers often discussed what they were doing and why. Some speculated that the underground chambers would provide protection should there ever be a cataclysmic nuclear attack or natural catastrophe. There was at that time a strong realization of the potential for human folly in relation to such matters. The group's spiritual studies had shown them that the forces of the Enemy of Mankind could steer people towards destructive acts. So the first section of the corridor was built in an S-shape in order to form a barrier against any outer radiation. Practical measures were also taken to ensure the self-sufficiency of Damanhur and its citizens, with the use of home-made bread, natural plants and herbs, hand-woven fabrics, and so on.

The spiritual idea that forcefully motivated the group was the notion of direct contact with the universe by means of Mother Earth, there in that underground place which had never seen the light or welcomed a human being. When the moon was full, those coming out of the excavation used to lie on the floor, looking up at the stars and feeling strangely nourished, in an atmosphere that seemed unreal.

There were also practical tasks to be done, such as finding uses for the excavated earth. Around this time the many potholes along the track that led to the house were filled in.

The digging remained secret, of course, because the group had no planning permission. Not that it would ever have been given. There are no regulations for digging into a mountain and any application would have been turned down flat, especially by a regional authority with no laws to regulate for underground buildings and structures. Also, it was thought that a refuge should, in fact, be secret. This refuge in particular should not be known to many people.

The builders were extremely careful. They never made loud noises or shouted when they were outside. They were also very good at hiding the entrances to each of the chambers – in fact it is hard to find them even now. They would make the main entrance appear to be just a wall with some steps and other pieces of equipment piled up in front of it. When they started work, they simply removed the steps and equipment, opened the fake wall and went into the temple. When they finished, they covered it over again. They did not speak to anyone outside the work group about the project – at first the temple was even kept secret from newcomers to Damanhur. One of the great delights, I was told, was taking a relatively recent arrival to the temple for the first time and showing it to them.

Underground, everything was quiet, everything still. Those digging would pause a while and listen to the strangeness of that eerie silence, while large water drops, slimy with clay, would run along the jagged walls.

Nobody was expert in building, but they all did their best. Soon the first corridor and chamber were excavated. Small pyramid-shaped niches were cut out of the walls to hold candles. The walls were plastered directly on the wet earth, the builders mixing the plaster outside. Sagging sections of the corridor were reinforced with layers of brick. Finally the floor was laid with a mosaic of Luserna stones.

With the first stage of the work complete, it was time for celebration. Fruit and vegetables were freshly picked from the gardens and orchards, and bread baked in the wood oven of the house. Everything was shared among those who had worked under the mountain, while in the middle of the underground chamber a fire was lit.

The walls were rendered, designs prepared and painted on them. Almost as soon as the room was constructed, it was dedicated as a temple, and once the altar was ready, rituals and meditations were performed related to the initiation path. This first chamber became known as the Blue Temple.

Then the group moved on. 'When we thought we were ready,' recalls Condor, 'we made an entrance, a doorway, under the place where the altar was and we carried on with the excavations.'

Gradually, other people joined the work group. At its peak, there were about 150 people working in the temple, a great step on from the initial group of 15–20.

The temple was always built in such a way as to guard against the possibility of being discovered. Each part gave the impression that that was as far as it went, so you could only go on if you already knew you were able to. As Condor explained:

> That was our security. We were digging downwards, knowing that it was going to be bigger, but at that time we did not realize how big. However, as we were digging, we soon realized that it was getting – big! There was an even greater amount of earth and rock to take out. We were very careful, only taking it out in the trucks at night, making as little noise as possible, being very careful to use the debris wisely, to not despoil the surrounding environment, being very careful never to be discovered.
>
> Gradually we managed to finish a second chamber and to install an altar in there. This chamber was to become the Water Hall.

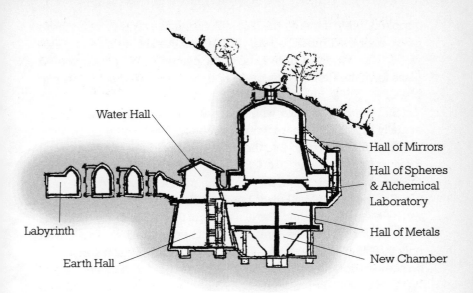

Figure 1: Section through the Temple of Mankind

This was in 1983, five years and almost a million buckets of earth into the project. The Water Hall has a particular magical centre – through its altar a direct link has been established with the synchronic energy lines of the Earth. Writings on the walls relate to 12 different alphabets, forming many ancient and sacred languages at various levels, explaining the history of the awareness of Mankind. The Damanhurians have adopted one particular sacred language that can be written in symbols, numbers or Arabic letters. Discovered and developed through Oberto's researches, this language, which has eight levels of complexity, is defined as sacred because it enables communication with the divine, both inside and outside individuals.

Originally, the chamber had a cupola painted as a sun with 365 rays coming from it, surrounded by stars showing the position of the constellations at the Summer Solstice. However, in the summer of 1989 it was replaced by a glass dome, though the first ceiling is still underneath. This was the first of the superbly elegant glass cupola domes made by the Damanhurians in a style that they have made their own, modelled very closely on the Tiffany style of glasswork. Thousands of individually cut pieces of brightly coloured glass form the dome, each piece copper-edged and soldered into place.

Still the only people who knew about the temple were those actually building it. There were even people at Damanhur making artefacts that would go into the temple who did not know just what their work was being used for. Usignolo Mirica, another of my guides, was at Damanhur for two years before she knew of the temple. She saw people all dirty, but thought they were doing forestry work – even at midnight! She just thought they were crazy. That was back in 1981, when the temple was still comparatively small, with only the Blue Temple complete, but Usignolo was still taken aback on seeing it for the first time. Soon she was digging herself.

Those who had most recently become Damanhurian citizens were assigned to dig the passageways towards the large chamber that would eventually become the Hall of Mirrors. Those who had been there longest, who had already worked on the Water Hall, drew an opening in the wall north of it and from there made a new assault on the mountain. The floor of Water Hall was removed to begin the excavation into the next chamber, which was to be exactly underneath it, but much larger.

Huge strength came from working together on this monumental task. The earth was sometimes very soft and crumbly – which created its own problems – but sometimes hard rock which required great effort to dig through. There were ropes and pulleys to haul up the buckets, and another human chain to remove the earth up staircases, through the Blue Temple and along corridors to the outside. Pick and paddle, buckets, pick and paddle, chisel and hammer, buckets...

The excavation continued non-stop for nine months, by which time the diggers had reached a depth of seven metres (23 feet), with a diameter at the base of nine metres (30 feet). Twenty-three metres (75 feet) further down and it was finished. This was to become the Earth Hall.

The group acquired a second cement mixer, capable of mixing 200 litres (44 gallons), to make concrete reinforcements and create the hall's large ceiling. Four beams of reinforced concrete were anchored two metres (six feet) into the rock from the floor of the Hall of Water, which was also to become the ceiling of the new hall. Along the vertical corridor running out from the intersection of the beams, transport of the extracted material continued. The daily average was 2,000 bucketsful, but there was often double that quantity, a total of over 12 cubic metres (424 cubic feet) of rock, dug by hand.

An excavation toward the lower part of the hall freed space for the first four columns (there are eight in total). Measuring 40 cm (16 inches) in diameter, they were set in reinforced concrete with special adjustable steel plates, which kept them in a state of tension with the beams of the ceiling, and secured into plinths set under the level of the floor. Construction of this huge hall, built with great will but without specialist skills, was an enormous achievement.

Round the outside of the columns runs the hall's circular wall. The cement for this was sent down from the Water Hall through a special freight elevator via a pulley. The smooth plastering of the walls was a job that was decidedly problematical and fatiguing: the first layer of plaster-cement had to have a regular thickness, with a net inside, electro-soldered to thin sweaters. The next layer of plaster-cement started to define the smooth curved surface and was applied with a mix of fine plaster produced by a small cement mixer, transported to the inside and made up of fine cement, fine sand and microsilica to guarantee a high degree of waterproofing. Finally, a finishing layer of white cement was added to produce a perfectly smooth surface. All of these processes would have been difficult enough under normal circumstances, but working in a newly dug pit some 50 metres (165 feet) underground and hampered by exceptionally damp conditions proved enormously difficult. It was impossible to employ the building materials in the usual ways.

Damp and water drainage were perennial problems. Under a niche to the south a well was dug out into which a pump was set for the drainage of excess water. It passed through a system of pipelines into an awaiting reservoir. Now water systems permeate the whole of the temple structure, carrying unwanted water flows to more suitable locations. The drainage and condensation control in the Temple of Mankind have been studied and admired by many architectural engineers, and even by the military, who were fascinated as to how the rooms were kept dry enough in such a subterranean location to allow murals to be painted on walls and for them to remain there! Once again, the Damanhurians showed great strength of character by overcoming all the obstacles placed in their way and producing superlative results.

Next a spiral stairway was built to join the Earth and Water Halls, an umbilical cord linking the two rooms spiritually as well as physically. When the walls and the columns of the Earth Hall were completed and the cement laid for the floor above, arches were built for the glasswork. In the centre of the floor of the Water Hall a reinforced structure was electro-soldered into place with a trapdoor containing connections for the neon light to illuminate the painted glass centre of the ceiling below.

This whole assault on the depths of the earth had been grandiose. The builders now felt a strong common motivation and the great satisfaction of working together. Indeed, their work often seemed more like play.

The depths of the mountain formed a natural connection with the strengths of the universe. This was amplified by means of Selfica, complex structures used for accumulating and storing subtle energies. The ancient science of Selfica has now become a major area of research at Damanhur. It has been recovered, developed and adapted through modern technologies. The aim is to concentrate and direct intelligent energies through the use of metals, spirals, circuits and alchemical processes. This is discussed more fully in Chapter 14. About 300 tons of Selfic structure were built into the fabric of the temple, but also the cement itself was coupled to a special Selfic energizer as it was being prepared for use, thus widening the field of action and forming a larger Selfic network that constitutes the whole complex. Selfic energy surges throughout the rooms of the temple, strengthening the direct connection to the synchronic points and forming a web of energy that complements the natural energy placed in the temple by human activity.

Again, once the construction of the hall was finished, decoration of the walls began, together with the fitting of the ceiling and the dressing of the columns in ceramics. The very first workshop courses in ceramics happened about this time, producing some extremely proficient and skilled craftsmen.

The floor of the Water Hall was completed in mosaic, whilst on its underside, the ceiling of the Hall of Earth was painted with an elaborate design. As in the Water Hall, a small portion of bare rock was left exposed. This was eventually done in every chamber to remind the Damanhurians of where the temple had come from, and of their own link with the Earth, the digging into the Earth and the digging deep inside their own souls.

The next chamber to be built was the largest of all, the Hall of Mirrors, dedicated to the element of air. This was huge, bigger than any had ever dared dream they would build. An enormous amount of cement had to be mixed to make it structurally secure. There was an increased desire to be vigilant on the safety aspects of such a large construction. Again, in the concrete was an enormous amount of Selfic structure, collecting subtle energies.

The group also built a small apartment to house people who were involved in intensive research work in the temple. Adjacent to this apartment is the Hall of Spheres, where experiments with energies and with Spheroselfs now take place, connecting directly with the forces of the synchronic lines. To either side of this chamber an alchemical laboratory and a room housing a large Selfic cabin define this area as the nerve centre where much of the more specific research work is carried out.

Next came the building of the Labyrinth, a series of connecting passages with niches for works of stained glass. Construction of this part of the temple is still underway. Here you can see where the building stopped at the end of an alcove. The bare rock still has the marks of the hammers.

The next part of the temple to be completed, the Hall of Metals, is situated underneath the Hall of Mirrors, with the Hall of Spheres and the small apartment sandwiched in between *(see Figure 1)*. The Hall of Metals is also directly above yet another chamber, which is still being constructed. Both of these latter chambers share a common support pillar that runs right through the centre of them.

The Temple of Mankind was finally revealed to the outside world in 1992 following an incident when one of the original group who had left Damanhur many years before suddenly began to ask for large amounts of money and to threaten the community. The full story of this particular incident is told in Chapter 6. However, the immediate result was that the temple was under threat from the local authorities and all construction work had to stop.

Damanhurians had mixed feelings at the time. As Condor put it:

> [The temple] was so close to us, so much a part of our essential spiritual selves. However, when it came to letting the world know about it, well, there was a great feeling of relief that the world could at last be shown this great work of art, which we were so proud of. The world was getting to know about the rest of Damanhur, so why should they not know about this also?

When Oberto was asked if he would have preferred the temple to remain secret, he answered in the affirmative, because the work was far from complete. In fact, only 10 per cent of it has been built even now. But the builders were perhaps relieved to have a bit of a break from clandestine construction – and now the need for secrecy was gone, might they start using pneumatic drills?! Synchronistically, they felt sure they would find the right moment to resume the work. Indeed, they do now have permission to continue limited building. They are allowed to finish the parts already under construction, for safety reasons. They do not, however, have permission to continue building *per se*. In fact they have to spend large amounts of money on monitoring the structure that is there, having all manner of stress tests and seismic and structural tolerance readings carried out by geophysical engineers. But all the surveys have shown the temple is perfectly sound and stable. In fact, the engineers have been amazed by its structural qualities.

As one of them said, 'This is some structure…!'

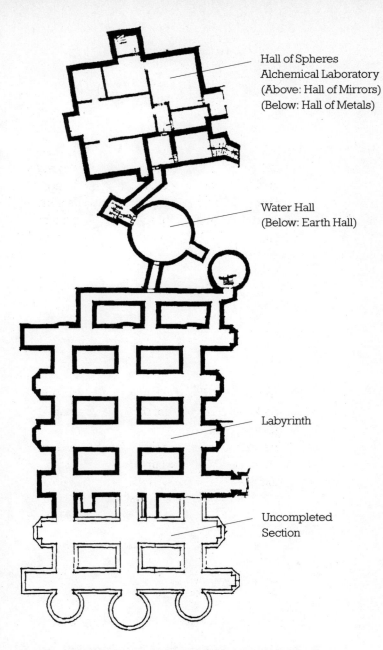

Hall of Spheres
Alchemical Laboratory
(Above: Hall of Mirrors)
(Below: Hall of Metals)

Water Hall
(Below: Earth Hall)

Labyrinth

Uncompleted
Section

Figure 1a: Plan of the Temple of Mankind (second level)

chapter 2 – incredible artwork

---

*We had a great deal of strength, a great deal of enthusiasm
and some great ideas.*

Piovra Caffè

Standing in the temple on your first visit is an awesome experience. Passing through the innocuous courtyard door, down the corridor to the Egyptian chamber, you already feel that something
very special is happening to you.

If you want to see the Temple of Mankind, the Damanhurians are
perfectly happy that you do so. Ring up and they will make arrange-
ments for you. But they want you to be ready, so they lay on a special
preparation day: an hour or so of inner harmonizing, then working
through the words of a couple of sentences in a sacred language
and giving it an interpretation in dance, walking circuits on top of the
mountain, meditating in spiral walkways … and then into the temple.

Prepared in this way, heightened in awareness, you can really
appreciate the temple. You can share something of the feelings that
were experienced by those who helped construct the chambers,
furnish the decorations and make the artwork for this unparalleled
place. You can participate in the spiritual experience of the site.

I remember on our first visit passing through the Egyptian chamber, with its elaborate mosaic floor concealing the message 'This is a fake temple hiding the real one', and trying to find the break in the wall amongst the Egyptian hieroglyphics, the secret entrance that will allow access. We were a party of about seven and, try as we might, not one of us could find the semblance of a crack that might lead anywhere. Then we were presented with the first of the magic treats – magic in an understandable sense, but magic nonetheless – when Oberto flashed his remote control, causing a huge slab of stone to glide back, forming an opening. We were struck dumb with awe and amazement. As Daniela Biancolini, architecture inspector for the Italian Heritage Ministry, had said, 'Nothing like this exists outside the films of Indiana Jones.' This was not the recommendation the Damanhurians were particularly looking for, but Ms Biancolini did also write a glowing report on the magnificence of the structure and its attendant artwork for the Beaux Arts inspection of 1994.

Sliding back on an unseen trackway, the slab of stone revealed the entrance into a new corridor. Stepping through is like entering another world. The walls here are filled with all manner of signs, symbols and writings in an unfamiliar language. Round a bend, another entranceway leads into the Blue Temple.

THE BLUE TEMPLE

The Blue Temple is so called because it used to be painted blue and because, as the first chamber to be built, for a time it *was* the temple. Also, it now houses the large Blue Sphere, one of the nerve centres of the temple. It is not only a sacred place in itself, but also contains the secret entranceway to the Water Hall and the rest of the temple beyond.

The first decorations here, painted in brightly coloured acrylics, related to figures demonstrating the chakras, the human elements of spiritual evolution. The ceiling was of stars. 'Every man is a star' is an old saying that gradually came into the Damanhurian culture and in one star, with five points, the figure of Man was specifically depicted. This expressed the central activity of human evolution: communication with the divine.

For many years the precise function of this chamber was unclear, but as the Temple of Mankind developed, the purpose became focused. Now, the Blue Temple has been transformed into a place of meditation, particularly on social themes. The walls are in the process of being completely repainted, with a new design of arches and colonnades, porticoes for prayer and meditation, and figures in idyllic pastoral scenes.

The mosaic floor features a very large female figure, of Rubenesque proportions. A smiling goddess of a woman, with flowing black hair and the crown of a princess, she lies there in all her naked splendour, almost too soft and sensuous a figure to have been formed from such hard materials. She represents Tarot card 17, *Stella*, the Star, she who pours the Waters of Life from two great ewers, expressing eternal youth and beauty. She is practical intuition; she communicates with the heavens and the elements.

Figure 2: The Star

However, this is not the most remarkable thing about the floor. Another flick of the remote control and a section adjacent to the woman's torso starts to descend into the earth, forming itself into a stairway. I have never been shown just where these stairs lead to and have always been too polite to ask. I guess this information remains, as the Damanhurians will sometimes politely say, 'reserved'.

Just to the left of these stairs is an enormous throne, an exquisite piece of claywork, with dolphins on the arms and a huge shell-shaped back. The idea of the throne was conceived on a long spiritual journey that many Damanhurians undertook in 1983 and was realized in Castellamonte terracotta by Passerotto Olmo some six years later. The story of the journey is symbolically carved into the throne, together with stylized representations of the alchemical and fantastical elements of mythology. It is now located in an alcove opposite the Blue Sphere.

The Blue Sphere is the largest of the spheres in the Temple of Mankind, with a capacity of some 66 litres (14 gallons), and is a magical instrument filled with alchemical substances. Its function is to aid introspection, to boost the concentration of those meditating in this chamber. This is where the community leaders perform their ritual meditations when making spiritual decisions on behalf of the community and where others meditate deeply on social matters.

Down another passageway, the artwork becomes more elaborate, with symbolism and eclectic design features. The passageway comes to an abrupt end at a brick wall with stone shelves. Again, all is not what it seems. This is another disguised doorway, opening onto a set of steep stairs. You have to duck your head as you go through and watch your balance as you tackle the stairs. They lead into an alcove rich in marble. It also has the first examples of stained glass, which are elegantly made after the style of Charles Rennie Mackintosh. There are lots of Egyptian figures here too, so there must be another electronically-controlled door. Sure enough, at the touch of a remote button another huge block of stone swings open, leading to another passage.

All along the passages and down the stairways are rows of small statues, each about 50 centimetres (18 inches) tall and very individual in style. Sitting, kneeling, standing in strange positions, every one of these clay figures was made by a citizen to represent themselves, so that their spirit might remain present inside the temple at all times.

At the end of this next passageway is a door that for once really does look like one – a richly decorated, heavy stone door with a real handle! This opens onto what must be one of the greatest jewels of the temple: the magnificent Water Hall.

THE WATER HALL

The Water Hall is a very special chamber. It fair takes your breath away with its rich play of blue sea colours, a most impressive stained-glass domed ceiling, a floor of marble and onyx mosaic, and an intricate and unimaginable amount of text and graphic work covering almost every space on the walls.

Only 28 people, some of the longest-serving citizens of Damanhur, worked on the construction of this hall. The others continued to dig out other parts of the complex. But this small group knew they were creating something of special significance, right on the active energy points of the synchronic lines.

Excavations began behind a door concealed in the altar of the Blue Temple and proceeded vertically towards the lower part. The weight of the mountain was supported by means of beams of iron. Looking at the incredibly beautiful artwork in the temple now, it is hard to imagine the feelings of those privileged few digging out the raw earth. But the idea that animated all of them was that of creating a secret place with their own hands, a special place to be used for meditation and enriched with beautiful art.

In the temple archives I discovered something of the meaning of the artwork in this chamber. The Water Hall symbolically represents the journey of each human being until, reaching the sources of the soul, it engages in spiritual communion with the archetype of the feminine, which presides over life and death, dream and vigil, knowledge and memory. The deities connected to this hall are all linked with the divine feminine.

Four large gold snakes dominate the chamber, serpent-dragons gilded with leaves of 24-carat gold. The circular walls are completely covered in signs, circuits, maps, Selfic drawings and figures that are deemed to have a magic-theurgic purpose, a direct application of the Damanhurians' esoteric physics. I also recently learned something not generally known at Damanhur – there are spiralling water channels *inside* the walls of this chamber, continuously generating energy with a flow of waters from all other parts of the temple. The multitudinous signs branch out uninterruptedly, creating particular aesthetic effects by way of their complexity and the colours they are so elaborately traced in: blue, red, gold, orange and black.

Between the sketches on the walls are many circuits connected to circles and spheres that represent the inhabited planets in the galaxy. Earth is represented twice, for the two hemispheres, appearing behind the tails of the two snakes. Damanhurian researches have identified a succession of planets on which life already has made an appearance and on which life could evolve in the future. The synchronic lines are also represented. These not only cross the Earth but also form roads of union with the many worlds of this galaxy, running between the near and distant star systems.

The four snakes trace these synchronic lines. They have open jaws, with magic signs in their mouths. Their movement represents the actual flow of the lines, corresponding to energies flowing through the viscous conductivity of the mountain.

There are also two altars in this chamber. The principal one is on the left of the door as you enter, set in a niche of exposed earth in direct contact with one of the major synchronic lines. The other altar is situated opposite, at the top of the marble staircase. Each of the altars houses a specific sphere, alchemically prepared.

The mosaic floor forms a circle within which is a six-pointed star. In each point are dolphins, sacred animals linked to the divine feminine. At the centre flies the flag of Damanhur. The rest of the floor is made up of onyx mosaic representing the waves of the sea. The wave effect is obtained by the particular tones and colours of the onyx. This was the first of the marble floors completed at Damanhur, when this art form was still a real experiment for the young artists. It is easy to forget that at the time they were working on the major artwork in the temple, the Damanhurians would largely be in their early twenties – young, idealistic and talented.

I talked for many hours with one of the artists, Piovra Caffè. She is now responsible for the Way of Integrated Arts and Technologies, one of the spiritual paths of Damanhur, and as such, has a co-ordinating role for all the artwork in the temple chambers. She knows them all intimately. For Piovra, they are her babies.

'Creation of artwork is very different now from when we first started,' she told me, 'The way we go about the whole process is different. And, without doubt, in the future, it will be very different again.'

The reason for this diversity is because, as with everything else at Damanhur, nothing remains fixed, everything is an evolutionary process. For Piovra, this is the first canon of art:

> At one time, the artists worked in an independent manner, following their own individual paths, based on the cultural associations they brought with them and the way in which they were used to working. But we were trying to find what we had in common, to produce things that were alike. We came together more when we were working on the large communal works.

One early major work which brought them closer together was the design and construction of the Open Temple. It was a huge challenge:

> …because in this region, there are a lot of traditional artisans who work with red clay. It is a major tradition in this area. We were just a bunch of young people, without a great deal of experience! But we had a great deal of strength, a great deal of enthusiasm and some great ideas. Nothing seemed too big for us.

The Open Temple is certainly large in both concept and realization, with enormous terracotta columns reaching up to the sky and an altar set in front of a huge panoramic screen *(see plate 5)*. It provided early challenges that the artists met by the enthusiastic acquisition of new skills. This would prove invaluable preparation for their work on the Temple of Mankind.

I asked Piovra if there was ever a firm design for the Temple of Mankind, a plan of what it was going to look like. She told me that Oberto had a very clear idea of how it should be realized, particularly with regard to architecture:

> ...which is, of course, one of the first arts, the cradle, if you like, of all the other arts.
>
> First of all we went in fits and starts. We would have some ideas, then we would stop, then we would have some new ideas. But Oberto had a much grander vision, so we learned to think on a much grander scale ourselves, to have a project in mind.
>
> It is important to mention that when we first started, it was only Oberto who supported the artists, because nobody else believed that the temple could be so beautiful. He really encouraged us and he enabled people to understand fully how important art is, as culture, as inspiration and as a statement of purpose in the temple.

I wondered how the process worked. Would Oberto come to the artists with little sketches or drawings? Or, more likely, would he come with an idea about the philosophy of the place? Piovra explained:

> Oberto alone knows what the function of each chamber is to be, and he gives us an indication of what symbology and design should be put into it. At one time, we would not move at all without Oberto telling us what to do. Now, for the new chambers, he is encouraging us to come up with our own ideas. However, they must mean something.
>
> After we have chosen the theme of a temple chamber, we work on it first by studying. We study all the Damanhurian philosophy in relation to that particular subject or aspect. We read, we study, we ask questions. We may ask Oberto questions. He will then encourage us to widen our questioning. This is the rational part, the thinking part of it. There is a more sensitive part that is to do with dreaming. We use dreaming a lot. If I do not dream at night I find I am lost the next morning as to

what to do, creatively. Every artist has their own method of working – there are some, for example, who open their minds to allow ideas to come into them, but the ideas come from the part of the mind that is non-rational. And then both parts are united and through technology, or through artisan workshops, the work is created. That is the final stage. Roughly 60 per cent of the work is planning it and 40 per cent realizing it.

Throughout the whole of this, we have constant contact with Oberto. If we are drifting away from the theme, he will put us back on course or throw in some ideas. Whilst Oberto knows what he wants to obtain, for any work of art to be any good the artists themselves have to feel and know what they are doing. So Oberto gives us the opportunity to put our own ideas and feelings into it. In fact, that is why it is a spiritual path.

The artwork in the Water Hall was actually arrived at somewhat differently, however, for this is the only chamber in which Oberto himself had a major practical involvement. As Piovra admitted, 'We only painted the serpents on the synchronic lines.'

The chamber is one of mystery, of complexity. The walls are covered in writings in 12 different sacred languages, which, it is commonly acknowledged, are difficult to interpret. Oberto is the only one who understands them all, in all their complexity. This is a lesson in acquiring knowledge, rather than being given it. So there are those who study the languages and claim to understand part of the writings. With regard to the complexity, Piovra believes they are not even a fifth of the way towards understanding it. Many levels are represented and sacred language has eight levels. 'But we struggle with it, even at the first level. It must be very difficult for Oberto to have students like us, who can only write the first few words.' Then she added with a charmingly impish laugh, 'He must be very patient.'

She went on to tell me of her own contribution:

My work, after Oberto had done his writings, and the serpents were in place, was the cupola. And that is a lot easier for people to understand, because written on it, round the sides, in signs, is what the chamber is for.

Another thing to remember is light. That is very important, because it is linked to colour. Colour, by itself, has a frequency and a vibration. It has an action on our bodies. So while we have contact with higher forces, it is as if colour becomes a messenger to put us in contact with them. In all the chambers light coming through glass has this function.

In this chamber, the vibration is blue, light blue and white. That is why it is easy for women to use it, because these are the colours related to the feminine aspect.

The dome was the first large-scale Tiffany artwork; at that time it was the largest work of art the Damanhurian artists had undertaken. I thought it magnificent, but Piovra surprised me by saying that she now sees it as very basic, very primitive:

Look at where the lead joins the glass together – there are only two signs of the sacred language there. In later works there is more complexity, with up to 150 signs on the same surface.

I am always critical of the work.

Piovra is adamantly self-deprecating, but she smiles another of those impish smiles.

Behind this cupola are some very amusing stories, too. I will tell you one. Have you noticed that the cupolas are curved? In order to make them, we rested all the pieces on wooden frames to link them all together. It was the first time we had done any curved glass work and we were really enthusiastic. But when we looked at it, we slowly realized that we had done it the wrong way round. This stained glass has two sides, one smooth, the other rough. When we had soldered it on, we did it with the smooth side facing us, but it should have been the other way round. We were in despair. Anyway we took some heavy books and put them on the glass to try to make it curve the other way. We locked the door of the workshop and nobody could enter for days, while the dome went round the other way!

Not long after that, we made the more complex cupola of the Hall of Mirrors. We made sure that we got that one the right way round!

I get a very strong feeling that the Water Hall is a place just to be. I have always been a great collector of books, but I don't read them, I just have them. There is something about being surrounded by texts that create a space where your own mind can intuitively open up. It is as if you can read them without opening them, by a form of osmosis. The Water Hall is like that. Besides the languages on the walls, it also contains schema for the synchronic lines and even magic formulae. The texts on the walls are like a library of books, where it is possible to describe the library but not say, without assiduous study, what is in each of the books. These complex walls can also be seen as a form of meditation and some of the writings have a similar function to a mandala. It is a spiritual exercise just to look over them, without conscious understanding, or even pass over them with a pointer. In Damanhur, you often see people passing their fingers or a special pen over schema on card or paper for their personal meditations. It is a way of allowing understanding to come through the unconscious rather than the rational mind.

Though the Water Hall represents the female principle, the chamber is not used primarily by women, but by both men and women exploring the feminine sides of themselves. They do this through meditation and ritual, making contact with the feminine forces of the universe. The hall is also linked to birth, to reproduction. Pregnant women often perform meditations in there.

Piovra showed me the niche of bare rock, the point through which synchronic lines flow, and told me that that point of energy was the real reason for the temple being built there. Through it the Damanhurians can send suitable thought forms into the synchronic network. Piovra explained that it was important to spread positive and harmonious thoughts, because thought has the power to create. In the Damanhurian constitution everyone is responsible for their own thoughts.

Like every chamber in the temple, the purpose of the Water Hall is essentially the giving out and the receiving of ideas. Each of the halls has certain energies, but the channels of intuition, through which ideas arise, are not just linked to one chamber.

THE EARTH HALL

And so into the Earth Hall, via the spiral staircase umbilical cord from the womb of the Water Hall. This remarkable hall is probably my favourite chamber in the whole temple. On my third visit to Damanhur I asked if I might do some writing in the temple and I chose to sit in this hall. This was what I wrote, on 30 December 1996:

> Sitting in the Earth Hall of the Temple of Mankind, writing about the temple in the temple.
>
> Eight white columns, rising from floor to ceiling, all individual, whilst all in the same style – gold embossed images in relief on white china glaze ceramic. Sacred symbols, divine images – serpents, birds, a scorpion, mermaids, statuesque figures, mythical symbolism. Crowning the columns are *capitelli*, each with its own specific imagery.
>
> These columns stand majestic, symbols in themselves of the steadfastness, firmness, solidity of this Earth Hall and of the people who built it. As I sit writing this, I am aware of a hammer drill in another part of the temple, as the construction work goes on. Only 10 per cent built, with an age of construction work in front, as further doors are opened into the soul, into the universal psyche of Mankind...
>
> Working in the Earth Hall alongside me is Cincillà, painting the latest fresco of the many in this chamber, one that represents the Hall of Spheres. This panel is rich in its symbolism and an important reminder of the importance of the work carried out in the other halls of the temple. The walls of the temple are meant to be read in much the same way as you would read a set of Tarot cards – read, interpreted and meditated upon.
>
> I look up. The ceiling is a fabulous splash of colour – six circular bands of rich variety. I know that everyone at Damanhur had a hand in painting it. That is important. Oberto had told me

that there are even many paintings underneath the paintings that can currently be seen, that the Temple of Mankind is not just the artwork that is on the surface, but that which is under the surface, but is never revealed. Like the ancient Egyptians, who always painted the reverse side of the sarcophagus, under-neath the frescoes of Damanhur is painted a whole history of the community, no less potent for no longer being seen.

The outer ceiling ring is orange, save for the places where the columns meet, the *capitelli*, where it fades to white. An intricate design has been painted into this orange ring, inter-locking circles of red, green and gold. A piece of the roof, left in its original state of bared craggy rock, cuts into the orange band, as well as into the next band of deep purple. This is the reminder of the cutting into the bare earth, a point of spiritual contact between the temple, those who built it and those who come to share it.

The purple is a darker, more prominent colour. Painted into this ring are diamond and angular shapes. The next band is a deep green, at the blue and turquoise end of the scale. This is the widest of all the bands, with six rings within it, most-ly of a red colour, like berries in abundant foliage, and includ-ing a prominent band of red heart shapes. Inside this, separated by a band of intricate red diamond shapes, is a strong band of royal blue, a lush, vibrant colour, with lotus flower shapes painted into it. And, finally, a band of rich red completes the design, a maroon red with star shapes and leafy patterns.

They tell me that the symbols in this ceiling are actually ideograms in the sacred language, spelling out the words of a song: *ERIJA BET LEBAJ* ('We Arrive at the Awakening'). The whole of the song is carved into the marble all around the room. It is a song to the reawakening in the new body, with all the memories of former lives.

The final band is multi-coloured and is in illuminated Tiffany glass. Green and purplish blue, it culminates in rip-pling bands of colour. And in the centre of all these rippling bands, a montage of seven faces, and in the centre of them, the sun. Who are these faces? Surely they are divine...

The gods... The gods... The gods – those who are about to fall asleep – reunite. They know that, for them, the large wheel of the Kaliyuga draws near, at nightfall, and that, for a long time, victory will go to the Black God of the Stellar Vortexes.

The Great Major God of the Superior Circle, Three Times Ra, summons the three gods who are still awake, who are allied to Mankind: Horo, the Goddess of the Waters and the Mysterious God. These three immense gods sit down shoulder to shoulder, as if in the centre of a great arena, and they look outwards, into the eye of the Great God of the Superior Circle. It is so vast that all three gods, whose own sight is exceptional, perceive only the pupil that fixes them, bathing them with benevolence and respect.

A mighty voice tells them that they will awaken again only if a new city rises up out of the alliance between gods and Mankind, on that point where, one day, thousands of years in the future, new vortexes, knots and synchronic lines will pass, a city which will be able to save Mankind, which will, in the meantime, be tried and tempered to see if it is worthy of its destiny.

And only with the awakening of the gods will Mankind undertake the right way. The times will have to be precise and perfect, and be born from the desire and the force of Mankind.

This future sacred place of this alliance between Mankind, the gods of Mankind and the God of the Superior Circle is land now entrusted to a small gnome called Soffio. The alliance will be possible only if the masculine and feminine principles unite, tantrically producing the androgynous amongst Mankind.

Horo goes north, to the land entrusted to the small Soffio. He is tired of the journey, of the multi-millennia struggle, and is getting weaker and weaker. He digs a handful out of the mountain, as if it were fresh snow, making a comfortable seat, settles down, reclining his head, resting it on the palm of his left hand, and falls asleep.

The Goddess of the Waters, in order to rest in the same place, turns herself into three sources. Where she places her knees, large lakes are formed, and where she places the fingers of her hands, small lakes are made. Where she places her head becomes the sea.

The Mysterious God arrives at the same place; he is the tiredest of all. He lies down on the earth and sinks into it, as into a most comfortable mattress. His elbows are mountains, his hair green woods, his throat a deep volcano.

Now, to the gods, only the dreams are left to give substance to their Maya, to Mankind, their protected.

Only the dreams are left... Only the dreams...

I shake myself, as if awakening from a deep sleep. I am looking up at the ceiling and contemplating the rich flow of life, the ripples we make on the surface of reality. My eyes are drawn to the seven faces in the centre of the concentric bands of colour. My dream thoughts have been drifting around one of the Damanhurian myths that has been related to me, 'The Myth of the Sapphire Masks'. Now I remember, these seven faces staring down at me represent the seven original races of the Earth. The sleeping gods are to be reawakened here in this place, through this work. This ceiling symbolizes the dedication, the diligence and the sense of purpose of the Damanhurians. What binds them together is what keeps them together. The interlocking structure of the ceiling painting is a reflection of the close and interlocking nature of their lives.

From behind one column, I see Time peeping out at me. He is tall and dignified, with long grey hair and beard. Barefoot, he has a robe of gold, with green silk edging and red inside lining. In his right hand he holds a small hour-glass, in his left he holds high a glass sphere. He looks out into the vast space of the chamber, taking care of Man's temporal needs, holding his future in his hand. Time is a great softener.

I am happy here. I don't know what it is, exactly, but I feel an affinity with this place, I feel at home here.

As I gaze around the hall, the next large figure I see is female. Maybe she is Mother Earth. She is certainly pregnant. Her almost naked body is draped in a turquoise chiffon garment, transparently covering her shoulders and part of her torso. Great waves of flowing bright red hair, with strands of beads and shells woven into it, enhance her beauty. Her arms are outstretched, one palm facing up, the other down. The

Damanhurians have told me that this is a sacred dance movement and that sacred dance is used with pregnant women as a
preparation for birth. This woman is stepping into a scene of
truly epic proportions, the conflict between Mankind and the
Enemy, the conflict of Damanhurians overcoming adversity.
The faceless grey form of the Enemy is represented by vast
numbers of oncoming figures. Pitched against them in battle
are the Damanhurians. I recognize some of them. These are
the people who have become my friends on my many visits.
Look, there is Tapiro and there is Fenice. There are Caimano
and Gau and Ara. There are Coboldo and Antilope Verbena. I
notice Condor with the body of Superman and I have a quiet
laugh to myself. The battle is raging, but the Damanhurians all
have determination and forceful aggression on their smiling,
laughing faces. These are people who will win; they will not let
the faceless forces of darkness overcome them, not allow anti-
life negativity, which may even be their own, to be the victor in
this conflict. This is a fight for life, no less! It is on behalf of all
Mankind and must not fail. As a grim warning, over the chif-
foned shoulder of the Earth Mother-to-be is painted a scene
representing universal darkness. This is what could be, if the
Damanhurians fail in their task. But the smiles and the determination on the faces of the Damanhurians show you that they will
not fail. They will fight until their last breath. They are a people
of joy, of resilience, of fortitude, of a determined certainty.

To be sure, this is a fight of fantasy. But it shows the character of Damanhur, the forcefulness and certainty of this group of
people, vigilant and courageous defenders of the destiny of
Mankind. And if that sounds a little bit over the top, well it is, but
in this place that seems just a normal part of life!

I notice that flowing from this scene is an abundance of
water, running from beneath the feet of the expectant Earth
Mother into the Moon Door (see plate 16), behind which lies
an underground reservoir of water, a source of nourishment
and vital energy for much of the work carried out in the Temple of Mankind.

On the other side of the conflict scene, maybe representing a period after the conflict, are three figures. Another

female figure looks at the battle, her hands also in a gesture of the sacred dance. She is completely naked save for flowers and ribbons entwined in her hair. On her body, her arms, her thighs, are painted, like tattoos, animal figures that represent the Damanhurians, all close together, as the Damanhurians themselves are. Above the woman's head, suspended, is a Grail chalice, floating on a silken yellow cloth.

The second figure in this grouping is a large androgynous being, the golden body of Mankind, the tallest figure in the whole chamber at around 5.5 metres (18 feet) tall. Without hair or defined sexual organs, at present it looks more like a man, but soon another figure with more female characteristics will be painted over it in a special paint that can only be seen in ultra-violet light. So the coming together of man and woman will be represented, the unification of the spiritual principles. Once again, the figure's arms are raised in one of the gestures of the sacred dance, right hand down, cupped upwards, left hand up high.

To the right of the androgynous figure is a male youth, his hair ablaze with celestial happenings, like a myriad of fireworks all going off at once. His arms are in the gesture of a book in the sacred dance and he blows onto them. They are becoming transparent, and more celestial bursts emanate from his hands and out into space. He is the Demiurge, not a divinity, but a being who takes archetypes, ideas, and throws them out into the material world.

The next figure of epic proportions is a running man. Again he is naked. He holds his left hand out in front of him in a 'Stop!' gesture. The space between him and the next figure in the series is not yet filled, but his gesture does appear to be directed towards the very large sinister-looking dark grey figure facing him. This figure represents all the negative forces, the negative energies associated with the Enemy of Mankind. He is a gaunt and awesome figure, but far from attractive, a man of stark posture and stern, scowling features. He has the thick neck and the bulging muscles of the bully. He would have you, if you did not have him first. He is someone you hope not to meet and yet might meet, one day, as a reflection of yourself.

The final large figure is the two-faced god Janus. Astride an as yet incomplete arch, his golden bronze faces stare in opposite directions. I have recently learned that this will become the doorway into the new chamber currently being excavated. This is the work that I can hear going on now, the sound of pneumatic drills ringing through the mountain structure.

A series of painted panels depicts the spiritual paths of Damanhur, the ways *[see Chapter 4]*. Each of the Damanhurians follows a particular spiritual path associated with their own interests and it seems only natural to represent these in the temple.

It still intrigues me to see people I know well depicted on the walls of a temple. I recall another situation in Italy. I had taken a youth theatre group to the Spoleto Arts Festival, in the Umbria region, in 1977. We had decided to work on a visual piece to overcome the barrier of language and had devised a drama based on David Bowie's *Diamond Dogs* album and incorporating other Bowie songs. At this time punk was a dominant style in London and the piece showed a not-too-distant apocalyptic future in which young aggressive punks had subjugated the older grey people, treating them badly with whips and chains. It began with a ragged procession with burning firebrands depicting this sorry scene. As the young actors reached the stage, they were greeted by a prophet figure, who sang *Five Years*, holding his hand up, fingers spread, in a sign of caution, or five. He was warning them that they had only five years to sort out their differences. The next scene, based on *Cygnet Committee*, showed the two sides sitting down to heal wounds and resolve conflicts. Over the next few scenes and songs the situation once more deteriorated and a vicious battle ensued. Some of the young people had learned how to fire blow on a circus skills course and this was put to great visual use during a final spectacular scene, with a lone figure singing *Rock 'n' Roll Suicide*. We performed this piece all over Umbria, in town squares or open theatres, and the Italians loved it. One of our performances was in Orvieto and whilst there we visited the cathedral, which is famous for its splendid Signorelli frescoes, painted around 1500. As I was walking round looking at these evocative frescoes, one of the young people came running up. 'Come and look,' he said, breathlessly. 'Our story is on the walls!' He took me to another chamber and, sure enough, there was a procession, with punkish-looking people subjugating greyish people with whips and chains. There was a prophet figure holding his hand up in a gesture of caution, or five. There was a group of people sitting in counsel and there was an enormous conflagration, with angels flying overhead, *breathing fire!* The whole scene had been painted over four centuries before.

Now here I am in the Temple of Mankind, in another part of Italy, looking at people I know painted in panels around the Earth Hall.

First is the panel that Cincillà is still working on. In the middle is a group of children, children from all the nations and continents of the world. They are holding hands in a dance of union. In the distance, a naked couple stand face to face, their hands stretched out in front of them, touching. They are the Esoteric Couple. This is the spiritual path of caring, of nurturing, dedicated to the uniting of the children of Mankind. It is a possible way forward for the world. The children are dancing partly in the Hall of Spheres and partly in the Water Hall, symbolically embracing, in this way, the safe haven of the feminine principle. This fresco panel is rich in its symbolism and is a reflection of the importance of the work carried out in these two other halls.

The next panel shows an atmospheric Open Temple, bathed in blue moonlight. Sirena Ninfea stands at the fire altar, conducting a ritual ceremony for the Way of the Oracle, the spiritual path of communication with divine forces. Next is a picture of builders in the temple transporting the many buckets of earth, a human chain of high-powered action. There is Picchio, and there is Alce. These people are on the Way of the Knights; they have taken on a specific responsibility for construction in the temple and for security in Damanhur. The Way of the Monks is represented by a scene of meditation and ritual in the temple, showing Cicogna Giunco and other monks and nuns in devout spiritual contemplation. In another panel, dominantly blue, Gabbiano sits, book in hand, explaining the finer points of esoteric physics to a seated circle of avid listeners. This represents the Way of the Word. The panel for the Way of Integrated Arts and Technologies is, as yet, unpainted, but all the artwork in the temple is testament to this particular spiritual path.

As I read over my notes now, vivid memories come flooding back. My time in the temple was inspirational. I came out feeling quite refreshed, revitalized. I later learned that the Earth Hall is situated exactly in the middle of a synchronic line, so in this chamber a person is in physical contact with the Earth forces. No wonder I felt at home.

An interesting thing happened just before I was to come out. A party of visitors was being shown round the temple and one of them, a German woman, walked into the chamber, looked around and immediately burst into tears, completely overcome by a wave of emotion. She was comforted and soon calmed down, but there was no doubting the strong feelings that just walking into the chamber had invoked in her.

With all these thoughts in my head, I resumed my discussion with Piovra Caffè the following day. I told her that I had decided that what I would really like to do would be to live in the Earth Hall. I would just stay there. And sometimes Piovra or one of the others would bring me bread.

'That's okay,' retorted Piovra, 'but only if you want to paint!'

It's true that I have never been in the temple when painting was not underway, particularly in the Earth Hall, where scaffolding is almost permanently erected. Piovra recalled how the ceiling of that hall had been painted:

Try to imagine what the temple was like just after it had been dug out and plastered, when all the walls were uniformly plain white. Then, all of a sudden, from the white walls, there was this ceiling, painted in all those bright colours. It just stood out. I will always remember how that ceiling looked.

We built scaffolding right up to the ceiling, with planks on it that you had to climb up, going round and round in a circle. We painted lying on our backs. When the light went out, as it often did, we would have some quiet little naps. Because we were working so close to the ceiling, every once in a while someone would say, 'Let's move these planks down, so that we can have a proper look at it.'

What was so impressive about the energy of this ceiling was that all the Damanhurians contributed towards painting it, all 170 who were here at that time. We made three secret lists of people – those that were good at painting, those that were reasonably good and those that were absolutely useless. We called the useless ones 'artichokes' and got them to fill in the backgrounds, do the easy things. The lists remained hidden right until the completion of the work, but then one day I forgot about them and left them out and one of the useless ones found the artichoke list! So everyone found out and lots of them were pretty annoyed. No, they laughed, really! Remember, this was the first thing painted in the temple, even before the paintings in the Blue Temple and Water Hall were finished.

The pattern of the ceiling is based on the numbers 33 and 66, following a formula in the sacred language. It begins at the centre, which is painted luminous glass, with the awakening of the three gods as outlined in 'The Myth of the Sapphire Masks', then the rest forms a huge spiral, with lines spiralling out 66 times. It looks like a simple repeating geometric pattern, but there is a more elaborate design, with writings and symbols in the sacred language spelling out a meditative text.

I asked Piovra about the portraits of the people at Damanhur in the Earth Hall. They are represented in three different ways: first as body-paintings on the large female figure, then as faces on the figures in the battle and finally in the panels of the spiritual paths of Damanhur, each person being on their appropriate path. Piovra explained that the citizens of Damanhur take animal names and every time a new animal name is taken, the animal gets painted on the woman. Then, if somebody leaves Damanhur, they no longer need their animal name, so they are painted out. It is the same with the faces in the battle. Only fair, I suppose!

Painting sometimes has to stop in summer because humidity is a big problem then. As the paintings are very delicate, it is very important that the walls are completely dry. So the painters lay down their brushes and make plans for the winter, when it will be dry inside the temple. They can foresee several years of work in the Earth Hall alone, although, as Piovra went on:

> In one sense, it will never be finished, because as things develop we can see more complex ideas, new situations. We have really only just started. It will be an immense work when it is completed. It will be like an encyclopaedia, explaining esoteric physics and the history of Mankind, as the human race, as well as telling the story of Damanhur and providing divinations. It will be many things. So the planning of this work has only arrived at a certain point and gradually it will increase in complexity. The more we know, the more complex it will become. Plus, not everything is explicit, some things can only be understood from within, some pieces are confidential in the esoteric sense. Going to the chamber and trying to understand it will be a form of study.

This is in fact one of the functions of this chamber. Every chamber has several functions and each is dedicated to a specific element – not just the material element, but also everything connected to it, every form and concept. As for the Earth Hall, I had always thought in terms of Mother Earth, but Piovra told me that the equilibrium of the hall is most closely related to the male principle. So the artwork there echoes the male and female principles and by contemplating the figures you are actually going through the process of balancing the male and female principles inside yourself. The androgyne represents the meeting of the two sides.

Piovra explained that this showed something of the spiritual value of art:

> Art is something that allows you to refine the soul. To some people it is just beauty, but for us, it is following a path towards the evolution of the soul. All art has this foundation and I cannot put it any other way than to say that art has an

'added value' for human beings. To me, it is a means of talking with the gods. Some commune with the gods through nature, but for me, art is the means of communication. And art is also a metaphor in that as you create beauty outside, so you are beautiful inside.

Next time I visited the Earth Hall, the walls were virtually filled with images. The new paintings continue the theme of the myths of Damanhur. The big grey figure now has symbols painted all over him. It appears that these are signs of the sacred language, used as a form of cage. This is an indication that the negativity inherent in this figure must be kept at bay. Also, there is a new painting that looks like a representation of the Open Temple in Atlantean style. There are three long slitted windows which were amongst the earliest of the glasswork, before the Tiffany style was developed. These windows are dedicated to Horus, Bastet and Pan, three very important concepts in Damanhur. Near these windows are representations of the various human civilizations: a stone circle, an early fortress city, temples of the Egyptians, Incas and Mayans, and scenes from Atlantis. Certainly the Earth Hall holds some of the most powerful images in the whole temple.

THE HALL OF METALS

It was in this chamber, the newest in the temple, that the Damanhurian artists really came together. It was a major step forward in the evolution of the artwork and therefore of the people. For me, this hall shows an emerging Damanhurian style. It is a most satisfying room, with a languid quality of tranquillity and a serene ambience, with a feeling of space, of airiness.

A major feature of the chamber is the human form. On the walls, paintings that look like enormous charcoal drawings show male and female figures, bold and confident images, full of life and vigour, while in the centre of the hall is a single column with embossed copperwork figures, larger than life. I had seen these being made in the workshop of Picchio Abete, who has devised a technique for pushing the copper out way beyond what are considered normal limits for this kind of relief work. The figures are very stylized, but dominant and powerful.

Four other columns connect a floor resplendent in mosaic imagery with a ceiling of terracotta bas-relief. These columns are complex, with multi-layered symbols twisting round them and a beautiful bronzed metallic finish that highlights the natural colours of the glazes. I had witnessed them in all their stages of development from raw claywork in the studio through first firing and early glazing to sectioned construction in the temple itself, and feel particularly close to these pieces of work.

The ceiling carries the terracotta work a stage further with bas-relief figures, warriors and dancers, beautifully coloured in beiges, brilliant whites and golds. The floor is even more distinctive – large figures, superbly drawn in mosaic, depict the various vices that afflict humans. Carelessness, with her eyes closed, jumps into the fire. Pride is locked in chains. Egotism, envy and lust are also depicted.

The stained-glass windows will eventually depict the ages of man. Only two are finished, those of an old man and a child, but their fine detail shows what a high level of craftsmanship the glass workshop has reached. They are painted in glass, the tiniest fragments of glass, delicately cut, being used to put the finest detail into the portraits. The old man is a strong and prominent image, the glass leaded in place. The image of the child is soft and gentle, with no leading round the glass pieces. There will be experiments with the other windows so that each will have its own distinctive style.

Piovra had told me that this chamber symbolized fire. I asked her to tell me more:

> Even if not in an obvious way, there is fire in the central column. Notice on the side columns, the four elements are represented – earth, fire, water and air. To work metals you need earth, because you find metal in the earth, fire because you need to melt the metal with fire, water because you temper the metal and air because you cannot have flame without air. There is another element, which we don't talk about very often. That is ether. To us, ether is the union of all the elements, it is thought, a spiritual vehicle, thus the fifth element and most

important. We are not familiar with it. We can touch the earth, we can be burned by fire, we can feel the wind on our faces and breath the air, we can bathe ourselves in water, but ether is something quite alien. However, our principles are based on thought and ether is precisely that.

I also spoke to another of the artists, Cobra Alloro, who is in charge of the terracotta workshop. Cobra first came to Damanhur when he was 21. He had been a railway worker, but his first creative endeavours in the community were with wood. It was only when large columns were needed for the Open Temple that he attempted claywork. So he found out about terracotta by acquiring the largest kiln available and making huge sections of 6-metre (20-foot) columns. His favourite works are the ceiling pieces his workshop did for the Hall of Metals. Far from easy to make, they represented two years' developmental work. For Cobra, this was not just an aesthetic project, but a human story of struggle, of conquest, of discovering how to collaborate with other arts laboratories. Great friendships were developed during the work, powerful personal links established. It was as if the Hall of Metals marked the coming of age of the Damanhurian artists. Working on it was an experience beyond just art – it was a human experience. The artists knew that something really special had come out of it and the Hall of Metals is indeed a fabulous achievement.

Yet, as Cobra confided in me, none of this would have happened without a lot of hard work, both on the artwork and on the human relationships:

All human beings have their limits and their contradictions. There are contradictions within me. Many times one can be egotistical or jealous. We are only human. There can be big differences between how I would like to do something and how others might wish to do it. Ultimately, such conflicts are resolved here, but it is not always easy. However, the fact that we are here for a specific purpose means that we have to resolve conflicts in order that it can happen. As you resolve them, you grow inside. You have to confront certain parts of yourself. This is the way of spiritual growth.

We use the analogy of a river with lots of stones in it and as they all rub against each other, they smooth off the rough edges. Here, all the people, all the materials, all the sharp edges, all the sharp angles, they rub against each other and smooth out naturally.

I liked that analogy. It explains how they all manage to rub along, how they create together, how such monumental amounts of work get done. Work for the temple, devotional work, over and above daily employment, is there to help fill out the spiritual dimension. For Damanhurians this is work that gives as much as it takes.

Cobra reiterated that Oberto Airaudi often intervenes in the planning, because he has a clear vision, but the artists can put their own ideas forward. The workshops then hold meetings and come up with collaborative ideas. This way of working has now become a regular forum, a constant pattern for working together, not only on the temple, but also when organizing exhibitions outside Damanhur. Such co-operation and collaboration have not come about by accident, but as a result of the spiritual path the artists follow.

The work that he had helped create for the Hall of Metals had obviously had a profound impact on Cobra. I could sense the emotion in his voice as he spoke of it. Piovra also felt it had been special:

I am proud of this work. We have worked on things together, we have grown together. So we are all a little bit in love with this chamber.

She agreed that it showed a developing Damanhurian art form:

This is in fact an aim of ours. We are trying to rid ourselves of conditioning. You have to become children again, then clear your head out and become grown-ups once more. It's pretty difficult.

Something that also proved difficult was expressing the Damanhurian philosophy in metals for the first time. Piovra found herself studying chemistry and physics, even though she admitted to being pretty bad at such subjects at school and not at all interested in them:

> Gradually we began to get a few ideas and I remembered things that Oberto had said maybe 16 years ago that began to have some meaning. He was giving us leads and we began growing together and doing research together, and so we worked out communally what this chamber should be.
> Each chamber has been progress not only in terms of spiritual endeavour, but also in terms of technical realization.

Giant steps were certainly made in technical realization with this hall. The ceiling is in a unique terracotta with a particularly vibrant finish, the mosaic on the floor is made of very tiny pieces, the size of a fingernail, while in the glasswork the faces of the old man and the child are each made up of some 4,000 pieces of glass, all put together to create the shading and the form of the face. All the workshops overcame their own limitations and developed new techniques for this hall. It is indeed a landmark in the development of the Damanhurian artists.

THE HALL OF SPHERES

Down a corridor from the Hall of Metals is a very important chamber which acts as the nerve centre for the whole of the temple.

Here rows of spheres are set in niches along the walls and rows of chalices are set on stands between them. The stands are carved with ornate figures of couples entwined. These were the first examples of figurative art made for the temple. Above them, rich deep red marble panelling appears to create an aura around each of the chalices.

The paintings in this chamber are strangely naïve, large figurative portraits of Pan, of the goddess Bastet, of a young Horus. Each is placed in a mythical setting, with smaller background figures acting out incidents related to their lives, and over the whole of this lies an opulent panoply of gold leaf, entirely covering the ceiling and coming part-way down the walls.

'The Hall of Magic!' Piovra exclaimed.

The most amusing thing about that chamber was doing the gold work. We had just learned how to do gold leaf, from a man who was completely crazy and should have been locked up. He said that before he died he wanted to show us how to do the work because the craft was dying out. However, he taught us how to do it on tiny little pieces of wood, whereas we wanted to put a whole lot of gold up on the ceiling! And, as gold is usually laid down flat, relying on the laws of gravity to hold it in place, putting it on the ceiling was very difficult. We ended up covered in it and every time a bit fell on you, 10,000 lire were being thrown away! It was incredible.

With this type of work, it is usual to put on face masks, because gold leaf is so fine that even if you place it on the table, it tends to float off. If you try to pick it up, it will just break up in your hand. However, with us being up there on the scaffolding hour after hour after hour, we wanted to talk our heads off, so we just did what we wanted. We changed the use of gold leaf!

Under the golden ceiling, spheres sit in their niches, strangely marked, Selficly linked to other energy sources active in the chamber, in the temple and beyond. They are filled with alchemical liquids, aqueous substances that have been developed at Damanhur over many years. Each column supports a chalice, some made at Damanhur, some collected from elsewhere. These chalices are Grail symbols, potent images in a chamber particularly related to subtle energies.

Two doors are on opposite sides of the room. One leads to an alchemical laboratory, the other to a room housing the time cabin, an elaborate structure which functions as a powerful accumulator of subtle energy and a potent link to synchronic flowlines.

THE HALL OF MIRRORS

Lying nearest to the surface of the mountain, the largest chamber in the temple, the Hall of Mirrors, is devoted to light, to air, to sky, to the sun and to life. It is symbolically associated with Horus, the hawk-like divinity associated with sun and sky, and is approached through a drawbridge mechanism, perfectly disguised in a wall of granite above the stairs in the Egyptian corridor. Another entrance is positioned in a side niche and connects the chamber with the small apartment where those engaged in extended research sometimes stay.

On entering, there is an immediate feeling of spaciousness. Usually, the lights are low and the cupola dome is the first thing to attract your attention. Around 8–9 metres (25–30 feet) across, it is made of rings of intricate Tiffany glass. It is illuminated from behind with special curved neon lights, giving the impression that above it is open sky. Gold, the dominant colour, relates to the story of the sun and the other radiant colours each symbolize one of the attributes of the Horus divinity.

In the four corners of the room, beneath the dome, are beautifully sculpted birds. They are lit largely from behind, creating powerful silhouetted images. All round the top of the chamber runs a balcony with an intricate filigree balustrade. It is an impressive spectacle.

Normally as you enter music is playing – beautiful female voices, serene, delightful. The acoustics in the room have a distinctive clarity, raising the singing to the near-angelic. As the lights come up, the effect is complete. For the first time, you become aware of being completely surrounded by mirrors. As far as you can see there are reflections of yourself, and of everything else in the room, including the other mirrors – reflections, within reflections, within reflections, to infinity. The Hall of Mirrors is a truly awesome experience.

The floor is in red granite, in the centre of which, corresponding to the centre of the dome, is a circle of black marble, edged by an elegant mosaic in red, black, blue and yellow – a dandelion, the symbolic flower of Damanhur. To the sides, under the mirrors, run narrow drainage canals, carrying away excess water, and four niches, representing earth, air, fire and water.

To attend concerts in this chamber is fantastic, as it reflects sounds as well as the figures of the dancers and musicians. 'The colours in that chamber are reflected thousands of times,' enthused Piovra, 'because of the colours of the cupola. They are reflected to such a degree that it is like a colour bath. You can actually change your body.'

This cupola is the largest stained-glass cupola dome ever constructed and the Damanhurians are currently trying to have it ratified by *The Guinness Book of Records*. It is made up of beautifully-coloured, high-quality glass panels on a huge ironwork structure. The centre of the dome represents the sun. Immediately around it run two different bands of snakes, forming a spiral, the basic form of the universe, and symbolizing life. The next band represents the stellar hawk with super-elongated wings which contain the universe within them. The outer band contains a prayer in the sacred language, composed of 66 signs, repeated three times and interrupted by four winged scarabs. The hawk, the snake and the scarab are all symbols of the Horus divinity.

The centre portion of the cupola has magical signs coming together. In the middle of it all is written the purpose of the chamber: to reflect all things. This links with the function of mirrors – to broaden your mind. A mirror reflects your face, for example, but how do know for sure that the face you see is not that of another world?

The four seasons are also represented in this chamber, on a perpetual calendar, four large panels of glass mosaic *(see plate 2)*, showing the lunar and the solar cycles, the Solstices and Equinoxes, together with the days, months and years. Each of the seasons is also linked to a force: one to water, one to nature, one to the heavens and one bringing together all the other forces. An animal is also linked to each force – dolphins to water, a huge bull with wings to the earth, birds to the heavens and then all the animals together. The symbolism of the walls is very complex and worthy of prolonged study.

Also on the walls are the prayers used by the Damanhurians in their spiritual meditations, a prayer for each month of the year:

PRAYER FOR THE MONTH OF MARCH
May our dream be the guide
may our will be strong
may spring bring new energies
to the plant of which I am a part.
May Damanhur be like a strong oak
full of living buds.

This work – the seasons, the prayers, the constellations and the
perpetual calendar – was the first mosaic placed on the temple
walls. Piovra explained the connection between the mosaic and the
cupola dome:

> What we have done is to take the image used in the cen-
> tre of the cupola, which represents the rays of the sun, and
> reproduce the same design in the mosaics. The colours were
> done in a graduated way, so that they are lighter nearer the
> cupola and gradually get darker towards the bottom of the
> mosaic. This represents the fact that light passes from the yel-
> low to the darker colours. It shows that light is coming down
> towards the Earth.

To stand underneath this cupola, in this chamber of reflected
imagery, is to feel as though you are in touch with fundamental
divine forces, a positive linking of the inner world of spirit and the
outer world of community. When you stand on the black marble circle in the centre of the room and look into the mirrors, you feel as
though you connect with the entire universe. Each person is an individual and is simultaneously in relationships – each in a universe,
each part of a universal spirituality. Looking up to the dome above
amplifies these feelings. Piovra said this was linked to the function
of the mirrors:

> Mirrors are very important. They reflect, and when you
> reflect, you multiply. Considering that like responds to like,
> you also begin to reflect back again. Mirrors have many signif-
> icances. They also reflect not only the things you see, but all
> thoughts and actions.

She told me about the construction and development of the dome:

> On the one hand, making it was very quick, only nine months of work, that is, the physical construction of the glass, apart from the planning of it. Once again, lots of Damanhurians participated in this work. On the other hand, the choice of colours was a long process. A whole month went by without even touching any glass. This is because colour is linked to the Damanhurian philosophy and is a form of knowledge. And it is one of the keys to reading the meaning of the dome.

This dome is a beautiful example of creative complexity.

THE LABYRINTH

Work still goes on in the temple – a Labyrinth is in the process of construction and another chamber is being dug, one that had only just started to be excavated at the time the temple was revealed. You can often hear the distant sound of drills, deep in the heart of the mountain.

Much of the Labyrinth is in place, enough to show what it will look like. When complete it will be a series of nine connecting passageways. Some of these are already finished and the walls rendered in plaster. There are some experimental paintings on the walls, large figures, men and women. I gather, however, that these will be no part of the finished artwork, but the images underneath the images.

At the end of each connecting passage and in various places along the corridors are a series of three-sided window niches, straight at the base two sides curving to an apex. Eventually, each of these niches will have a stained-glass panel, a Tiffany-style setting with a painted image of a face in its centre. They will represent different divinities that human beings have adored over the centuries. Some are already in place: Pan and Bastet, both key elements in Damanhurian philosophy; Anubis, the jackal-headed Egyptian god of the dead; Cebile, the Roman goddess of the more savage aspects of nature, counterpoised by Gaia, the goddess of the Earth; and Brahma, the Hindu god, with four faces all facing in different directions. Other window panels have still to be put in place.

All the artwork in the Labyrinth will be dedicated to telling the history of Mankind, according to the different divine forces that have featured in that history. The mosaic floor will also be linked to the many divinities and there will be figurative terracotta all over the walls, with male and female figures touching each other across the archways at the junctions.

There is much work yet to be done as I write this, but by the time this book is published, I have little doubt that the Labyrinth will be nearing completion. A few days ago I was in the mosaic workshop, watching them putting together tiny pieces of marble to make a complicated design. Imagine how astounded I was to see the very sections I had seen being made already in place in the Labyrinth just three days later. Action is the first principle at Damanhur.

A NEW CHAMBER

On one of my later visits to Damanhur, I heard of a new chamber. On the last day of that visit, I got to see it. Work on the chamber had been interrupted when the legal wrangles about the temple had first started, but now it could be completed. Excavations had only just been resumed. A small amount of rock had been dug out and there was some evidence of construction – a couple of pneumatic drills, some support propping and buckets, those famous buckets...

When I was next in Damanhur, five months later, I was once more shown into the new chamber. It was virtually finished, along with a new tunnel forming a new way out of the temple. The entrance to this corridor is through a stained-glass doorway from the Earth Hall. Drilling and digging are still in progress and it is a bit of a scramble to get through the doorway, but it will no doubt be easier when complete. There is a little trackway for trucking out rock and earth. Electric wires and pneumatic lines run along the walls. The sound of the drills is deafening. Deep incisions have been hacked into the raw rock. This corridor is to be left bare, so that when people come to visit or meditate in the temple, they will have a real contact with the Earth on their way out. We go on, past the buckets, the water running freely down the walls, the puddles on the floor, and into the new chamber.

Raw, earthy, this new chamber is full of energy. Entering it is like going inside a sculpture, inside something that has been physically carved out. Now I know something of what those early pioneer diggers must have felt as they first cut into the mountain. At present the chamber is rough, unformed, but no doubt Piovra, dreaming artist of Damanhur, is already planning the artwork that will soon be gracing it. I was right. Later she told me:

> We already have plans, so far plans that Oberto has developed, but I have some ideas of my own that I have already started having lots of dreams about. When that happens, I have to remember the dreams. Such dreams have many more colours than my normal dreams. I dream about halls that do not yet exist. Then I get up and I draw them. But every hall also requires a certain amount of study, as preparation. Instead of letting intuition run wild and just following my dreams, I have to go and study, and then link study and dream together.

I wondered if it helped Piovra living on top of the temple. She said:

> I think I am here for that very reason. Before, I never remembered a single dream. The first few days I lived here I did not dream, there was too much energy. But after that, I balanced myself out.

A similar thing happened to me. I very rarely dream, but at Damanhur I had many dream experiences. Whilst staying at Magilla, a Damanhur property up in the mountains on the site of an old Celtic settlement, I dreamed almost every night. Others also reported an increase in their propensity to dream in this place. Then, whilst on my second visit, there was a dream project, the aim of which was to meet with others in the dream world through an out-of-body experience. All that needed to be done was to put your name and date of birth on a list, and then visualize the colour green before going to sleep. I did this, though it was none too easy, and although I did not meet anyone in the dream world, I did have the most amazing visual dreams. For nights after that I dreamed lucidly. However, when I moved to live at Ogni Dove, the house on top of the mountain containing the temple, the first night I could not sleep. It was as if I were being propelled beyond dreams. But after that I did not dream. Whatever energies are at play in Damanhur, they are potent and powerful.

Piovra said:

> You probably had dreams, but did not recall them. When the energies are stronger, it is more difficult to remember and to remain lucid. This is one of the most suitable places to dream, once you learn to harness it.

I asked her what her dreams for this new chamber had been about.

> Well, the new chamber will be linked to the Earth Hall by means of a figure 8, which is also the infinity symbol. Not only that, but 8 is also the symbol of Earth and of Pan. It links to the forces of the Earth, to the universe. With this connection in place, the function of the Earth Hall will be complete. This chamber and the Earth Hall will literally form a figure 8 shape. One will be slightly above the other, but together they will form an 8.
>
> The new chamber will be about knowledge and the central feature will be a Tree of Knowledge, represented by an upside-down tree. It will be formed around the central column. The roots will be sculpted in terracotta on the ceiling, all the roots of knowledge spreading out over the whole of the ceiling. It will have Selfic qualities, as well as the 'added value' of the art itself. There will also be glasswork on the ceiling, though probably not illuminated. The branches of the trees will spread out over the floor, with the leaves and the spider-web twigs in mosaic. Union will be a concept, a labyrinth of ideas.

With the completion of the new chamber the first 10 per cent of the Temple of Mankind will also be complete. This means that the project is on course and all the functions of the temple will be magnified. So, dear reader, you may have the opportunity to visit a Temple of Mankind even more amazing than the one I am writing about here.

THE MYTH OF THE MAGIC WAR

Many millennia ago a great magic war broke out, in which Mankind was defeated, losing knowledge and awareness of its own divine nature and becoming imprisoned within matter. Legend has it that the Enemy was not just satisfied at having won, but wanted to destroy Mankind completely, being afraid that it would arise again to form another empire extending across the galaxies, bringing civilization and knowledge and spiritual union among the different forms of life, in contrast to the Enemy's plan, which was to impose the homogeny of just one race.

In order to avoid its own annihilation Mankind devised a plan to save at least a part of its knowledge. It entrusted this legacy, this memory, to the thread of reincarnations it programmed for itself and for similar forms. With the future lives there was the possibility of recalling, by reawakening, the past knowledge.

Now able to guarantee spiritual revival for itself, Mankind was defeated and went back to the Age of Stone. Our small planet was forgotten, relegated to the extreme borders of the galaxies by interstellar civilization until such time as envoys were sent to the Earth with the seeds of a new civilization: the knowledge of fire, writing and mathematics.

Centuries went by and new civilizations bloomed. These were the civilizations of Mu and Atlantis. Over time they expressed the objective of the reawakening of Mankind more and more strongly. The ancient Enemy saw once more the threat of expansion and once more started a work to eliminate it. The Earth became yet again the scene of destruction and catastrophe. Mankind forgot its origin and the priests lost contact with the gods. The few who were able to safeguard the knowl-

edge took on themselves the task of leading humanity again towards the primeval end. Yet even at this time Mankind managed to safeguard some emergency planes of existence that would start in the case of a new defeat to guarantee the future reawakening of the human race.

So, the legend goes on, from that time onwards, the strength of men has been in resurrection from one era to another, through reincarnation. The Enemy had conquered the synchronic lines of the planet, through which it is possible to control the flux, the flow, of the souls. So Mankind laid plans to reconquer some of the lines and, in the confusion of the Enemy defeat of the Earth, began to operate a selection policy, choosing those souls that were best suited to safeguard the planet to go on again up the mountain of the lack of awareness to Mankind's divine origin.

The Masters came, and they taught, and they still teach, how to recognize the true nature of Mankind inside oneself, how to fight to free the human beings who have become unaware and prisoners of the Enemy.

part two

from group to nation and beyond

It began as a project, as a vision of how the world might be.
This was our vision of the whole world.

Orango Riso

Given that the Temple of Mankind is such an astounding achievement, what of the community that built it? The social structure developed by the Damanhurians turned out to be every bit as remarkable as the temple.

The first thing to be very clear about is that this is a place of spiritual, philosophical research, not about the creation of a new religion. Here they research spirituality, here they research social philosophy, here they research living. The citizens of Damanhur are always happy to tell you that the apparent success of their experiment in living is based primarily on balance, a balance of those three aspects: spirituality, social philosophy and life. The fundamental social structure of Damanhur is based firmly on them. As Caimano Salice, one of the leaders of the community, summed up, 'There are three aspects: the School of Meditation, the social aspects and the Game of Life; the three bodies of Damanhur.'

The School of Meditation is a long-established body in which spiritual principles are thrashed out and discourse and research are avidly undertaken. The social aspects of Damanhur are completely demo-cratic, have undergone many changes over the years, but are well-established in formal structures. The Game of Life is a unique and radical form of social interaction that helps keep life at Damanhur vibrant and refreshing.

I asked Orango Riso what brought these structures into being. His answer was illuminating:

> It began as a project, as a vision of how the world might be. So we had a vision of a world peopled by small communities, autonomous, independent, with a harmonic relationship amongst them.

If all this sounds a bit too good to be true, let me just say that after staying with these people, living with them, experiencing the nature of Damanhur's social structure as it functions in people's daily lives, there is no doubt in my mind that the reality comes close to the vision.

Damanhur means 'City of Light' and is named after an Egyptian city located 160 km (100 miles) northwest of Cairo in the middle of the western Delta, which was once the site of the ancient city of Tnm-Hor, dedicated to Horus. It is now no longer a simple community, but a federation of communities with a highly sophisticated administrative structure that manages to integrate the spiritual, the philosophical and the dynamic aspects of social living into a unified entity. Every aspect of life seems to be fully integrated into every other, so that economics, for example, has a profoundly spiritual dimension, while the building of the temple is fully integrated into the social functioning and the devout spiritual sincerity of the citizens of Damanhur goes hand in glove with their entrepreneurial resourcefulness.

THE SOCIAL STRUCTURE

Caimano Salice and Orango Riso are the two *Re Guida*, quite literally King Guides, of Damanhur. Their names are, of course, Damanhurian, literally meaning 'Cayman Willow' and 'Orang-Utan Rice', respectively. Once individuals embark on the spiritual path of Damanhur, it becomes evident that there will be one or two radical changes in their lives and at a certain point along their pathway of inner growth, the person takes the name of an animal. To change the name is a reminder that everyone lives with change, a reminder not to be too rigid of soul. Taking an animal name means connecting with an animal race; the name of a mythical creature or a spirit of nature may also be taken. The new name also connects an individual quite purposeful and positively to other Damanhurians. Similarly, at a further stage of inner development, a plant or vegetable name is taken to further strengthen the numerous connections. Consequently, Caimano Salice and Orango Riso regularly debate on spiritual matters with Formica Coriandolo and Fenice Felce, or Poivra Caffè regularly shares her design ideas with Gorilla Eucalipto.

As for the roles of the *Re Guida*, these are two elected posts that head up the federal responsibilities of the three communities of Damanhur. The term 'king' here is used here not in a monarchical sense, but more in a way akin to the priest-kings of ancient yore, kings with a spiritual responsibility for their people. The King Guides do deal with constitutional matters, but they also serve the spiritual needs of the people. Everything is connected.

Though it might sound a bit bizarre to have the two heads of state named after a tropical alligator and a giant monkey, that is only one of the disarming aspects of a social system that, for over 20 years, has guided this blossoming community. The central importance of games, life games, in both the social thinking and functioning of the communities is another aspect that outsiders often have some difficulty in understanding, yet it is the one dynamic aspect of Damanhur that has probably done most to ensure its success.

In the early days the social structure of Damanhur more or less took care of itself. When there were just a few dozen people, living on the one site, only the most basic of social conventions were necessary. As spiritual master and visionary inspiration, Oberto Airaudi obviously held a more central role in these earlier times, but even then, the overriding philosophy was everybody pulling together for everyone else, building their lives as they built the temple, with dedicated effort and unselfish co-operation.

As the community started to grow, more defined social processes became necessary. Once there were 100, 150 people living in the central part of Damanhur and in houses throughout the valley, there began to be discussions about constitutional matters. Social stability, based on co-operation and synergy, on combined action and collaborative effort, was a realizable goal, but needed a stable structure. How were the finances to be regulated? How was the community to function in economic and practical ways? As numbers grew, it was time to bring processes into play that would ameliorate the potential difficulties and unwieldy nature of a large number of people living alongside each other without restricting their needs and desires.

First, two communities were established, each with their own democratic processes and economic systems. Later, a third was developed. At that time, a federal government was established to link the three communities socially, spiritually and economically. Over the years, this structure has become increasingly complex and sophisticated.

The current overall social structure, which has been revised no fewer than three times whilst I have been writing this book, has the two King Guides squarely at the centre of federal matters, two well-established communities, Tentyris and Etulte, and three embryonic regional groupings, Rama, Damjl and Valdajmil (see Figure 3).

The King Guides are heads of the Federal Government, the School of Meditation and the Game of Life project team, and oversee the communities, the spiritual paths and the other organizational functions. The Federal Government has the major responsibility of regulating the financial and administrative processes in order for work to continue on the Temple of Mankind, making sure the necessary resources are available to the work teams and to the artistic laboratories. It is also responsible for the Treasury and the offices of registration and archives, foreign affairs and international relations, and legal and technical services.

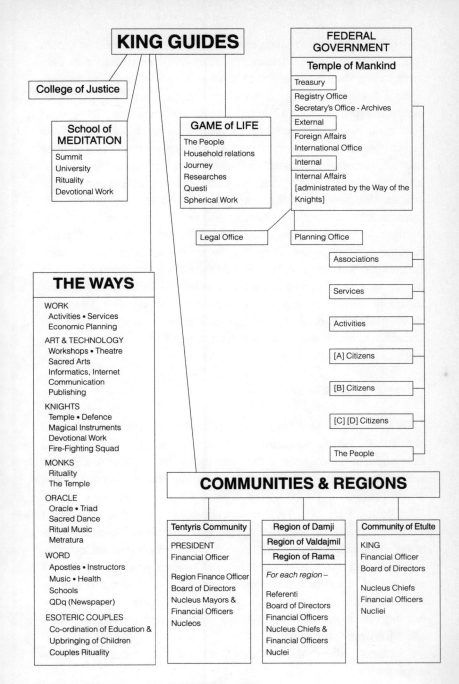

Figure 3: The social structure of Damanhur

The communities and regional groupings have their own autonomous status and their own forms of local government. Tentyris has an annually elected president, whereas Etulte has an annually elected king, acknowledging the weightier spiritual emphasis placed on a territory that includes the Temple of Mankind, the sacred wood and the monastery at Ogni Dove. The regions each have *Referenti*, people who are elected to help steer these new social groupings towards community status. Each of the communities and regions has its own board of directors and finance officer. Within each of the communities and regions there are a number of households, called *nuclei*, or nucleos. These are normally made up of around 12 to 15 people who live in large houses, sharing living expenses and all social responsibilities. Each nucleo has an elected head of household (called a mayor in the Tentyris community) and a person responsible for the household finances. Similarly, there are people responsible for overseeing the active development of each of the seven Ways, the spiritual paths of Damanhur, which will be fully explored in the next chapter.

THE FEDERATION

I wanted to take a closer look at the federal structure, starting with the *Re Guida*, so I interviewed the two King Guides, Orango Riso and Caimano Salice, in their office, a small room tacked on the end of the mosaic and clay workshops, just round the back of the Open Temple.

Orango Riso is a fiery-looking man with a flame red beard and a full mane of orange hair, yet he is as gentle as a lamb, as wise as an owl. Caimano, clean shaven with classic good looks, is equally mild-mannered, equally erudite on matters of state and matters of spiritual well-being. Together, they are a formidable spiritual team, with probably a greater understanding of Damanhur and its mysterious processes than anyone except perhaps Oberto Airaudi himself.

I asked about the formation of the Federation. Caimano explained:

The decision to form distinct communities was taken when the number of citizens rose above 250, because we found that around 200 or 220 was enough for a number of people to form a cohesive social group.

This was a key passage in Damanhur, because it set the direction for the future and the direction was going to be, having smaller communities. The Federation that we have today, in relation to the Federation that we imagine, is still a small reality of what we can achieve.

Orango added:

It began as a project, as a vision of how the world might be. This was our microcosmic vision of the whole world. The choice, at that appropriate time, of turning Damanhur into a Federation was a reflection of our idea for the whole of the planet. And, of course we are on the lines here, so what we do here could be a start for the rest of the world.

The first autonomous regions formed themselves around 1986 and, following the Damanhurian principle of experimentation and refinement, the communities of today have evolved from them. Each of the communities has a particular direction related to the individual characteristics of the environment in which it is situated. For example, Tentyris is centred around the family, whereas Etulte, with the temple and the sacred wood in its midst, is the spiritual research centre. When I first visited Damanhur, there was also a third community, Damjl, but now three smaller regions have been formed from it. One of these regions has taken on the responsibility of acting as a reception centre, welcoming people from all over the world who visit Damanhur, eager for experiences.

The total life of Damanhur is one of bringing together the technological, philosophical and spiritual. On a practical level, for example, at Etulte they carry out research on green ecology and low-impact technologies. Some of the households there have actually been producing the electricity to light and heat their houses via water or solar power. Orango explained:

People today have needs that are different from what you might imagine. We need the coming together of nature and technology. If it is properly used, technology can be a major step forward. And it has also helped us in developing our own social structures. First of all, it has improved our communications. It has also allowed us to increase the amount of experimentation that we are able to carry out and has been the basis for our esoteric physics. We consider ourselves to be a people who study a lot and thanks to the technology we have been able to develop new philosophical thoughts.

The interconnectedness of life at Damanhur is also reflected in the Federation's role in balancing the different needs of all the communities and in creating an intercommunity plan for development. In this way the impulses of each community can not only be used, but also become common wealth. Orango continued:

Every year we have what is known as a letter of intent of the communities. They draw up their principles, the way they are going to develop, in order that everyone can see how they are going to go forward. Then they adapt it to their own needs, their own way for realizing their plan. This allows them to widen their concept of life and this is very important to them. And any individual can find a way to express themselves and create their reality within that of the greater organization. This is pushing beyond the vision of the egotistical. It is what led to the birth of the People.

The People of Damanhur are a wide constituency of supporters much broader than the communities of Damanhur. They have all been to Damanhur and taken part in a short ceremony in which they ask to become a part of the People and are given a pink silk bracelet as a sign of belonging.

Those who live and work at Damanhur are called the citizens of Damanhur. Some are fully part of Damanhur, others not. They are referred to as citizens A, B, C, and D. Citizens A were originally those who lived full-time in Damanhur, sharing all resources. Now there is a process underway known as 'economic harmonizing'.

According to this system, every family unit decides what to share and the rest is kept by individuals. Citizens B live in Damanhurian homes at least three days a week, but might contribute a fixed amount. They mutually decide what to contribute. Citizens C live wherever they want, not in Damanhur, but like the others, they are part of the School of Meditation and they pay a contribution every month. Citizens D, a class now more or less defunct, live anywhere, but are not part of School of Meditation – they are similar, in fact, to the wider People of Damanhur, those who want to be loosely associated, but spiritually linked.

THE CONSTITUTION

Over the years a number of basic social principles have evolved at Damanhur and have now been collected together as a constitution. The King Guides are responsible, as guarantors, for ensuring that this constitution is followed. Every two years or so, its 21 Articles are updated and reprinted in booklet form. Normally there are two or three subtle refinements each time. Whilst I was at Damanhur on my second visit, my interpreter Elaine Baxendale and I helped to translate the principles that form the current constitution *(see Appendix 1)*.

The constitution covers such aspects as the reciprocal trust and respect of citizens, the spreading of positive and harmonious thoughts, the nature of community life and a move towards self-sufficiency, the equal value and dignity of all working tasks, a harmonious respect for the physical body, social responsibility and a spirit of service. There are practical principles, such as living in communion with nature by avoiding all forms of pollution and waste, research and education in art and sciences, taking care of personal living spaces, marriage and responsibility for bringing up children, as well as the general responsibilities of being a citizen of Damanhur.

The constitution is supplemented by community regulations which are devised in local forums and might be thought of as similar to British bye-laws. These regulations cannot, however, countermand constitutional principles. Changes to these are matters for the whole of the community nation to decide. Since the first corpus of community rules was established in 1980, there have only been seven major revisions, the most recent of which, and the most radical, was establishing the federal structure in 1996.

In the early days of the Damanhurian social system, Oberto Airaudi had a more pivotal role, but now he is simply a common citizen. His function is seeing that everything works from the point of view of the citizen. Most matters are now under the guidance and jurisdiction of the King Guides, who are elected on a six-monthly basis by the full constitution of citizens, though they may be re-elected any number of times.

So, in brief, there are two communities and three regions linked by a federal government, with a well-developed constitution and a sound and secure economic base. But how does it function in practice? I sought further assistance from King Guide Orango, enquiring of him just what were the responsibilities of the Federation, in terms of employment:

> The Federation is not an employer. It utilizes the services of specific individuals, who are, in return, taken care of out of the common purse. The Federation, on its own account, allocates intercommunity work, the work of connecting communities. In the past, it was a very complex organization, but with growth, some of the services it used to administer have become autonomous – the schools, for instance. This is because we have an enterprising vision about work, preferring that, wherever possible, a service becomes self-regulating. That way, we feel people actually realize themselves and create a better politic, a better way of working.
>
> Another example is the health system. It used to be completely organized by the Federation and people who contributed their services to the internal health services were taken care of out of the common purse. Now, the people of Damanhur contribute directly towards the health services they receive.
>
> There are only a few services that the Federation directly administers. It now tends to back a project when it is just starting and help it get going, then it can become an autonomous, an independent enterprise.

This slimming down of the practical responsibilities of the organization will allow the Federation to play a more active role in the spiritual development of the community nation. At the moment, however, it still has quite a lot to do with the regulation of the communities. I asked Caimano what sort of legal framework was necessary for this:

> The College of Justice, that is our legal system. It guarantees the administration of our rules and law, and its officials are elected by the people, not chosen by the King Guides.
>
> Whenever we want to put forward a new law, or change an old one, our suggestions are brought to the College of Justice to be assessed. Whenever we have any problem, any quarrels or disputes, or anything that is hard to interpret, these things also go to the College of Justice.
>
> There are just three elected people in the College of Justice. Theirs is a very specialized role. They have no direct relation with the King Guides. If the King Guides want to promulgate a new law, first they give it to the College of Justice, so that they can check it and have it presented in the right way, so that it conforms to the constitution and to the tradition.
>
> So the College of Justice is not a law-making body, but a law-interpretation body. They do refer to written law, but more so according to tradition, according to precedent. In this respect it is much closer to English law than Italian law. In the Italian system tradition has no role, it is all based on written laws.

THE SCHOOL OF MEDITATION

As already mentioned, the directives on which Damanhur is based are three: meditation, the social system and the Game of Life. The King Guides are also directly responsible for the School of Meditation and the Game of Life and can either choose people who will manage them or oversee them themselves.

The School of Meditation is at the core of Damanhurian life. All full citizens of Damanhur are initiates and as such have access to ancient esoteric traditions. The School of Meditation is the means by which such access develops. At meditation meetings everything to do with the spiritual aspect of humanity and its contact with the divine is discussed. At these meetings initiates wear robes, long single-piece garments not dissimilar to a monk's habit. There are different levels within the school, with different colours of robe for different ranks. White is the initiate level, red the second level and yellow the third level. I had noticed that those wearing yellow robes carried out most of the specific function during rituals, lighting fires, closing circles or presenting chalices. These colours have nothing to do with power, only with a level of spiritual growth. The higher ranks help the lower and the King Guides act as the bridge with Oberto, although all the initiates have the possibility of direct contact with Oberto.

The knowledge gained in meditation is then applied in everyday life. This is one of the important and original things about Damanhur. But it works both ways: the knowledge that derives from meditation is applied in the social system, and the social system throws up things that can then be applied in meditation. Everything is interlinked. The School of Meditation also has control over some of the rites performed at Damanhur, as Caimano explained:

> The rites that have a direct link with the School of Meditation are those for the Solstices and Equinoxes. They are major collective rites that are very important. The Solstice rites happen in June and December. For us they are a moment of contact with the powers and the forces that are expressed in and on the planet. There is also a moment when the synchronic lines open, in relation to other spaces in the universe, through the rites of nature itself, and also through the collaboration with the plant forces.
>
> These important rituals also happen in symbiosis with the divine forces, and have been carried on, without interruption, for at least 6,000 years by groups present on the planet. And at this moment in time, the Solstices are important and so we have, in past years, undertaken journeys throughout the world and performed these rituals in different places and then carried back here the fundamental essence

of these rites. That is because of the synchronic knot that is here at Damanhur.

There is a basic ritual form that remains throughout time and there are other aspects that can be developed. However, the message of the ritual, in its fundamental aspects, is always the same.

The School of Meditation supervises the ritual and checks out all the different groups that take part, the work that they do – the musicians and dancers, for example.

Talking of ritual, I asked Caimano why I had seen pictures of him wearing a crown and pictures of Orango wearing a crown and carrying a sceptre. Thanks to my studies of medieval history, I associated these implements with a powerful ruler, possibly a despot, a manipulator of diabolical mischief! I told Caimano that I found this a strange image in the context of Damanhur.

I can see that you have learned much from studying the machinations of kings throughout history! But you do know that King Guides are elected? Being elected is a measure of the recognition that others can give to you, not only socially, but also in the heart. Therefore, it is a very different respect from that given to the kings of history.

And the role of the King Guides is to make contact with the subtle forces. The crown and the sceptres actually help in this work, because they serve as bridges to make these contacts and amplify the energy. They are ritual instruments which can amplify and direct an action or a gesture. They are all charged with energy and can carry out very precise functions.

On several visits, I stayed with Caimano in the nucleo household where he lives. It was a revealing experience. Like any typical Damanhurian nucleo social unit, there were some 15 people living in that household, but in the four-week period I was there, I think that they only came together once. This was not by choice; these are people with very busy lives. Most of the household would leave early in the morning and very often not return until late in the evening. They would all try to come together, however, for nucleo meetings, where all manner of household problems were discussed. One of these meetings, that I attended as a guest, lasted for almost four hours. Discussion was often heated, but never less than amicable. They appeared to have discussed everything in the universe by the end of the evening, but everyone was smiling and all problems seemed to be resolved.

TENTYRIS

I also spent some time out at a property called Magilla, high in the mountains above Lugnacco, some way from the administrative base of Damanhur, and part of the community of Tentyris. Magilla is a large residence, currently being extensively restored. The house is built on the site of an ancient Celtic settlement, of which there is still archaeological evidence to be found, particularly rocks with special slotted holes, in which the Celts would place firebrands in line with the stars during their ceremonies. In the grounds, there is also a spring, a sacred place, where weddings and other ceremonies are held.

For many years, the house was the residence of an old Piemonte lady, the only survivor of a wealthy family who had lived there for generations. In later years, this huge house had proved far too much for her to cope with alone and it started to fall into rack and ruin. The old lady sold it to the community of Damanhur and moved into more suitable property, still in the valley. So the restoration of Magilla began.

Life at Magilla is a modern form of harmony with nature, where technology may be used, but only if a natural solution cannot be found. For example, the house uses some solar energy and a little water power, by way of a stream-driven turbo. I was taken down a ravine, away from the house, cutting through thickets and shrubbery as dense as any jungle, to where the turbo had been constructed, at the point where the flow of the stream was at its greatest. The turbo blades turned inexorably, in perfect rhythm with the natural flow of water from the magic spring – an idyllic means of generating electricity. It had proved adequate in the early days, when a just few settlers were living at Magilla, but now that 30 are in residence, extra power has to be taken from the electricity supply companies. However, such power is used wisely and is always supplemented by the natural energies still available.

At Magilla there are two nucleo family groupings in quite separate parts of the very large house. Within these groupings are, of course, natural families, but, as in Caimano's household, it is in the nucleo group that all the economic and social dynamics are worked out. Sunday is the day when all members of the nucleo family units at Magilla try to come together over a special meal.

Magilla forms part of a plan for the main settlement of Tentyris, a vision of beautiful buildings in abundant natural settings, with cascading waters and dancing fountains, rich varieties of flowers and exotic vegetation, with the majority of food requirements being grown within the community and the largest wine cellar imaginable. The latter is already in place, as is the first water feature, a round receptacle waiting for the cascading waters. The whole scheme has already been visually realized in a large colourful painting to be found in the office of the President of Tentyris, Gorilla Eucalipto.

The dream that is Tentyris is also embodied in its name, which means 'City of Women'. One of the main projects here is the restoration of a house to be known as *Porta della Luna*, Doorway to the Moon. This will be the Tentyris equivalent of Porta del Sole, at Etulte, the house that incorporates the entrance to the Temple of Mankind. In Tentyris the forces are those of the moon, water and the feminine spiritual energies of the planet.

The other important aspect of the Tentyris dream is that this will form the base where the main international settlement of Damanhur will take place, with people coming from all parts of the world and either embracing the Damanhurian way of life completely or running their own ecological, esoteric or social living experiments alongside those of Damanhur.

People are already starting to come to the valley, though Damanhur is not a proselytizing community. Far from it – the Damanhurians are more likely to tell people how difficult it is to live there and impress upon them what sense of commitment and dedication is necessary. Damanhur is not a place where you can come to be introspective, to contemplate your proverbial navel, but a place where demands will be made of you, where practical, purposeful actions are as important as inner reflections. It is a place where the work of the hands is as necessary as the workings of the heart but a place where the rewards are significant. Consequently, people from all over the world are hearing about Damanhur and going to live there for trial periods, and some do settle there.

Magilla is a magic place, a feminine place. The people who live here, as elsewhere in Damanhur, work extremely hard to create a comfortable living environment from the dilapidated remains of former dwellings. The effort is rewarded in many ways. It gives the people a resilience, a degree of insulation against life's traumas, an ability to transform negative pressures into positive energies. It also leads to a gradual increase in the quality of life, as the residence becomes a luxurious dwelling. Magilla signifies the spirit of determination that is the focus of the 'city of women', the dream that is Tentyris.

I was still not clear, however, which properties belonged to which community or which region. I knew about Magilla and Porta del Sole and that the community had some houses in Baldissero, some in Vidracco, in Castellamonte, and others in the woods above the temple. But I had no clear picture. So I headed for the office of Gorilla Eucalipto, President of Tentyris, in the basement of the main administrative block in Damanhur. He told me something of the history and location of the various communities:

It started out with just one community, called Damanhur. Then, in 1990, that was split into two: Damjl and Etulte. Damjl kept the settlements in the lower valley, Etulte the houses and the wooded area on the hill of Vidracco. In February 1995, there was the official beginning of the community of Tentyris.

Tentyris has rather a long history. It began with a single property, Magilla, way out in the mountain area, and it was this area that was originally called Tentyris. Then, the three nucleos of Damjl, called Aria, Rama and Aurora [Air, Rama and Dawn], established an association with the new nucleo at Magilla and Tentyris, as a larger entity, was born.

But these communities, the three that came from Damjl and the new one at Magilla, at heart and in truth, did not fully form a community as such. Then Valdajmil, up to that point also part of Damjl, decided to leave, and at that time the other properties of Tentyris asked for it to be annexed to them. So they all joined together and it was at this point the community of Tentyris, as it presently exists, was formally ratified and established.

Then, in May 1997, the community of Damjl was completely revolutionized. Several nucleos split off and formed a region known as Rama, and Valdajmil itself became an autonomous region, leaving a third region known as Damjl. Damanhur is thus composed of five distinct social groupings, each with a different political status.

Wow, it's a complicated business, forming a community! I asked Gorilla about the administration of the individual communities:

As well as the Federal Government, every community has its own government. It is a government that has its own power, both in terms of territorial rights and the economy. So far as Tentyris is concerned, there is an elected president, who has absolute power, then there is a council, which has an advisory function. Each of the nucleos has its own head of household, called a mayor. A gathering of the mayors of the various households makes up the council of Tentyris.

The nomination of the mayors is made by the president and the president is elected every 12 months by the people of the community. It is possible to serve more than one term of office – this is already my fourth term.

One of the responsibilities of each community is also to help administrate the financial resources of that community. This involves not only economic factors, but also territorial factors – being responsible for the land, the houses on it and the social aspects, the relationships of the people within the community. President Gorilla emphasizes:

We try to develop positive relationships amongst ourselves. In addition to the constitution, each of the three communities has its own set of rules and its own aims. The aim of this community is to create a village, which will be called the Village of Tentyris.

Families are the basis of our philosophy. We talk here of a very minimum of six people, but more like 10, 12, 15 people, in a family group, the nucleo, groups that are strong enough to be able to put the needs of the community on their shoulders. Solidarity and sharing and mutual support, these are the fundamental aspects of the community. There is a lot of room for growth and at the moment this is the largest community. Etulte has the most land, but we have the largest number of people.

The Village of Tentyris will be an international village. We cover a wide territory and there is a lot more land that we want to buy. There are lots of properties that we could buy, all over the valley. As there are lots of people coming here from all over Europe and other parts of the world, we are suggesting that they buy houses in this area, renovate and rebuild them, and help to create the international village.

You have to keep pinching yourself to remind yourself that this Damanhur way of living spans only two decades and that some of these sophisticated social structures have only come into being within the last couple of years or so.

Gorilla and Husky, his fiancée, took me on a trip of the Tentyris territory, the day before they were due to get married by the spring at Magilla. From Magilla it is a short drive further round the mountain to a settlement that consists of three dwellings. The first of these is *Porta della Luna*, a magnificent property set in the most beautiful environment. Across the way is another well-situated property, the House of the Couples, a property in its very early stages of restoration, nothing more than a shell at the moment, but glowing with potential. And then there is the Baita, the magic Baita. This had originally been a dilapidated mountain shelter, but had been restored with such special care and high level of invested energy over many years that it is now regarded as one of the most spiritual of Damanhur's premises. I had heard so much about it, now here it was, in front of me. People come here when they are engaged on some particular spiritual mission, when a period of profound meditation and spiritual preparation is necessary. Oberto visits the Baita a great deal.

ETULTE

Next I was off on my way to the top of Vidracco's hill, to the fraternity of Etulte. That's a good word – it makes you feel good when you say it: Ay-tul-tay. All I knew about Etulte was that it was a bit special. It had, right in the centre of its territory, the Temple of Mankind, also the sacred wood on the hillside above the temple and the Damanhurian monastery at Ogni Dove. It was at the latter that I interviewed Elfo Frassino, the king of the community, who told me something of its history:

> Etulte was born as a community before the others. It was the first community to establish a separate identity. Before Etulte, there was just Damanhur as a single unit. But we had already realized that the time would come when Damanhur would divide into different groups. Etulte was formed on a small scale in the same way that the original community had been formed on a large scale. But from the beginning it had a very strong character of its own, an experimental character. In fact, at first Etulte was an experimental laboratory within Damanhur.
>
> When Etulte was established, the temple was still a secret and so the people who began to live in this area regarded themselves in certain respects as custodians of this land and felt that living here was a great privilege, in as much as the community is an extension of the temple. Just as, in the past, a village would quite naturally develop around a temple, so this has grown as a territory. Many houses and properties have been bought and renovated. First of all the properties were divided up, but now we have managed to get them all into one body. This is the high part of Etulte, but Etulte is also composed of another nucleo, in Cuceglio. That is Aval, short for Avalon, the house where Oberto and 13 other people live.

The other strong aspect of the community, besides the temple, is the wood. It is both a sacred place in that little by little it has been made sacred and also in that it gives us substance. A few years after the formulation of the constitution of Etulte, the heating system in all our houses became a wood-fire system. So the community became self-sufficient, from an energy point of view. This was a great step forward, economically. We were also pleased and proud, because this gave us the opportunity to achieve a symbiosis, a spiritual relationship, with the woods.

Within the woods, we are carrying out some projects that are of interest to the European Union, projects of regeneration. The original owners had been cutting everything down in these woods for years, right down to their roots. New shoots would grow up, then, after about 20–25 years, they would be cut down in turn. And this has gone on for years and years. So what we are trying to ensure is that these young trees are allowed to live, to grow, for much longer, say, 100 years. It is a lot more difficult than replanting. It is not starting from scratch, but you have to calculate the potential life of the tree right from the beginning. It is very tiring work, but it gives us a great deal of satisfaction to bring dying trees back to life.

I remarked on the mile after mile of stone circuits, spirals, complex schema, being built out in the woods *(see plate 5)*. These circuits are constructed by way of huge amounts of labour and a veritable mountain of stone. They are defined by stones, each of them larger than a canonball, just about able to be lifted by one person; tens of thousands of such stones make up the vast complicated circuit network. Elfo explained:

What we want to make happen in the woods is what we call 'the Wood Temple'. Just as we have created a temple under the mountain, so we want to create a temple on top of the mountain – an extension into the open air. Within the wood, using the same logic as we did when constructing the temple, there are certain particular environments, certain places that have their own characteristics, their own specialization and different uses, just like the halls in the Temple of Mankind. For example, there is an area where we celebrate the Solstices and the Equinoxes, there is an area dedicated to feminine energy and another for masculine energy. The circuits we are building now will link together all these different areas.

From a social point of view the plan is to form a settlement of about 200 people here. At the moment, we have several habitations, but we do want to create some new ones. We are already interested in building houses made of wood and stone to put inside the wood to create a village. In the meantime, we are busy buying as much of the wood on the mountain as we can.

At first, there were only about 20 people at Etulte; now there are about 100. When there was a very large community at Damanhur and only a small community at Etulte, the people at Damanhur would say, why do these people want to be different? But after a time, more and more Damanhurians came to identify themselves with the territory and it became a particular path, and then other communities were born.

Now there is a relationship of solidarity and reciprocal respect between Etulte and the other communities. We even work together on common projects. Each community is quite distinct, however. It is as if Damanhur were experimenting with three different types of community, three different models. As more time goes by, each one develops a more distinct character and this is a rich source of wealth. It enables us to take what is good from each experiment and to pass it on to the others.

One of the themes that Etulte is exploring is the idea of the journey: the journey outside Damanhur, the journey to the woods, the journey of everyday life. The experience we have acquired whilst travelling has become the inheritance of everyday life, leading to the growth of interpersonal relationships.

Ultimately, we plan to make a small community within each of the extended families at Etulte. For example, Ogni Dove will have its own government and its own lands, and will rule itself, will have the dignity of autonomy. So the objective of Etulte, even if it will take several years to realize, is to pass from being a community to being a federation of communities – a federation within a Federation.

I asked Elfo about Ogni Dove. As a monastery, was it not very different from the other nucleos at Damanhur?

Without a doubt, it is a unique place. This is the only household, for example, where those who live there are all part of the same spiritual path. But there are other places, with different characteristics, that also have unique qualities. For example, the household where I live, Porta del Sole, is unique because that is where we have constructed the temple. It is not a monastery, but the presence of the temple is a very strong element in daily life, therefore it characterizes our life there. And, to take another example, Aval, that is the house where Oberto lives and that is obviously a very strong element in that nucleo household.

Each household has its own characteristics, its own potential, its own richness, that can then be developed in the direction of its own uniqueness. There are important social and administrative aspects, but it is the particular energy that is here that is such a motivating force.

DAMJL

There also used to be a third community at Damanhur, Damjl. I even interviewed Nibbio Origano, then President of Damjl But things can change very quickly at Damanhur. And in May 1997 they did just that. Overnight there was a revolution and the citizens living at Damjl had to move out of their homes. There was a complete restructuring. I had to tear up my 16 pages of text! As Nibbio had said to me, in the one remaining relevant bit of the interview, 'The situation changes, it always changes.'

In the restructuring, most of those living at Damjl had to move out, and all the young people of Damanhur came together there to form a new group. The people who live at Damanhur, who have dedicated their lives to the community, have to be prepared for such drastic changes. Change is an important principle. When it comes there may be a certain amount of imposition for individuals, though such changes will have been much discussed and prepared in the democratic organizations with a responsibility for social cohesion. While still in its initial stages this new social grouping will be known as the region of Damjl, rather than a community; indeed, it has recently been annexed to the community of Tentyris. Two of the young people, Lira and Gambero, were elected as *Referenti* of the new region. Still in her teens, Lira was as surprised as anyone to see herself propelled into such a responsible position, but she was able to tell me something of the reasons behind the sudden upheaval:

> Things changed because on this territory there was a structure that had no dynamic. We did not have strong objectives, common objectives. And we did not have the focus to realize our goals. Little by little, the situation got worse. The people here were all beautiful, but they were not together, they were like a jigsaw puzzle with the wrong pieces in it. So, Oberto and the Guides had the idea to give this place to all the young people in Damanhur. That is, young people in age, but also in Damanhurian life, those that were new to the community. So there may be 40-year-olds here, but we are all people who arrived when Damanhur was already realized.

In order to bring the group together, Lira and Gambero decided to make them actually fight to win their territory – though only with water, flags and handkerchiefs:

> Gambero and I decided to ask Oberto to organize an attack on this territory. We did not know what we were starting off, but we felt it was important in order to unify all the people. In just two days, we organized this battle. It was young against the older people.
>
> We divided our territory into eight zones. Each zone had a flag of Damanhur and the attackers had to conquer each zone and capture the flag there. We fought with water and what we call *scalpo* – a kind of handkerchief that hangs from

your trousers. If you take another person's handkerchief from them once they are wounded and twice they are dead.

The actual battle lasted from 11 at night until a quarter to midnight. The older ones, they knew all the techniques, all the tricks. They had played games like this many times before. They also knew how to break rules, and so on. In the end they won all our flags.

At the beginning, Oberto and the King Guides said that if we lost, we would have to move out of the territory, but as we had put up a good fight and defended our territory, all that happened was that we had to do seven hours work each, work on the territory, that is. And the others, because they had broken the rules, had to do three hours work each, painting all round the Open Temple, laying circuits and doing renovation work.

Such battles have been used before in Damanhur for various purposes and are part of the Game of Life *(see Chapter 8)*. In this case, fighting for their own territory brought a strong sense of common identity to the young people of Damjl. Now they are working with the more experienced people of Tentyris to make their contribution to the overall community of Damanhur. As Lira so wisely says:

When you teach a baby to walk, the first days you will stay with it and hold its hands. But finally, it will walk alone. The others have experience, we have enthusiasm. We have to dream and dream our hopes for this region. The more you dream, the more you realize.

LIVING AT DAMANHUR

There it is, then, the social structure of Damanhur, in all its magnificent complexity.

It is important to remember that Damanhur is not a revolving-door society. People who live there have chosen to do so after carefully considering all the implications and it tends to be a life-long decision. New people do join Damanhur, but not until they have got to know it well and until the Damanhurians have got to know them. It is one thing to read about Damanhur and to be fascinated with the idea of it, but it is yet another thing to share the work, the engagement, the difficulties of everyday life. Damanhur is no wonderland; being spiritual means working very hard, in a practical sense, to turn dreams into reality.

More important, Damanhur is a society of initiates, totally devoted to the evolution and uplifting of the whole of humanity. It is a huge and very proud mission. People at Damanhur have chosen to always put collective interests before individual ones. They do not claim to be perfect: they are learning as they grow, refining themselves through their errors, changing constantly, just as life changes constantly. For this reason, Damanhur cannot be understood or explained only through words and ideas. It is a living being, a deep and fulfilling experience of transformation, of bringing out hidden or latent talents.

The life rhythms of Damanhur are very intense and fast-paced, and at first people who come there – Italians and foreigners alike – often feel a bit disoriented. Experience has proved that it is much better to approach Damanhur's reality in a gradual and progressive way. Newcomers are encouraged first to come and visit, joining one of the many programmes that the Damanhur Olami Association offers. During such visits, if people then feel close to the project, they can take the further steps necessary to become part of Damanhur's spiritual people and possibly eventually become full citizens of Damanhur.

VAL DI CHY

Not everything at Damanhur proves immediately successful. An idea currently being developed, called Val di Chy, will allow people to settle in the valley, to be close to Damanhur and to share something of the spiritual ideals while still keeping their social and economic independence. Some small steps have taken in establishing Val di Chy, but without success, as yet. It is one thing to come to Damanhur full of wide-eyed optimism and with personal vision, but it is another thing to make it work. Whilst I was in Damanhur, an English family arrived, a couple and four children, ranging in age from two to 13 years. They had not really resolved the practical implications of coming to Damanhur, about where they would live, how they would survive economically, and so on, and they felt that they did not get much help in settling down. In actual fact a great deal of time and attention was given to them, but it did not necessarily fit their own agenda. Damanhur is not an easy place to settle in, however one comes there. It involves struggle, dedication and the giving up of personal interests for a community awareness. Also, to settle in the valley and be connected to Damanhur but retain independence has its own difficulties, primarily financial ones. In theory, the English family knew all this, but found it difficult in practice.

Also in the Val di Chy project were Jan and Jonni, from Belgium. They had bought one part of a medieval semi-detached dwelling in Vidracco. An elderly brother and sister had lived in the two parts, but the sister had died. It was her part of the property that Jan and Jonni had bought. However, the old man, now in his seventies and regarded locally as a bit crazy (though no one had spoken to him for more than 20 years), had been living in the sister's part of the house for over 30 years and Jan and Jonni had to persuade him to move out. They bought a caravan and were living in that whilst they tried to renovate what bits they could get access to of their own property, as well as cleaning-up the old man's part. To make matters worse, he had been collecting junk for over 50 years!

The story of Jan and Jonni is one of unimaginable patience. Eventually, they cleaned out the old man's own property and got it back into a habitable state. Then, over a couple of days, they persuaded him to go back to his own home, and a team of Damanhurian friends moved into their property and stripped it of the junk accumulated there. It was some sight. The courtyard was filled with all manner of old stuff: broken toys, discarded household goods, old wheels, bottles, tins and loads of old magazines and newspapers. Finally, Jan and Jonni could move into their new home and start the real restoration work. In other words, they were back at square one, and it had taken them almost six months to get there.

Jan and Jonni demonstrated the exceptional qualities of fortitude and tenacity that are needed to make life work in this valley. Yet even they did not survive long enough to become a stable part of the development of Val di Chy. Jan specialized in computer graphics and Jonni was a calligraphic artist. They both had an interest in Taoist therapy and had planned to run courses alongside those of Damanhur. For many reasons this seems not to have worked out. The practical means of turning dreams into realities can sometimes be tough. So Val di Chy is yet to be fully realized, as the English family did not make it either, though they stayed longer than I thought they would. The right level of practical, inspirational and spiritual determinants just did not click into place for them. They moved on in search of another dream. Val di Chy still awaits those with just the right finely balanced attributes of self-discovery, dogged tenacity and sound business sense needed to share the Damanhurian vision without adopting the Damanhurian life.

Speaking for myself, I feel that I want to do this inner search because I want to make contact with divine forces and I can feel that there is definitely a powerful presence here.

Melusine

Citizens of Damanhur are initiates. Consequently, citizenship carries with it certain spiritual responsibilities. As well as personal development within the School of Meditation, each Damanhurian chooses one of seven spiritual ways to follow, though many of these interconnect. Citizens are free to leave one way for another, but are encouraged to persevere with their initial choice and to work through any philosophical difficulties. There is a deeply held principle at Damanhur that if you start something you should see it through. This is not totally inflexible. It is principle, not dogma. But the overcoming of personal hurdles and inhibitions is a fundamental part of personal development. The seven ways are intended to help people develop inner strength, to realize their spiritual identity within the context of the day-to-day world that they live in.

Each of the ways has a person with the responsibility to guide, to advise, to counsel other people on that particular path – not a leader as such, but a helper. In order to find out more about the seven ways, I went to speak to the people with responsibility for each of them.

THE WAY OF THE WORD

This is the way of communication. Citizens on this path might teach in schools, run the newspaper or the internal broadcasting network at Damanhur, or deal in external relations. In short, they try to make Damanhur understood, both by its inhabitants and the world outside.

The Way of the Word has several different strands. Essentially there are three main ones. The first is the pathway of the apostles, which is the primary path. That is because the apostles take the word out, in the biblical sense. They spread the word of Damanhur. The two other strands are the pathway of music and the pathway of health. These two take the word out in another sense – in music, because it is a vibration, a sound, just as the voice is a sound; and in health because this deals with communication between people.

The person responsible for the Way of the Word is Albatros Ebano. He told me:

> The Way of the Word was born around the idea of apostles and one of the tasks is to take the word out to those who might want to come close to Damanhur. It is therefore important to have many people who can witness and communicate accurately what Damanhur is all about.
>
> Working together with Oberto, the path has developed a study course of communication. People have grown in such a way that they can now hold conferences without being afraid of speaking in public. Conferences have been held in Holland, Germany and England. People have also learned to hold courses and to communicate with journalists, to speak on television. For us Damanhurians, it is a point of experimental research to be able to develop communication skills, to communicate effectively with each other and with the outside world.

For people on the Way of the Word, this taking the word out of Damanhur is an essential and primary spiritual path. However, it is also necessary to take the word into Damanhur and to create a culture within the community. So the Way of the Word also has the task of developing new ideas, opinions and debates. For example, the daily newspaper *QDq*, which is a central feature of intercommunity communication, is managed, administratively and spiritually, by those of the Way of the Word.

This illustrates how every aspect of life is intertwined at Damanhur. Damanhurians believe that they grow spiritually when they do something materially, productively. 'For us,' Albatros said, 'action is the first movement.' So the spiritual path that someone is on is normally closely related to their occupation.

As regards the newspaper, in making strenuous efforts to get around 16–20 pages of news out daily, the followers of the Way of the Word deal not only with the cultural aspect of communication, but also with the administrative aspects. So, as Albatros said, 'For us, the material and the spiritual are intertwined.'

Music

Albatros also explained how other strands of the Way of the Word fitted into the picture:

> Musical research started several years ago and developed in two directions: the vocal direction, with choral work – the choir is one of the oldest groups in Damanhur – and then the direction of the musicians. There has been a lot of experimentation with music. In our concerts, the music is developed by both the musicians and the dancers, for they need music to dance to. We try to develop new music, new compositions. A lot of this research has been done within the temple.
>
> Music is also a very important part of the rites that are celebrated here at Damanhur. This is a very different kind of music and is composed in different ways from the concert music.

On a separate occasion I spoke to Lepre Viola about the music. She is the person responsible for this particular pathway within the Way of the Word. She is also a teacher of music in the Damanhurian schools and develops much of the music for the concerts in the temple.

> There is a little path, that is the Way of Music, inside the Way of the Word, and I have a part of the responsibility for this, for the people who use music as a means of inner growth.
> The people who play music, or sing inside the temple, have to be on this path for some time. It is different for each person. These tend to be people who use music as a spiritual path, because the music of the temple is a particular kind of music. When you are inside the temple, you are in connection with it, and you have to be clear of mind and focused in order to sing and play.

I was interested to know if there was a particular way of composing for the temple.

> Certainly we have a particular kind of composition – we compose together, not group improvisation as such, but truly communal composition. Other musicians cannot believe it, but we do all work together on a piece of music. We use a lot of meditation and prayer – inner harmonizing.

Lepre believes, like Rudolf Steiner, that people who make music in a spiritual way have a strong connection to the divine. She herself has studied spiritual music, and it was on these researches that she based a musical style for Damanhur. In her book, *La Via della Musica*, Lepre refers to *la dimensione del suono, le musiche per ognuno per ogni momento* (the dimension of sound, the correct music for everyone in each moment). She pointed out that the music in the temple is just as important as the stained glass or the mosaics, for it fills the air with sound and gives the physical body of the temple a certain resonance.

Steiner believed that there is a plane of existence where music and colour live, or, more precisely, the vibration of music and colour. Any musician who wants to have a spiritual contact with music could be in connection with this plane, transforming those vibrations in the music.

Lepre herself has also done a lot of research on the different peoples of the world and how each has their own particular form of spiritual music.

Health

The other strand of this spiritual path is health. People associated with this pathway are involved in wide-ranging research covering all aspects of healthcare and therapy, both from the point of view of spiritual research and practical, day-to-day healthcare. Daman-hurians view illness as an opportunity to learn something, to look at the process of healing, to study its manifestations. They are believers in natural rem-edies and therapies, but not to the extent of turning their backs on conventional approaches to medicine, should they prove necessary. Esperide cleared up some points for me:

We are not fanatics in our approach to healthcare. In Damanhur, we use a lot of natural medicines, especially prana-therapy, but also herbs, colour therapy and now acupuncture. But what is most important is that we also use traditional, conventional medicine. We are not against conventional health-care. Should surgery be necessary, we would wholeheartedly endorse it, if it were the only solution. But where it is possible to use non-invasive therapies, we do so. When it is necessary to combine natural techniques with conventional medicine, we do that as well. It is never a fanatical attitude.

For us, health is a way of life. Being healthy is the environ-ment, it is the thoughts you have, it is the forms around you. We have a holistic approach.

The pranatherapy that Esperide mentioned is the main healing method in Damanhur. Pranic healing is actually one of the oldest and most widespread methods of treatment for physical illness. Based on a form of laying-on of hands, without actually touching, it takes the form of a flow of energy from healer to patient. The healer uses a type of energy called *prana*, which is the undifferentiated energy of life that is always present in the universe. This energy can be consciously directed by the healer toward the patient, using what is known as *chakras*, a Sanskrit word meaning 'wheel'. These are subtle energy centres that vitalize and control the physical body. The patient's aura receives the energy, which serves to vitalize the physical body, especially those organs which most need to regain physical health. Pranic healing is known as the queen of therapies, because it heals on all levels – physical, emotional, mental and spiritual.

Damanhurians do not regard healing as a special gift, but as something that anyone can do if they can access the right energy planes and act as a channel, so they have set up a school of healing that is open to anyone. There are also study centres outside Damanhur, for example in Berlin, Milan, Bologna, Modena and Palermo, and a new centre soon to be opened in Rome.

Most Damanhurians take pranatherapy as a preventive form of medicine, usually about once a fortnight, and more often if they have an illness.

Antilope Verbena, who is co-ordinator of the health programme, has been working in this field for 14 years. Engaged professionally in health services outside Damanhur, having held a number of senior nursing posts and with a current responsibility for a large geriatric care centre, she is able to make comparisons of health statistics and has found a much lower incidence of serious illness within Damanhur. Antilope said:

> We have a clinic here with daily opening hours, in much the same way as a doctor's surgery or any clinical centre. Nurses run the health programme and once or twice a week a doctor comes, a very good doctor, a specialist from a hospital in Turin. He has a regular surgery. There are other doctors we can call on, either day or night. We also have other qualified health professionals based here: two obstetricians and people who work in analytical laboratories.
>
> Nobody works full time here at the moment, though in the past we have had full-time medical people. Damanhur changes, but we try to organize it so that there is always someone patients can be referred to. I work outside Damanhur and

if I am not here, someone else takes over my role. I am also a pranatherapist in Florence.

We also have a diagnostic method, based on processes developed from our Selfic researches, as well as diagnosis by radionics. I do such diagnostic work for people. For us, health is not only a matter of healthcare and research, but is also a means of spiritual growth, hence the fact that we have a Way of Health.

As Esperide had explained, Damanhurians are open-minded with regard to healthcare techniques, but they give prime importance to all natural therapies, which they try to integrate with pranatherapy. In addition, they are doing a great deal of research into the healing use of esoteric physics. People normally walk spirals as a form of meditation, but these can also be set up to have specific healing purposes. Other healthcare techniques use the magical technologies developed at Damanhur. There is no extreme position. If there is one way to cure, it is used; if there is an easier way, it is used instead. The constitution actually states that drugs should not be used; however, in acute cases conventional medicine is considered. At Damanhur they choose whatever they consider best at the time. However, they feel that much allopathic medicine only relieves symptoms, whereas an alternative therapy is more likely to focus on the cause of an illness.

Everyone always has a choice. If they want to use the clinic at Damanhur, they can; if they choose to use outside doctors, they can. Whilst women are encouraged to give birth at home, they do not have to, and can go into hospital should they choose so to do.

There is also a more advanced, futuristic way of healing at Damanhur, developed over years of research in the temple's laboratories, which uses Selfic cabins and instruments. In a room in Damanhur's central area there is a Selfic cabin and a newly developed scanning device which are used for diagnostics as well as remedial treatments. This is a technology based on esoteric physics, which comprises alchemy, Selfica and conventional scientific knowledge. These devices were tested on Damanhurians for many years before they felt confident enough to open them up to a wider public. But the results, even on very serious illnesses, have been so promising as to induce Damanhurians to set up a proper, fully equipped 'Selfic clinic' that is open to anyone. The cabins are also used as a form of preventative medicine.

Every Damanhurian has detailed medical records, including their genetic background. Using such information, the most likely genetically inherited diseases can be predicted and measures of prevention taken. It takes a lot less energy to heal such illnesses at the pre-development stages. Also, when people marry, the genetic backgrounds of the couple can be examined to see whether there are any potential risks to their children.

Damanhurians believe that the soul has a centre around which different personalities are accumulated. These are distinct personalities, with many different aspects, and all combine to make up a person. This theory is examined in greater depth in Chapter 12. However, an affinity is postulated between certain obvious personalities and particular organs of the body. For example, when you say someone has a 'good heart' or that someone is a 'brain box', the reference is to specific personalities within. Such ideas have been finding a recent resonance in the world outside Damanhur.

During my very first visit to Damanhur, in March 1996, I bought an Italian edition of the magazine *Focus* which contained an intriguing article about doctors having discovered a 'second brain' in the stomach area. A news report in *La Stampa* of 27 August 1997 highlighted new research whereby each of the organs of the body is associated with its own particular nervous system. Esperide also showed me a report about a young woman who had developed very different personal characteristics after having a heart and lung transplant. It was a review of a book entitled *A Change of Heart* by Claire Sylvia (Little, Brown, New York, 1997). After the operation she noticed that her attitudes, habits and tastes had all changed. She started behaving in an aggressive and impetuous way completely new to her. Five months after the operation she had a dream in which a young man appeared who she was sure was the donor of her heart and lung. She undertook investigations and discovered she did have the organs of an 18-year-old man who had died in a motorcycle accident. Her experience was causing something of a sensation in medical circles, but for Esperide, it was all readily explainable in terms of the Damanhur theory of personality. If personalities reside in the organs of the body, change your heart and you change one of your personalities.

All these personalities may not, of course, always live harmoniously together. One of the main purposes of being in this present life is to link them all together in a way that they at least get on well, but when there is imbalance, even at a physical level, it might be because the different personalities are competing with each other, each trying to gain control. Such conflicts can be the cause of illness. You might experience stomach pains at night, but not during the day, or headaches in the day, but not at night. These could be linked to different personalities trying to take control at different times of the day. So healing research undertaken at Damanhur attempts to integrate the different personalities. If there is a weakness in one particular organ, they try to work on the personality that is linked to that, integrating that personality with the rest, so that there will be a resolution of the inner conflict. With illnesses such as cancer, there is not the time to do such painstaking analytical work, however. For such serious illnesses, they use the Selfic cabins.

The finance for such research is provided by the Damanhurians, who pay for their health needs. In this respect the Way of Health has to function like a business. Albatros restated the entrepreneurial nature of the communal life:

> Damanhur would not have been able to exist if it were only conceived of at a mental or a spiritual level; it has to have this practical level, the means of self-sufficiency.

Yet it is always part of the spiritual path to anchor the spiritual research into everyday life.

Teaching, Theatre … and Responsibility
The Free University of Damanhur is also run as a business and the Way of the Word supplies teachers who help administer it and develop and run specific courses. Not everybody who teaches courses at the university belongs to the Way of the Word – there are some specialists in other subjects there too. However, the Way of the Word oversees the management of the courses. There are no

fixed compartments at Damanhur, no single way of doing things.

Again, schools are part of the Way of the Word, although not all the teachers are on this path. For some, it is their main path, but others have a secondary involvement, alongside their participation in their first chosen path. In every path there are different levels of belonging. In this way it is possible to belong to more than one path and all the different paths interact with each other.

This is also shown in regard to theatre, which in the past was one of the directions for the Way of the Word. Then this particular strand broke up, with some theatrical people remaining in this path and some going into the Way of Integrated Arts and Technologies. Always at Damanhur, things change.

Another part of the Way of the Word is the public relations department, because its major task is communication with the outside world.

Albatros was the first of the people responsible for overseeing one of the spiritual ways that I had spoken to and I was keen to find out from him just what it meant to be on a particular path, how it related to other aspects of Damanhur.

In the beginning there was the School of Meditation and the spiritual paths were formed many years afterwards. The paths allow people to grow in a way that is closely related to what they do, to their daily life concerns. Everyone has their own spiritual development, everyone has their own different way. There are those who are most suited to developing it through the word, those who would find an artistic way more useful, those who can do it through research into ritual, and so on, and so on...

The responsible person has to think as widely as possible about all the aspects of the path. I have to speak with people in order to stimulate them and see beyond the present, to have a vision of where we might go. I need to put together all the different parts of the way so that it comes together as one organization. I have to organize meetings and even celebrations. I have to create a movement within the organization, just as if it were a human body organizing all its different parts so that they function together. And I have to bring out the best in individuals. It requires a lot of energy to maintain contact with all the various strands, with all the people who are involved, and maintain an overview of it all.

THE WAY OF THE ORACLE

If each of the ways is the spiritual expression of one of the aspects of Damanhur's life, the Way of the Oracle is that part devoted to the contact with divine forces. It is a demanding way because it requires total devotion, inner refinement and a particular form of self-discipline. The principle embedded in such an essential transformation is that of bettering oneself in order to become a channel to the divine. It requires a particular calling, a certain predisposition, a vocation.

The operations carried out by the Way of the Oracle are a constant magic interaction in the daily life of Damanhurians. As far as I can gather, 'magic interaction' means a series of precise and well thought out actions, based on the knowledge of laws that govern things and events in this material world. All Damanhur's actions are constantly contemplated, as are all the cycles of life.

As the Way of the Oracle is specifically directed to the spiritual, magical and sacred, it provides access to a vestal and priestly level. It also utilizes processes and researches at various magical levels, according to exacting ethical rules, all directed towards the positive evolution of humankind.

The way is named after the Oracle of Damanhur, apparently a group of divine forces involved in 'time prospecting', which is described as 'an investigation in time able to move and modify events'. Damanhurians claim to have 'reconquered' and resurrected these investigative pro-cesses in 1985, some 2,500 years on from the Oracle of Delphi.

I spoke with Sirena Ninfea, the person responsible for the Way of the Oracle. Her somewhat charming name means 'Mermaid Water-Lily'. She told me something of the Way of the Oracle:

> This way is the ritual body of Damanhur. For many years we have been working on the sacred rituals and how they

relate to the lives of the people in Damanhur. Here we do not separate the spiritual and the social aspects of life. They are intertwined.

Each month there are many rituals to make contact with the divine forces, to prepare the way to the Oracle, to receive the signs sent to us. The rituals are all linked to the phases of the moon, particularly the waning moon, the last quarter. Then there are specific rituals related to the black moon, the new moon and the crescent moon, the first quarter. These are reserved for initiates, for people who are prepared, who are activated to these contacts, but the ritual for a full moon, which you saw, is a public one.

Sirena was referring to an event that had taken place a couple of nights before we spoke. I had been a privileged observer of the final part of an Oracle ritual. This is a precise, detailed ritual incorporating sacred contact and unwinding, as Sirena had said, during all the four lunar phases. It requires specially prepared and consecrated places, so that questions can be forwarded to the Oracle and the answers can be 'felt'. It is the women members of the Way of the Oracle who are specially prepared for contact with the divine forces and they are called 'Pythias' or the 'Oracle contacters'. Questions can be asked by anyone from Damanhur, not necessarily those associated with the Way of the Oracle. People who do not reside in Damanhur may also consult the Oracle.

The rite of delivering the answers is performed each month, at the time of the full moon, in the Open Temple of Damanhur. All the citizens of Damanhur and any guests who so desire may be present. So we assembled in the appropriate place, as directed, at around 8.30 p.m. I remember that then there was no moon, but the general lighting around the temple and the fire that burned in front of the altar steps illuminated the proceedings in an eerie fashion. There was excellent drumming and the Damanhurians all wore their meditation robes, in the usual white, red and yellow. Sirena Ninfea was leading the ritual, dressed in a blue robe.

There were lots of different stages to the ritual, involving moving sacred instruments around the fire, readings and incantations, and the preparation of questioners. The night we were there, three people asked questions of the Oracle, or rather, received their answers, for they had asked their questions prior to the ritual. They were called, one at a time, into the heart of the temple, guided by one of the Oracle members who carried a candle. The answer to their question was then read to them. All this was to the constant accompaniment of the ritual drumming and flute music. It was a strangely moving experience.

There was a lovely moment when I saw people looking up into the sky. I looked up too. There was a beautiful, big, shining, full moon, radiating its light over all the proceedings.

All three questioners had their answers delivered and the ritual ended as the drumming subsided. The Damanhurians took their robes off straightaway and we headed down to the cars to be transported back to their homes. As we were loading up the boot, I became aware that the only light was that from the street lamps. I looked up and there was no moon at all in the cloud-filled sky.

Later, I asked Sirena about the questions that were asked at an Oracle ritual. She explained:

A reply is passed to the questioners through the ritual, like the old Delphic Oracle. It is always different and depends on what we have received by way of answers. People sometimes ask for interpretations if the reply is not clear.

It is necessary to be in places specially prepared, isolated from the everyday world, in order to prepare for the rituals – not only Oracle rituals, but all rituals. As well as the Temple of Mankind we have other temples here in Damanhur, other sacred places, like the Baita. We stay in these places for several days.

When people consult the Oracle, it is because they do not know what to do, they have decisions to make, but they are undecided as to what direction to take. They are possibly not in tune with the spiritual nature of the question they ask. So they ask the Oracle for help. Groups also present questions and sometimes even the communities ask for some indication as to the line they should follow. The Oracle is therefore active in time, in as much as people ask questions and future events can be changed by the answer.

The reply comes from the work we do, the work in those sacred places, through making contact with the divine forces. Because the reply is in relation to the question, the question itself is very important. If it is not at a suitable level, there might not even be a reply. Sometimes an answer comes in a blinding flash, but at other times it may have to be worked on considerably. The person can only have a reply when there is a right opening for it to be given. Also, the vestal priestesses, the *sacerdotesse*, of the Oracle might have the reply quickly, but the questioner will have to wait for the Oracle of the full moon to receive it. That is the correct moment.

The questions are varied. They might be about family, or work, or how to guide the entire community. Someone might question how best to get insight into something, how they might express themselves better in words, whether it would be better to do one thing rather than another. There might even be questions as to how to help the dead. The only ones that cannot be asked are those with a material or egotistical aspect. I assumed that there would be no point in asking what will win the Gold Cup at Ascot next year! But this ritual of the Oracle is a most important celebration for Damanhurians and is highly respected.

The Way of the Oracle also operates in particular fields of high magic research. Theurgic magic is practised, which involves maintaining a constant dialogue with the divine forces, addressing and awakening their specific energies, bringing into play a controlled use of their powers and combining such researches with alchemical processes at various levels. According to the Damanhurians, this work can profoundly influence the fate of our planet in the struggle against the Enemy of Mankind. The major tasks involve the finding and carrying out of functions related to divinities and to time matrixes, via the operation of alchemy and direct magic. The main intention is to develop an attentive and sought-after rituality addressed to a Grail Force, which in turn is used in the theurgic researches of Damanhur.

Rituals lead to super realities, where events and forms that become creations of the mind are translated to maximum frequencies, changing the universe through the creating power of human being. People who carry out this ritual activity sleep in the places where it is celebrated because they are still in direct contact with it during sleep.

At Damanhur there are several temples in which the Way of the Oracle operates, in particular the Temple of Mankind and the Baita, as already mentioned. The Baita has been prepared over time for hosting high-level magical operations. It is a place of clean energy, where elevated thoughts and positive energies come more naturally. It was originally itself ritually prepared with elevated, constructive and harmonic thoughts that integrated all aspects of life. It is kept constantly and meticulously clean so that the physical and the spiritual can embrace. Here barriers are more easily overcome and divine contacts made.

In such places of spiritual retreat, everybody directs their attention very closely to every subtle aspect of the ritual. Each nuance of each action must be followed, wanted, sought after – dances, movements, words in the sacred language, ancient gestures, everything must be supported by the right energy, brought in by means of special magical instruments. The first magical instruments were made by Oberto and since then have evolved, little by little, over time, according to what was needed at particular stages in the development of Damanhur, as it progressed through many different magical and ritual phases. Rites are also only effective if the vestals and priests are pure, so that they can be free conductors for the evoked energies.

The people of the Way of the Oracle work with modesty and courage, strength and constancy, with the pleasure of serving their ideal and working in friendship. They carry out meditations and studies, including practices such as the observation of mindlessness, prayer, learning formulas of power, investigating the use of silence, of spirals, the potentialities of the mind. They also use dreams as tools to drive ideas and creativity, and to reveal hidden depths, leading to experiences with dimensions that cannot be contacted otherwise.

Dance has now become another part of the Way of the Oracle, although when the paths were first started, it was part of the Way of the Word, because it was related to the sacred language. A characteristic of Damanhur is movement, transformation, change. If something does not work too well, then it is changed. It is development, it is evolution, it is progress.

Time itself is researched as part of this path; experiments are conducted relating to previous existences. Many rituals are necessary for accessing the time roads and the matrixes of the different spiritual forces.

Another very important part of the work of this way is researching and refining esoteric traditions, rituals from every part of the Earth, from every point in time, every people, including the Native Americans, the Mayans, Aztecs and Australian Aborigines, ancient Greeks and Egyptians, Atlanteans and Stonehenge Druids. The ultimate function of the Way of the Oracle is to bring together these ritual practices, unifying the spiritual energies emanating from such specific divine sources. This will be more fully explored in Chapter 15.

Fire is the element of particular importance to the Way of the Oracle. It is guarded and nourished with special care, because it is considered sacred, a symbol of light and a particular vehicle for contacting higher forces. It is used as a part of all major rituals and often the ashes from fires are saved to help guide future rituals.

The Oracle also helps the defence and the magic safety of places, people and territories, for the well-being and health of single people and groups, communities and organizations. Synchronic forces are channelled through specific rituals, so that small and important actions are nurtured and protected.

Another function of the Way of the Oracle (together with the Way of the Monks) is to help the passage of dead persons through the different phases and levels they encounter on what Damanhurians call the 'Threshold', maintaining, through the structure of the People, a connecting thread to this life. New births are recalled and future rebirths programmed. The theoretical basis for this is explained in Chapters 12 and 15.

Basically, the Oracle at Damanhur is comparable to the circulation of the blood that allows an organism to work as a whole. It works actively for the formation and growth of the whole community. As Plato said, in a favourite quote of Sir Herbert Read, pioneer arts educationalist and active anarchist,

An aesthetic education is the only education that brings grace to the body and nobility to the mind.

Damanhur is a place where people grow, refine their creative natures and find the highest order of aesthetic education.

Here is a sentence written for me by Sirena Ninfea in the sacred language of Damanhur, in three different ways: in the ideogrammatic, in numbers and in script:

BE OLAMI CAO LAOR BAV DAMANHUR
EEJ ATALJI JAE CAO

I hope that your days in Damanhur
bring you very much help

THE WAY OF THE MONKS
(formerly the Way of the Monastery)

This is the way of reflection and retreat. Those on this spiritual path do, in fact, go on a sort of retreat for up to two years, or longer if they wish, focusing entirely on their own spiritual growth. It is unique, in Damanhur, in that most of those on this particular spiritual path also live in a common household, the monastery, currently a house known as *Ogni Dove* ('Everywhere'), situated next to the sacred wood and above the Temple of Mankind.

Ogni Dove appears, on the face of it, to be a normal household. The people there go to work, eat their meals together, laugh and joke more than most. There is even a pizza parlour built on to one end of the house. It functions like most of the other Damanhurian nucleo dwellings, but with a particular emphasis on self-discipline and spiritual meditations. Often someone will be going through a period of silence or a period of fasting. But austerity and solemn religiosity are not the norm here – the laughing and joking are plentiful and wholesome, just like any other Damanhurian residence.

Unlike monks in the outer world, the people on this spiritual path keep their normal day jobs and retain many of the links with normal life. However, it is a path that is very much centred on the individual, more than, say, the Way of the Oracle. In most of the other ways, people progress and develop as part of a group, with the structure of their work reflecting their group effort. With the Way of the Monks, the individual is central. The ideas pursued are those of individual silence and fasting, chastity, individual meditation and personal attainment. Being a novice and then becoming a monk is a very individual process. Groups of novices do not become monks together – though they do help each other!

The monastery did not start out as a spiritual path, but as a necessary part of Damanhur. It was created just a few years after Damanhur itself, about 1980, long before the idea of the spiritual paths had developed. At that time some people decided to get together at Porta del Sole to found a spiritual path and have a greater contact with divine forces. They were mostly men because only men were involved in the initial building work on the temple. They equipped themselves with a set of very strict rules: there would be no cars, they would walk everywhere; they could not talk whilst they were eating; they would eat out of wooden bowls and each one would have his own bowl; they could not use gas to cook on, only wood. They got up very early. They had hours of meditation every day. It was more like a monastery, in the conventional sense, then than it is now.

At that time the economic set-up of Damanhur also enabled the monks to live in complete retreat, because everything was put in common and the community financed them to work in the temple. They lived there. They worked there. When they came down to Damanhur, they walked down the hill. It was a very extreme experience, but in this way the monastery was born.

The idea behind the path of the monastery was the need to conserve the subtle energies which were generated in Damanhur. It was felt that a certain group of people could serve as the spiritual containers of the energy generated by everybody's actions.

Initially, this path was something that few people could actually follow. The first group of men really thought that they had made a choice for life. But as the years went by, they realized that they had been too strict on themselves. So the policy of renewal was introduced. At this point some of the men left the path altogether to return to a less harsh regime, but others stayed on. A new group of monks was formed, called the wandering monks. The idea was that they would not live in a monastery, but in the different houses of Damanhur, taking it in turns to bring their experience of the monastery to all the other households. So now some monks remained in the monastery while others went out to live in normal homes with other Damanhurians.

It was another six years before the feminine side of the path was developed and still another year before the Way of the Oracle established itself and set in motion the idea of spiritual paths for everyone. For several years the male and female paths were quite separate. To begin with, not many women wanted to follow the Way of the Monks – well, in fact there was only one. Monaca Gau had been at Porta del Sole when the original group of monks was there, but had not been allowed to take on the status of monk, largely because it was so tied to the building work in the temple. That was why it took such a long time for changes to be brought about. Even after six years, and after the decision to include women on the path, it was still difficult for people to join the Way of the Monks. They had to have already reached a certain initiatory level within the School of Meditation to apply to become a novice monk or a nun (not strictly nuns as such, as in Italian there are male and female monks, *monaco* and *monaca*). Gradually, though, as Damanhur grew larger, more people, male and female, began to ask if they might become monks. It was through this path that they could actually build themselves within. This path could form them. So the novitiate was created.

Each person on this path sees themselves as a container, which they create with their own discipline, so they become like a vase that can receive. They can then keep within themselves both the subtle energies and the ritual energies.

Cicogna Giunco is responsible for the Way of the Monks and I asked her about this idea of a person as a container. She explained:

We are both containers and subliminators. We collect and preserve all the energies produced in Damanhur, through rites and meditations, but also through everything else – people laughing and joking, happiness, sadness, everything. We transform these energies and reroute them as vital energy, which is used for many things, such as the rituals and the activation of the spiral circuits.

The energy is created by discipline and a continual confrontation within the monastery. What is meant by 'confrontation' is that once a week people on this path sit down and talk, and try to plan the inner self and how they see themselves as a body within Damanhur. On the one hand, the path is absolutely an individual path, because everyone has to find their own way of growth, but at the same time it cannot be completely separate from the group, because it is within the group that one forms oneself, measures one's progress.

Monks and nuns, as a rule, are mediators between the initiates and the higher forces. They act as a means of plugging into the higher forces. They have their own ways and means of carrying out this role. One way is by becoming a container, a vase. The other is by dreaming, not in the ordinary sense of having nightly dreams, but by using dreams as a sixth sense. This is a human talent that needs to be developed further. Dreaming is a nightly stage you go through in order to be relaxed, but it is more than that. It is an ability that humans have lost through time and are now trying to reacquire. It is a means of travelling in space, throughout the universe, a means of understanding what form is and of travelling on the Threshold. By developing this dreaming facility there can actually be a bridge with the divine.

This is apparently not like being able to go into a dream journey and letting go. A person directs their dream journey, knowing exactly what they are doing, where to go and what to get. It is all very lucid. This is something the Damanhurians have worked on for many years, with particular training exercises.

For most people, a monastery is a closed place, where people cloister themselves away and are very aloof from the world. It is not, however, the same in Damanhur. 'We could not be containers of the subtle energies of the people,' said Giunco, who likes to be called by her plant name, 'if we were not in contact with them. We would not be able to produce joy within ourselves.' The pizzeria right next to the monastery at Ogni Dove was deliberately placed there for that reason – to maximize the interconnections.

The monks and nuns do, however, have their rules and their path of discipline. For example, there are periods when they do not eat meat and there are other periods when they are allowed to eat it. There are periods of chastity and periods of contact with prayer, which for them is a further contact with divine forces and energies. Giunco explained the reasons behind this:

> The periods when we do not eat meat are in order to clean out our chakras. Chastity allows for the construction of the vessel. Silence is so that we who have to be in contact with others do not waste a word. These disciplines are for our development. But they are not fixed rules, they are like a path, a way to go. They are also about conserving history and tradition at Damanhur. This has two functions: one is to pass it on to the young people, and the other is to conserve it for the older people, to take it for the people and keep it for them.

I wondered about the sort of person who might be drawn to this path. Giunco said:

> There are basically two types: those who can awaken in themselves a creative foundation from which they can reach higher forces, and those who are drawn towards contact with divine forces and understand within themselves the principles and philosophy of Damanhur, how to bring them to life.
>
> This is a very difficult path, not just because of the general disciplines, but also the self-imposed chastity means that you cannot have anyone too close to you, with whom you have a deep and intimate relationship, with all those intense personal sentiments and emotions. You cannot even be married. That is very difficult.

Chastity has always seemed, to me, such a difficult personal discipline. Giunco explained its importance on the Way of the Monks:

> You cannot have that one loving relationship in your life, love in the sense of personal physical feelings, intimate personal feelings, sex. Because if you are not giving love to one particular person, it means that you have got that love within yourself, and you are able to broaden it within yourself, so that you can give it to everyone.
>
> Nevertheless, for us, love as an ability is an important part of our lives, because, when you are in love with someone then you understand them, you are tolerant towards them, you want to help them, to make everything fine for them. We increase those feelings within ourselves, so that we can carry them to everyone.

During my stay at Ogni Dove I had been aware that the community had a special warmth over and above the warm feelings normally experienced in Damanhurian households. This was an embracing warmth, the sort that takes even strangers into it. Most people in the outside world would view a monastery as a very cold place, full of isolation, of people cut off from life, but this was precisely the opposite. It is strange, but you very soon grow to recognize that this person is on a period of silence or that person is fasting. However, there were always smiling faces about the place and that particular warmth.

I spoke to Melusine, who lives there. She has a highly responsible position as a chemical analyst outside Damanhur and one of her internal tasks, I think a devotional one, is the making of particular fragrances for each room in the temple. Like everything else, this comes about after prolonged periods of meditation and research. She told me about what it was like to live at Ogni Dove:

> We have been in this particular house for three years, but I have been a part of the monastery for almost five years. I have been through the preparation as a novitiate and now I have reached a certain level as a nun. I helped to set up this house

here, at Ogni Dove. I was here when the male and female aspects of the monastery decided to come here, to live together. I lived through that experience.

This is a very intense life – happy, friendly and a great deal of fun. Yet at the same time we have to live within certain strict rules. When we are living amongst others, we have to become aware of our personal rules. Life can be a little intense, because there is both the spiritual aspect and the socio-political aspect. Also, Ogni Dove is visited by lots of people. So we have to look after the place and look after the people who come here. Part of our way is to live amongst other people, to be available for the people who come here, people who are searching.

Speaking for myself, I feel that I want to do this inner search because I want to make contact with divine forces and I can feel that there is definitely a powerful presence here. Even though it does require a lot of discipline, and though it is very difficult at first, with time you do realize that this way widens your perception. It does eventually enable you to feel things and perceive things that you were not able to before. It is a way of feeling and behaving towards others. You think less about yourself in order to think more about those who are next to you.

We are channels for the forces that flow through us. When we feel these forces, when the energies are flowing through, there is a real satisfaction.

The Way of the Monks is a path that leads to an equilibrium of many things, to a consciousness and awareness, the physicality of gestures and the nature of subtle aspects. The individual element is important. The plan now is for the monastery to open up, both with regard to hospitality and with regard to study. As Melusine said:

Through our own presence we transmit what we are and what we are learning. It is an important part of the Way of the Monks not only to feel, but also to know and transmit what is the word, through study and through research.

THE WAY OF THE ART AND WORK

This is the path for people who want to realize their spirituality by making sacred the work that they do. They also take care of the economic life of Damanhur and work out the financial strategy for the Federation. In fact the businesses are the lifeblood of Damanhur, both providing opportunities for employment and generating income. When people first come and see the Temple of Mankind, the Damanhur centre, the high quality artwork all around, they inevitably ask: 'Where does all the money come from?' The best answer is probably: 'What does it matter?' But I have been in Damanhur long enough to know that the workshops and artisan businesses make a significant contribution to the survival of the community.

Equally as impressive as the temple and the artwork, when one first visits Damanhur, is the trip round the workshops – the weaving looms producing cloth of superlative quality at Atelier Damjl, the cheeses all lined up at the Commune Buona Terra, the exquisite food production and packaging at Compagnia della Buona Terra, the special agritourism and farm restaurant at Tiglio, the marble, mosaic, terracotta and Tiffany glass workshops in Damanhur itself.

At every place of work there is a large Self radiating particular energy. Like those doing the work, it contributes to the process, introducing yet another 'added factor' into what is being produced.

Sparviero Ginkobiloba not only runs the Atelier Damjl, the high-quality weaving workshop, with his wife Lama, but also heads the Way of the Art and Work. So, with the sound of handlooms in the background, as the weavers produced many more centimetres of beautifully hand-woven cashmere, thread by thread deftly yet delicately put into place, I asked Sparviero how it all came about. 'It all started many years ago,' he told me.

We needed to make clothes ourselves. We had to learn how to make material and how to dye it with natural colours. We started out with small wooden handlooms, like the ones we still use in the workshop. This would be in 1983.

At first the weaving workshop did not take off, so Sparviero and Lama decided to turn it into a business and to take a determined look outside the community for business opportunities, whilst still, as Sparviero put it, 'living in harmony with the movement of necessity'.

They started to make contact with various designers, people in the world of fashion. They felt it was important to take with them the philosophy of products made by hand. It was necessary for them to see whether it was commercially viable for them to do that, for if there were no commercial potential there would be little point in doing it in this way. The same went for the natural colours, the natural dyeing. They put forward the suggestion to other, larger companies and designers and offered their dyeing services to people who were producing large quantities of cloth. It was the large companies that then sold the idea to the public. If you are a small workshop in Damanhur, you do not have the marketing resources to sell large volumes of cloth, however good it is. The large companies, on the other hand, have all the resources to market a new idea, to sell the notion of expensive, naturally dyed clothing to a wider public.

Samples were done for these companies, resulting in orders to dye hundreds of thousands of metres of cloth. It was work that came in great waves – the workshop was very busy at certain times, not so much at others. But this left time for research and development.

In recent years, the business has expanded enormously. But the problems with operating at an industrial level with what is essentially a hand-made product are actually much greater than if it were manufactured in an industrial manner. The problem is not getting the orders, but getting them done. The Damanhur workshops not only sell as much as they can make, but often their work is already sold before it is made. Earlier, they made stuff and then tried to sell it. Bad business. The finances were always precarious. Now, it is orders first.

'Look,' said Sparviero, 'I can show you this line for this company. Every day, this company takes in 18,000 kilos of wool. Every day. So you can see what type of business we are dealing with. We do a lot of work for this company.'

He showed me colour sample catalogues for the many major companies and large designers that they now deal with, exquisitely beautiful and expensively produced catalogues. The range of wools and cashmere is extensive. The most famous manufacturer of cashmere in the world has Damanhurian materials in his catalogue. Sparviero showed me the lines that they supply to this exclusive firm. They are of excellent quality.

When Damanhur first started out, all the businesses were centrally controlled, all part of the communal organization. But it did not work. Now, there is something like a communist business structure run by a capitalist mentality. 'Look, it is simple really,' said Sparviero.

> I am here for Damanhur. I am not here to work. If I just wanted work and to run a business, I could go anywhere to do it, to one of the flourishing centres of industry. But I am here because I am part of Damanhur. We are here to work, to study, to make beautiful things, to create wealth, to live a more interesting life. All these things are part and parcel of being here at Damanhur.
>
> If tomorrow 200 people come here, where do we put them? What do we do with them? We have to work hard. This activity can maybe fund and support the development of another activity, and in this way Damanhur grows.

In any nation there has to be a balance between income generated from outside and the amount that is spent on the national community. Damanhurians have had to come to terms with that reality. The way they seem to have done it is to make the businesses autonomous, while still keeping a shared ideal. Sparviero told me about their plans for the future:

> The future of this business is not production orientated, it is to be more creative. We are organizing ourselves so that we can have the production work done outside, sub-contracted. Here we will create, design and develop new ideas.
>
> At the moment we have two looms outside, with people we know. We have given them the looms and we send them the drums of mixed coloured cashmere and the technical designs, and they make the material. Our dream is to have 100 looms outside, working for us. Only 98 to go!

If we can provide work for many people in the valley, this will also help break down some of the long-term antagonism that some local people have felt towards us. It will help us form strong relationships.

This workshop is certainly a cracking example of how you can run a business creatively and still be financially viable. But how do those on this path manage to realize their spiritual goals through their work? Lama explained that through work, they are actually going on an inner journey in order to know themselves better, to become aware of themselves from their most superficial aspects right down to their deepest parts. Every person in every kind of work can do this. And every instant can be different from the one that went before it, even if you do the same work for 10 years. Lama was keen to give us an example:

> In Damanhur, you must have heard us speak of the journey. This is about keeping an inner dynamic condition, something that is not static. It is about attention and awareness, watching what comes out of yourself, through work, and being able to recognize this, accept it as it is. It is a mental thing, an attitude.
> Of course work is much better, much more satisfying if it is creative and if it is stimulating. But with the right attitude of mind, the right mental approach, even the most mundane task can become interesting. It is not repetition, even if you are only sending the spindle backwards and forwards...

I could understand that focusing on the work, understanding it with every cell of your body, with every action that you perform, would bring its own rewards. This helped make sense of why people would want to follow a spiritual path that was about work. An old film title popped into my mind: *Work is a Four-Letter Word*. Sparviero laughed mischievously:

> There are still a lot of people who think that evolution only happens when you do a ritual or develop creative ideas. But work is an occult path. Not everybody believes that, even here.

There are those who take this as their primary path and those for whom it is a second path, then there are those who, shall we say, are laterally involved in it. But work is a spiritual pursuit. And the more you are convinced that what you are doing is a really important ritual, the better.

The Way of the Art and Work is a down-to-earth path. But the worker acts as a bridge to the divine. The inspiration is spiritual but is transmitted practically to the material world. This is the best way to awaken matter. When the bails of cashmere arrive, it is just cashmere wool, but when it has passed through the spiritual work process, it becomes a very special sort of cashmere. The same would apply any other of the products. Understand that and you understand a lot about Damanhur.

THE WAY OF ESOTERIC COUPLES

People who choose to place their relationship at the centre of their spiritual life may choose this way as their spiritual path. These people are responsible for much of the child-minding, taking care of children in the broadest sense of the term: their education, health and well-being.

There is a well-developed attitude towards marriage at Damanhur. Couples wishing to come together can commit to each other for specific lengths of time. Others might choose to stay together, to bring up children, to marry in a much deeper sense of the word. This is not a lax attitude towards marriage. Just compare it to the general social mores in the West at the moment, that gives the option of marriage or living together.

In Damanhur, there are two different types of wedding, one standard, one esoteric. Both are for set lengths of time: one year, two years or three years. They are renewable, should the couple so decide. The Damanhurian belief is that a union of love is a precious gift, because a happy couple can bring harmony, stability and growth. The act of marriage is a serious business. That is why they renew their wedding bonds, so that being together is always a choice, a desired commitment, and never an obligation.

The standard form of wedding involves a ceremony in the Open Temple or in some other spiritual place in the presence of the People. More and more couples are coming to Damanhur to get married in this way.

The actual ceremony is a simple but touching one, open to people of all creeds and philosophies. The bride and the groom stand in front of each other, their hands united and raised in front of their chests. At their side, stand the two witnesses, who commit themselves to being an active support to the couple. The celebrant pronounces this ritual formula:

Stand one in front of the other.
Now join both your hands, palm with palm.

This gesture means 'I am with you'.
With it you manifest your free will
to unite your individual paths to face together
whatever the School of Life may confront you with,
helping and supporting each other for a period of … year(s).

May the Positive Forces, whatever be Their name,
be the witness of what you are accomplishing
and bless this union born out of your love.
May this bring spiritual advancement to you
and to all our fellow human beings.

Let a kiss be the seal of your will.
In name and on behalf of Damanhur and the People,
we accept and recognize this union.
May it bring growth, harmony and beauty, wherever you are.

That is the standard form of marriage, but then there is a deeper, esoteric marriage, which is magical in nature and in which the bodies of the two people are joined into one. From the energy that is given through the ceremony, a common entity is built from the two people who are being married.

In the standard form of marriage, there is no absolute insistence on being sexually faithful. It is left to the couple to decide such things for themselves. In the esoteric form of marriage, there has to be absolute fidelity, because otherwise the special body would be destroyed. This has nothing at all to do with morals, but everything to do with respect, respect for the celebration of this sacred form of marriage.

Again, this form of marriage is for a fixed period. But it is actually a very deep process. In the first two years the participants are required to verify and renew their marriage regularly, because esoteric marriage is a very intense experience. Moreover, it requires a great deal of preparation. There is a long period of sexual abstention, prolonged meditation and a sharing of karma. This path offers the experience of one as shared through the other. So there are people who take this path because they want to experience a completion, to put at the centre of their lives a union of the masculine and the feminine.

Whilst I was first at Damanhur, Ramarra Bucaneve was responsible for this spiritual path, but now it is Alapaca Lavanda. Both Ramarra and Alpaca have been married to their partners in this way for a long time. Ramarra has been married to Cormorano for 13 years, Alpaca married to Castoro for 12 years. There are many on this path within such marriages. Some come into such a marriage when they want to have a baby, because this gives the couple a better chance of creating the right body for an elevated soul.

During the long marriages, there is constant renewal, whenever couples feel the need to renew. All ceremonies are held in the temple spaces, either the prayer temple at the Damanhur centre or at the Sun Door in the Temple of Mankind. The esoteric wedding requires a place of particular sacred significance and the couples wear their ritual robes for it.

On a practical level, the prime responsibility of this particular path is to provide spiritual guidance for the children of Damanhur. The bringing up of children is the responsibility of all citizens of Damanhur, but the Way of Esoteric Couples is very active in everything to do with education. Together with those of the Way of the Word, the people of this path prepare special education programmes and are responsible for the spiritual elements within the school curriculum.

THE WAY OF THE KNIGHTS

Those of this way – mostly but not exclusively men – do much of the construction work on the temple. They also act as security guards and firemen, and are often called upon when there is a fire in the locality. They have received a gold medal from the Italian Forestry Commission for their bravery in fighting fires, dealing with floods and other emergencies, and their services are now regularly called on locally.

I spoke to Picchio Abete, leader of the Way of the Knights. He told me that this way is 'a big School of Meditation, a way of thinking by practical action'. It was established in 1990, along with several other of the spiritual paths, and came to express itself through the need to defend Damanhur and through the building of the temple.

At the start, the overall philosophy of this path, concerning the way in which a physical practical action corresponds to an interior movement, had already been laid down. So the path's initial main development was on a social, practical level. For example, as guards, those on this path dealt with matters concerning civil defence and protection – putting out fires in the woods, and so on. They also created a defence system that could guarantee the safety of the houses and the people. This path had people with considerable practical knowledge about architecture and the construction industry and they built a large part of the Temple of Mankind.

But along with all this practical work, there was also the inner, spiritual part of the path. As part of this, a form of magical defence was developed. Picchio said:

> I will try to explain the concept of magical defence in the simplest way possible. It is a model of approaching or taking a particular attitude towards reality, through which we can express certain actions, and there are certain events that we call synchronistic, that correspond to these actions, that magically produce a result. For example, you have seen the large gate at the entrance to Damanhur. That gate has no locks. From our point of view, closing that gate is a magical gesture. However, from a logical point of view, somebody could just open it. But from a magical point of view, it is a defence.

So, of course, there are many rites associated with magical defence, positive and practical actions that we take in order to make the idea potent. It is not just some superstition, something that happens by accident. We make ourselves aware of all our territories and we protect them with our thought. This has an effect on the events at Damanhur.

Set out that way it sounds very simple, but, because the practical aspect cannot do without the aspect of thought, of meditation, this idea is actually a very fundamental one.

Picchio explained that the research conducted by the Way of the Knights had led to some interesting discoveries in the temple:

We discovered a great deal working in the temple, a lot of things that can be communicated more with the heart than with the mind. I can tell you one thing that we found, that we call the '33 ritual metres'. It is a correspondence between the material excavation of the temple and the interior excavation in one's own soul.

Also, we discovered the difference between a group of people working together and people working individually. There is a profound difference between the work of the collective group and that of a single person. The work of the collective group would always be greater in quantity and quality than if the same number of individual people had worked for the same overall length of time.

So for example, the work that is done in the temple is really heavy work, but it has happened that people who have worked there in groups have gone away with more energy than they came in with originally.

I asked Picchio to clarify the idea of the 33 metres, as it was a term I had heard others use in relation to work in the temple.

This was an idea that Oberto came up with and we interpreted in our own way. It brings together the practical and the spiritual side of Damanhur. In order to build certain parts of ourselves, we knew it was necessary to build part of the temple. And Oberto told each of us that we had to build 33 metres.

At one time this was quite literally the case and people actually excavated 33 metres in the temple – 33 metres of rock, their own height and width. They even worked out how many buckets it would be and arranged competitions for getting the 33 metres done first. Picchio said that was because they were very young, then, in terms of their thought. Now, the 33 metres expresses the best qualities of each individual. If very good painters were to come to Damanhur, what would be the point of expecting them to dig 33 metres? It would be far better to have them paint 33 metres or do any amount of work equivalent to 33 metres of digging – putting a roof on a building, say, clearing dead trees from the woods or constructing a beautiful computer programme on the Internet.

Picchio's 33 metres are expressed in the area of security:

Damanhur had a need for security. The fires in the woods, for example, were sometimes started deliberately, especially in winter, by people from outside. The problem for people outside is that for many years Damanhur has been seen as different and therefore possibly dangerous. Public forces, such as the *carabinieri*, have been dead set against us. So, even though, for example, people have come into our car park and slashed all our tyres, we could not be seen to retaliate in any way…

We always reported such incidents to the police, though. And over the years, we have gradually won their trust. Nowadays, whenever we point out that something is wrong, they come to help straightaway. But we aim to prevent calamities, not suffer them, and we have our own emergency service. Our way of thinking is geared to prevention, rather than defence.

The biggest work Esperide did was in defending us from the attacks of journalists and it was more difficult because it was a legal attack. Around 1992 local public opinion seemed to be turning against us, with the help of some outside forces, the Church and some local politicians. Certainly, when the temple was revealed publicly, it was a very difficult time for

Damanhurians. Esperide used her 33 metres to defend us very effectively.

But the *cavalieri* form of defence is more physical than civil. We have a responsibility to physically defend our territories, but rather than resorting to aggressive measures, we use rituals to effect protection, first of all, with thought. We created these rituals ourselves. This was the work of the Way of the Knights.

I enjoyed meeting Picchio. He is a strong character, a man who gives off confidence. I would feel secure if he were protecting me. Life at Damanhur is good for Picchio and he is an ideal example of how effective this community actually is.

THE WAY OF INTEGRATED ARTS AND TECHNOLOGIES

This path is very important to those involved in creativity, in all manner of ways, whether creating artwork for the temple, creating the website interface with the world outside or producing artefacts that have a commercial potential. It is composed mainly of two groups: the artists, who create and take care of the visual art created in the community, as well as teaching it in schools and experimenting with new forms and imagery; and those who deal with the technology at Damanhur, setting up links on the Internet, implementing alternative technologies or maintaining computers, as well as working with video and the internal television channel.

Art and aesthetic research are at the heart of all the spiritual paths, but this one in particular. They are tools capable of giving substance to a creative expression that is most obviously displayed in the Temple of Mankind, but pervades many other aspects of life in the community. The sacred in Damanhur is a concrete reality, created by sharing, the offering of creative efforts and strength in the realization of a common ideal.

For those on this path the development of heightened creative faculties is part of a sublime process, a way of getting in tune with themselves at the same time as getting in tune with the divine.

The development of the art in the temple is a direct reflection of the quality of the meditation, the results of following a particular spiritual path. There is a quality about the artwork that raises it above the mere application of paint or the sculpting of terracotta. The emotion most people experience when seeing the temple for the first time is undoubtedly connected to the high level of spiritual energy that has gone into its creation.

Piovra is always ebullient, always ready to talk about the temple artwork. When I asked her what she thought I should write about it, she was profound:

What is most important is to put across a feeling of the complexity of it, not in a numerical or a practical sense, though the quantity of the artwork is in itself significant, but more in terms of the inner complexity of the experience, as it has been developed and as it will continue to evolve.

What I would like to happen is that when someone looks at the temple, they become aware that every millimetre of it has a significance and represents that inner complexity. I would like them to realize that every millimetre has some meaning, both for those who created it and for those who encounter it.

She had a special request for me:

If you can, in the book, please put forward the idea of just how much meaning there is in the temple. It is important, not only in terms of complexity itself, but also to remind people that Man has no limits. This is the significance of complexity, that Man has limitless potential. Possibilities are infinite. I hope that the temple will stimulate people to evolve their own selves, their own souls. That, I think, is most important.

What drives the people in Damanhur is a spiritual motivation that grows out of their studies in the School of Meditation, but which is honed and refined in their particular spiritual path, or paths, for some choose more than one. This motivation invariably results in a creative expression, best seen from the artwork in the temple, but also evident in all practical manifestations at Damanhur, be it the fabrics created in the weavery, the foodstuffs sold around the world or the agricultural innovations taking place on the farms.

The spiritual ways are the means whereby an individual is able to indeed exalt their uniqueness, their differences, to render them precious and irreplaceable. They offer the possibility of following very precise practical and spiritual objectives as well as developing individual capabilities. So Damanhur itself becomes richer and stronger.

*I had employment in industry, working as a chemical dyer
for eight years. I could not stand it any longer. The demands of
working in industry were absolutely crazy. So I came to Damanhur. Here I am free to experiment, to develop my craft. Here
there is an exchange of ideas.*

Lontra Bambù

An important part of the development of Damanhur has been
that of the companies and arts workshops, which not only provide
satisfying employment for many of the citizens of Damanhur, but also
help to stabilize the economy. Damanhur is a tightly knit community
of creative and talented artisans and entrepreneurs, producing a
range of high-quality goods, from foods, textiles and ironwork to
ceramic work, mosaics and stained glass.

I walked up the road from the main centre of Damanhur to an
ordinary-looking industrial-type of building. On the sign outside, in
a beautifully designed graphic, were the words *Compagnia della
Buona Terra* (Company of the Good Earth). I had heard about this
business and seen some of its products, and I could hardly wait to
see Tigre Ciliegio, the man in charge of it. I asked him about the

relationship between this company, the largest at Damanhur in terms of turnover, and the Federation of Damanhur:

> The Compagnia della Buona Terra is part of the philosophy of Damanhur. We have a philosophy about food that we call the 'Gospel of Food', which lays down elementary principles.
>
> The company was born in 1975, along with Damanhur. It aims to provide a service and to disseminate our philosophy of food. It was set up as an Aquarian Age business, with the idea that there should be an equilibrium between the way it is administered and the economics in terms of capital, and that everybody within it should be equal, but each with their own function. We also hoped to try to find an equilibrium between spiritual, personal and economic demands. In the outside world, many people are unhappy in their work, because there is no such equilibrium. We do feel we have found some sort of equilibrium here. However, we are still striving, still trying to realize an ideal.

The main work of the Compagnia della Buona Terra is selling produce to the outside world in order to bring finance back into Damanhur. Some 95 per cent of the total product goes out of Damanhur and of that 20 per cent goes abroad. They have sold to the top companies and some of the most select retail outlets in the world, including Fortnum and Masons in London, the Abu Dhabi Airport Duty Free and some of the largest stores in Italy, Japan, Scotland and Germany. They also have a direct sales network throughout Italy, Germany and parts of France, as well as 80 smaller shops in America.

For Damanhur this is a big company, though to put it into some sort of perspective, compared to others in the food industry it would be a middle-sized firm. Still it is one of the largest luxury food companies in Italy and for a community of 700 people this is an important achievement. Even on the simple business level, it is good news. But given that it employs people in a satisfying and rewarding way, it is excellent news.

It is not just that the Damanhurians decided the luxury foods market was where they could make a lot of money – it was something that evolved out of the way that they work. In comparison to industrially manufactured products, the standards at Damanhur are extremely high and this had to be reflected in where they would find markets for their wares. The same applies to the beautiful cashmeres and fine silks that come from the Atelier Damjl.

People go to work at Damanhur not so much in terms of how many hours they have to do, but in order to accomplish a task that needs to be done. The work is always carried out by hand, with spiritual guidance and in a happy working environment, utilizing Selfic instruments to activate the vital energies of the products.

Of course, there is a big difference in production costs between systems where everything is done by hand and those where products come off conveyor belts and machines in factories. You will not hear the word 'factory' in Damanhur. All the work there is carried out in 'laboratories' or 'workshops'.

In the BBC *Newsnight* programme that I mentioned in the introduction, there was an interview with Lontra Bambù which implied that he had been a master dyer in the world outside, but at Damanhur was doing the same work with no pay and was not even able to keep his name. Lontra's Italian was translated in the overdub into something completely different. He was upset and annoyed, and said he would never be interviewed again. However, I did manage to persuade him:

> For me, that interview was a great disappointment. Those television people had seemed so nice. In fact, the woman who did the translation said that she would try to read beyond my words and try to communicate what I really meant. Just the opposite happened...
>
> I had employment in industry, working as a chemical dyer for eight years. I could not stand it any longer. The demands of working in industry were absolutely crazy. I was never into money, I was not a bread head, so coming here to Damanhur was no problem. In industry, they have reached standards that are fixed and you just go down the same track each time. So I came to Damanhur. Here I am free to experiment, to develop my craft. Here there is an exchange of ideas.

There is some satisfaction, for Lontra, in being able to produce work that now goes into the most prestigious fashion houses of the world and finds its way onto the catwalks, yet is produced by experimenting with natural elements to produce the colour. Many people at Damanhur find similar satisfactions. They find ways of working there that they would just not have access to anywhere else and are able to work on a scale and to a depth that would not be possible elsewhere. They are able to experiment and occasionally may make mistakes, but out of this comes the opportunity to develop their craft to the highest standards.

All this did not come about by accident. Through the Way of the Art and Work and through the School of Meditation, careful thought went into the spiritual development of all methods of production and into the reasons behind such production. Tigre explained to me:

> Our real purpose at the Compagnia della Buona Terra is to teach the way to eat in accordance with our way of thought. This means eating with imagination and colour, changing the sorts of foods you eat regularly, avoiding all forms of pollutants and trying to use the finest quality foods.

Damanhurians do eat very well, using fresh and organically grown foods and giving a great deal of attention to the way they are prepared and presented. In the households, food preparation is a cherished task and cleaning up afterwards is equally pleasurable, because it is a gratifying way of sharing. Tigre elaborates:

> Something that looks good will taste good. Presenting the food well also shows respect for the product that one is eating. It is important to remember that it is alive. We survive, as a species, by finding additional sustenance in other forms of life.
>
> We produce food with love and we believe that if you respect food, then it will respect you. This is why we do everything by hand, because we feel that we have to have a relationship with the food we are producing so that it can transmit life back to us when we eat it.

Food preparation is just as much an artform as the ceramics or the Tiffany glass and is treated with as much care and attention. For example, work is currently being done on the design and production of the beautiful glass containers some foodstuffs are packaged in. At the moment they are made for the Compagnia della Buona Terra at the famous glass workshops of Murano. However, in the future, the company plans to start making them themselves. This is just one area of creative and imaginative development. At Damanhur they are always looking for such creative opportunities.

In the food workshop they follow a process that is called 'Selfization', in which the foodstuffs arrive at one end of the building and are stored there pre-process. Then they are brought into the food laboratory itself, where they are processed and packaged. Next they pass into a despatch area where they are boxed and crated. Finally, they are taken away to the shops of the world. At each stage, the foodstuffs pass through a Selfic process by way of a large Selfica panel high on the walls of each area, radiating subtle energies which revitalize the foods.

It seems to work like this. When food is harvested, its vital energy immediately begins to diminish. By the time it has been packaged, gone through wholesale and retail outlets, and taken home, it hardly has any vital energy left. If the food passes through the Selfic processes, however, it is recharged with vital energy and has the same quality as if it had just been freshly gathered. The final Selfic structure, in the despatch area, is the one that fixes this vital energy, the energy of life, the *prana*.

Tigre told me about some experiments they had done using Kirlian photography that showed renewed vital energy following the Selfic process. He showed me the photographs. And I can vouch personally for the only real test – just how good the food tastes.

Fifteen people are employed at the food laboratory, but at times when large orders need to be got out, such as at Christmas, many people go there and give of their time. This is something that people outside the community sometimes find difficult to understand. How-ever, the whole of Damanhur is a mutual reciprocal process and the Compagnia della Buona Terra plays its part by bringing a great deal of revenue into the community.

Cheese-making is another business carried out at Damanhur through a co-operative process. The wide range of excellent cheeses are all top-quality products, made in large vats out of milk from Damanhur farms, matured for varying lengths of time and all passing through the Selfic process to tap into the 'added value' that is a consequence of links to subtle forces. The cheeses are sold through the shop at Damanhur or marketed to a number of other local outlets. The smell of the cheese in the maturing store is a pleasure beyond belief and the quality of the cheeses is exceptional.

Agritourism – people staying as guests on farms in return for their labour or their agricultural skills – is another idea that is being developed at Damanhur, in this case at a very pretty farmstead called Tiglio. The very old farm buildings are being restored using natural materials, whilst all manner of crops and vegetables are being grown under organic conditions in abundant open fields and neat rows of greenhouses. Already, many people with radical ideas on agriculture have been to stay there and in turn have helped the development of the project. Tiglio also has its own restaurant, where the very best home-grown produce is served.

Fauno, who is running the project, is justifiably proud of it:

At Damanhur we are more entrepreneurial nowadays. We are independent, but we also work for the community. These are two sides of the same coin. I am working for Damanhur, I have no problem with that, but I also want to make my own choices regarding growth and development, investment and finances.

We believe in this project. It will cost a great deal to do the renovation work. But my big dream is that this will be an eco-logical island: ecological energy, from solar power and from wood; ecological food, grown organically; and clean thoughts. When people come to stay here or eat in our restaurant, we can serve good food, all produced here, without pesticides or anything. They can have hot water, too, without using electricity. We are in harmony with nature.

The workshops at Damanhur also have fine reputations and are making great strides in developing new techniques. The terracotta workshop is known for its specially made claywork and as a consequence gets many commissions to contribute pieces to newly built houses or to properties under renovation. Ornate supports for shelving or balconies, balustrades, caryatids, decorative stanchions and all manner of garden ornamentations are made there. The workshop has also collaborated with the mosaic workshop in manufacturing decorative bases for tables with inlaid mosaic tops. The mosaic workshop itself is producing high-quality mosaics for floors and wall panels, for which there is an increasing demand.

The copper and iron workshops also supply bespoke work for outside customers; in fact almost all the Damanhurian businesses are now engaged in extensive trade outside the community: Tiffany glasswork, jewellery, Selfica, publishing bookshop and restaurants, not to mention the Sunday open market inside Damanhur, which is now attracting many hundreds of visitors from near and far. Many of the workshops provide art and craftwork for sale at this weekly exposition.

All the Damanhurian businesses manage themselves, though they are invariably run on co-operative lines. But they are not profit-making organizations. There are no fat-cat directors at Damanhur, giving themselves huge salary increases, and there are no directors taking dividends on their shares. Where shares are notarized, it is simply to ensure a fair and equitable responsibility for resources, say in a co-operative where a number of people have invested. All the excess proceeds go back to the community in some form or other. Of course, it might be that one year the board of a company needs to spend some of its proceeds to reinvest in itself. Such decisions are made at the conclusion of each financial year. But all the businesses exist for the common good of the people of Damanhur. Tigre explained:

> We have to present annual accounts to the Italian authorities, just like any other registered business, and we go to great lengths to ensure that everything is in order with the Italian state. Any donation that we make at the end of each year to Damanhur is a voluntary one. There is no obligation that it must be a fixed sum, or a percentage of our turnover, or whatever. We simply work out what we need for investment into the

company for the following year in order to develop and grow, and then we invest the rest in what we are all here for: Damanhur and its people.

A further development occurred as I was putting the finishing touches to this book. A new system is now springing up in Damanhur, a whole new way of looking at work. Small groups of people have been set up to discuss how best it might be developed. There are 28 such groups, with eight people in each group, so that over a third of the resident population of Damanhur is involved in this enormous project. The overall objective is to put energy into this field, to rethink and restructure it. Like everything at Damanhur, work is a dynamic process. By the time you read this, the way work is organized in Damanhur may well be very different.

I am one of the founders of Damanhur and all I want is what is owed to me.

Filippo Cerutti

Over 250 officers stormed the place, with pistols drawn, machine guns at the ready and helicopters hovering overhead.

Coboldo Melo

The newspaper articles in the archives at Damanhur make very interesting reading. Up until early 1991, most of them, local, national and international, were about what the community was doing on a practical level: courses, ecological projects, experiments in social living. The articles are often a little tongue-in-cheek, making fun of the animal names, for example, like the national newspaper *Italia Oggi* of 18 September 1987 which, in an otherwise quite serious article about the way Damanhur was not a religious sect, could not resist remarking:

The head of government, slyly, is a woman, who of course has to conform with the ritual that everyone who comes to

Damanhur has to get a new name: she is now 'Little Pink Elephant' and trying not to lose her seriousness as a thirty-three year old researcher with a masters degree in political science.

or the local paper *Corrieredi Chieri* that reported on 13 July 1990 about two new citizens who had moved to Damanhur:

> It is very difficult not to lose the notion of reality when dealing with people who think that elves and fairies really exist, and that you can meet them. Not everyone can do that, but these entities can become concrete reality: elves, goblins, cobolts. For some, like children, it is easy to see them. Others can get in touch through their dreams. We have never seen them.

Then there was the 1989 report in *La Stampa* on the newly established community of Tentyris headlined:

> Sex will not be taboo any more.

What was the sex angle? Well, Tentyris means 'city of women' and the press release the journalists would have worked from would have explained that the first groups of people who had moved there had done so because there was a link with water and the feminine principle and that they had all gone there to explore the feminine side of their nature, to explore new ways of becoming better men and women. Obviously the headline editor could not grasp such subtle nuances.

There were more serious reports, too, including some on the Warm Oil project on self-sufficiency *(see Chapter 8)*. There were 118 people living in Damanhur at that time and *La Stampa* of 12 June 1986 explained that they were all now following the example of six pioneers:

> ...who have just finished the survival experiment in a farm, lost in the heart of Valchiusella. We see that in one year the little city will be totally self-sufficient, producing its own food, clothing and furniture for the houses.

Il Giornale also reported on the same project on 24 July 1986:

A dream it may be, but they assure us in Baldissero that it is not like that. Several months ago they started the survival project. One of the goals was to verify the necessities of individuals placed under extreme conditions. So for the clothing aspect, they studied which clothing was really necessary, because of its protective qualities and aptness for the environment...

The fields of the community of Damanhur produce little apricots, peaches, herbs and other delicious things, that without any chemical trace are packaged in beautiful vases. They have on top the label of one of the most prestigious shops in Milan.

The local papers took up the weaving theme of the project in particular, as weaving was the primary industry in Piedmont before the days of Fiat and Olivetti. So the idea of using old looms had a romantic fascination for the local people, involving the renewal of lost traditions and recapturing heritage.

At the time of the Chernobyl nuclear accident there was also a lot of interest in what the ecologically-minded Damanhurians thought of it and what measures could be taken to limit the dangers from nuclear fall-out. There were also many articles about the courses being run in Damanhur, the projects and the work in the forests. The general impression the press gave was of a community that was perhaps a little wacky but nevertheless working in harmony with the environment, with the technological, political and economic goals of self-sufficiency. The Damanhurians themselves were portrayed as serene and secure people who were generally friendly neighbours.

However, in 1991, the hard-line Cardinal Saldarini was sent from the Vatican to sort out the Turin region, which was felt to have become a resting-place for many groups with Satanic leanings. There were indeed a few groups in Turin that were openly Satanic, but the vast majority were what we would now call New Age groups as well as Theosophists, followers of Gurdjieff and so on. However, the new cardinal went about his task with relish, claiming, in a major article which appeared in the influential *Il Giornale* on 16 February 1991:

> Adultery, fornication, impurity, libertinism, idolatry, enmity, discord, enviousness, jealousy, drunkenness, orgies, witchcraft, sects, sex and gurus – these are the new magical and esoteric movements, communities put up by the ruthless Santoni [Big Saints], all dedicated to orgiastic rituals and free love. In Italy there are about six hundred such groups, about thirty in and around Turin... And the most populated in Italy is right on the hills of Valchiusella, next to Baldissero Canavese, and it is called Damanhur. There live five hundred people, who are together day and night, around a temple in the style of Ancient Egypt, and they hang from the lips of a self-declared prophet, Oberto Airaudi.

This was before the Temple of Mankind had been revealed, so the 'temple in the style of Ancient Egypt' refers to the Open Temple.

These wide-ranging and unsubstantiated accusations were just the start. From this point onwards, the cardinal launched a full frontal attack and all the Italian press – local, regional and national – followed suit, with a concerted denunciation of Damanhur as a highly suspect cult. In the news clippings box of that year, there is just one complimentary article, from Sweden.

Coboldo Melo was the Damanhurian press officer at that time. He told me that the press campaign against the community seemed to be highly orchestrated. After the attack by Saldarini, whenever there was an article on sects, cults, black magic or whatever other lurid piece of sensationalism that could be dragged out, Damanhur and Oberto Airaudi would be mentioned, even if there was no link whatsoever with Damanhur. But it was always guilt by association. Then another very strange thing happened: a demand for money was made.

Back in 1983 two original members of Damanhur, Filippo Cerutti and his wife, had left the community. They had been dissatisfied with some of the changes that were being made. Apparently Cerutti had often had different ideas from the rest of the group, being a little conservative and strait-laced in his whole approach to community life. In fact he never actually lived in Damanhur full-time, only during week-ends and holidays. He had invested modestly in one of the original apartments built in those early years, but when he had left, he had said that he was not interested in the property or the money. He was quite wealthy, and he and his wife had left on quite amicable terms. They remained in touch with the community, often coming back to concerts and events and always getting a warm welcome.

But then, in October 1991, a letter arrived from Cerutti, demanding the money that he had invested in the property. In all the years since he had left, in all the visits he made to Damanhur, he had never once mentioned money. But then the letter came, very formal, very cold, demanding the money from his old friends. It was not an excessive amount – about 30,000,000 lire, which was around £11,000 at that time – but it was the manner of asking that was so strange. As Coboldo explained:

> We were very surprised by such an abrupt, formal and detached request. We could not understand why he had not talked to us directly about it. For us, the core of the matter was not the money, it was the relationship.

In their turn the Damanhurians wrote back formally, telling Cerutti that they would get a surveyor to value the property. They decided to do it all formally and professionally to avoid any later disagreements. Coboldo told me:

> In Italy, this type of proceeding takes some time, but it would have been assessed on the accumulated value of the property. So Cerutti would have got the fairest possible deal. But whilst these negotiations were going on, he instructed his solicitor to deal with this in a different manner. His lawyer told us, in quite clear terms, that if we paid him a sum of 700,000,000 lire [around £256,000] he would drop his claim, and if we did not accept this proposal, they would begin a campaign in the press against Damanhur and that they might reveal details about our 'construction work'. At that time, of course, no one outside the community knew about the build-

ing of the temple, but as one of the founders of Damanhur, Cerutti knew all about it.

The Damanhurian lawyer, Cormorano Sicomoro, replied that they were willing to settle at the right and proper amount, but they were not interested in agreeing to these extortionate terms, for two reasons: first, the community could not afford such a large amount of money, and second, they could not accept the idea of blackmail with regard to something that was their life:

> Our reply was, 'No, we are not going to pay you that,' and their whole attitude changed, and they said, 'Remember, we know all about the temple.' We still said no, as from an ethical point of view, we did not want to respond to extortion.

After this, very strange stories started to appear in the newspapers and every time it seemed that Filippo Cerutti was the source. For example, in *La Stampa* of 4 April 1991, he claimed:

> I am one of the founders of Damanhur and all I want is what is owed to me.

This was apparently 130,000,000 lire – more than the value of his investment, but far less than he had asked for through his solicitor. The article stated that Cerutti was only asking for what he had invested, that the Damanhurians had refused to give him the money, that he was being led on and that he had been deceived. More articles appeared, all of a similar nature.

And then, that fateful day in October 1991, at 6.30 in the morning, the Damanhurians were woken by over 250 armed officers storming the place, with pistols drawn, machine guns at the ready and helicopters hovering overhead.

'They were waving a magistrates warrant,' Coboldo recalled.

> It stated that there was a possible tax evasion of 50,000,000 lire [£18,000] by two of our co-operatives. Usually, people from the tax department do not go round in uniform, with arms. Normally, they would come into your place of work and ask to

see the books. But they invaded us, with their weapons out. It was a big operation, not just because of the numbers, but because many of them were police and army. There were women officers, dogs trained in sniffing out drugs, three helicopters and telecameras videoing it all, from above, transmitting it live to Ivrea [a large town some 10 miles away]. It was a huge show of force. Even a major operation against the Mafia would normally only warrant some 100–150 officers.

The operation itself probably cost more than 50 million lire. 'One of those huge helicopters alone costs one million every five minutes,' Coboldo said. 'They had three up above for three hours.'

It was an extremely frightening and unpleasant experience for all the people at Damanhur. The officers conducted strip searches. They searched children's school bags. They looked in fridges. They took away samples of food and detergent. And all in the name of tax evasion.

Coboldo was particularly angry. He had been a journalist for many years before he came to Damanhur and knew how these things should be done. Although the warrant said suspected tax evasion, he knew that these people could not be investigating that, not with such a show of force. Among the investigators were people from the finance division whom he had actually known for years. He asked them the reason behind the raid.

They told him, in confidence, that they knew perfectly well there was nothing wrong with the tax. They were simply acting under orders. People had been called in for the operation from all over the region, the night before the raid, to a barracks where they had received an intense tactical briefing and psychological build up. Then they had set out for Damanhur at the break of day, armed and expecting to find a very dangerous situation.

When the agents finally realized what was going on – though that took them a little time – they were completely deflated. Laughing now, Coboldo said:

> There were police sitting everywhere, their pistols and machine guns drooping, all utterly disappointed and wondering why they had been sent here. They were disillusioned,

tired and not just a little angry themselves. They had never experienced anything like this and they could not understand why it had happened. It cost us a fortune in coffees.

I myself could not imagine any situation in which such a heavy-handed action could be justified against the community. However, the reasoning behind it was provided the very next day. It seems that the whole operation was orchestrated with one aim: to discredit Damanhur in the eyes of the public. When local people saw the helicopters flying overhead and the large numbers of police vehicles, read about the raid in the newspapers and saw it on their televisions, it confirmed all their worst fears about Damanhur. It was a scandal, and it set the commu-nity's public relations back to less than zero. The local papers didn't help by exaggerating the story, saying the Damanhurians were evading more than a milliard of taxes – 1,000,000,000 lire (£375,000).

Coboldo saw a pattern emerging:

Attacks by a cardinal to set the scene, news stories such as Cerutti saying that he wants his money and we will not give it to him, a blitz raid by the tax authorities, a community that is making money but not paying taxes, tax evaders – all of it is playing on people's worst prejudices.

There was only one factor missing: sex. But that did not take long. Only a little while later came the headline: 'Sex, free love and children involved at Damanhur. Sex in the City of Light.'

Once more, the source of this story appears to have been Cerutti. It stemmed from a document that he had from back in the 1980s, concerning a suggestion that within the nucleo groups it might be a good idea if the birth of children was regulated, for financial and social reasons. In many ways, these are just the sort of things that any family discusses when deciding whether it can afford to support another child. At Damanhur, the discussion is just that bit more public, because the nucleo family groupings are larger. This, of course, was interpreted in the press as the heads of Damanhur controlling everything, right down to the birth of children.

'On the one hand,' said Coboldo, 'there is an implication that there is unrestrained sexual freedom, on the other that there is so much control you cannot even have children.'

The one thing that the journalists had apparently overlooked, however, was that the document they used for their story had been signed by Filippo Cerutti himself when he was still with the community. He had erased his name and date from the document before giving it to his lawyer to pass to the press and they had naturally assumed it was one of the documents taken from the tax raid. As Coboldo somewhat acidly remembers:

> It was a very naïve form of journalism. But such stuff was of interest to the higher authorities, by which I mean magistrates, politicians, people high up in the Church. These were the people who were behind the things that happened, who were prominent in asking for an attack against us.

Yet no charges were ever actually brought against Damanhur, even after the tax raid. It had all been for show. As Coboldo had realized, the aim was to undermine Damanhur's reputation by skilful playing on the classical fears – money, sex, harm coming to children, tax evasion, lack of Catholic faith, and whatever other horrors you care to think of. The only exceptions seemed to be treason and drugs! Coboldo laughs again:

> It was lucky that we had been able to establish such a sensible attitude towards the use of drugs. All it would have taken was a small amount of drugs in the muesli or the detergent and we would all have been in jail. But they did not even find a cigarette.

In early 1992, the community tried to restore its reputation by taking Cerutti to court. Oberto put his name to an action accusing Cerutti of spreading defamatory stories, but the Turin court declared his accusation had no basis. Coboldo was also in court:

> We said it was absurd. We wanted it to be made clear that our community was not at all what was being implied. In court

they called for several witnesses, but it soon became clear that the court itself was against Damanhur. The accused was Cerutti, but the authorities were really against us. The judge implied that Filippo Cerutti has every right to accuse us of whatever he wanted to. He would not listen to our case. We argued that everything Cerutti said was exaggerated, out of context or based on outdated documents, that his accusations were unfounded and were defaming our characters. The judge declared that Cerutti was an apostate, someone who leaves a group for reasons of 'faith', and as such, he had a right to exaggerate. It was just outrageous.

In April of the same year, there was a report in *La Stampa* about an ongoing custody case involving a couple who had separated. It was a private matter, as these things always are. But for the journalist, it became a public matter, because the woman was at Damanhur. The headline read: 'Take the child away from Damanhur' and there followed an article implying that the community was not a safe place for children. It was another classic situation, one that would resolve itself, sensibly and amicably, some time later, when a team of inspectors declared Damanhur an ideal place in which to bring up children, but at the time it was used to fuel all sorts of irrational fears about Damanhur.

Eventually a case brought by Damanhur against *La Stampa* and the journalist in question was more successful, though it was not until some years later that it was finally settled. Meantime, the damage was done.

A constant stream of news attacks followed throughout 1992. At one point the Bishop of Ivrea implied that he was close to having the Damanhurians excommunicated, with: 'Dear Damanhurians, you are no longer Christians.' Excommunication from the Catholic Church is a serious business in Italy. It is normally only carried out by the Pope, but it is possible for the bishops of a region, if they are all in accord, to carry out the procedure on his behalf.

I asked Coboldo how serious this would have been for the Damanhurians. With a smile, he replied:

It would have been a pointless gesture, because we do not consider ourselves to be Christians, though we see much wisdom in what Christ said and stood for. Where there was a little trick in all this, where the bishop was being very clever, was in the effect it would have on others. The bishop and his political friends knew that excommunication was pointless in our case, but what he was really suggesting was that if anyone had anything to do with Damanhur, they might also risk excommunication. That would hit those that we deal with, the people and businesses that we trade with. It would affect those who came to our courses, to our open market, everything. It was another attempt to isolate us.

The headline in one of the local papers actually ran: 'Who goes to Damanhur leaves the Catholic Church' and some suppliers stopped dealing with Damanhur because of it. They were Catholics and they were worried about their own position.

Soon after this, frustrated that Damanhur had not bowed under his demands for money or his public attacks, Cerutti played his biggest card: an anonymous letter was delivered to the local *carabinieri* station, telling them that there was a secret temple hidden at Damanhur.

A group of *carabinieri* visited Porta del Sole, demanding to be shown into the temple. They had a map, they knew there was a temple, they knew where the entrance was. They went into the corridor and along to the Egyptian room. They looked around, wondered what all the fuss was about and went away. The ruse had worked.

However, there was more to come. That July the *carabinieri* organized another raid. At 7 o'clock in the morning, armed again, they went to Oberto's nucleo and took him to the temple entrance, telling him they knew that there was more to it than the other officers had seen. Going into Porta del Sole, they searched all the rooms, looking for another entrance to the temple. But they could not find one. The information Cerutti had provided them with was limited, out of date. But they did know that there was more of the temple than they had already seen.

The state prosecutor, Bruno Tinti, arrived, a stern, powerful judge and minister of justice who was quite notorious in the region for being brusque and tough. It was he who had ordered the tax raid against Damanhur. He had a map and other plans of the temple, and said that he would order the drilling of holes all over the mountain if the Damanhurians did not show him how to get into it. Coboldo and Oberto looked at each other.

'We thought for a moment what to do,' recalls Coboldo.

Then Oberto took the decision to show them into the temple. We could have risked leaving them to find it, because it is hard to find. But we took the decision to face up to the risks of showing it to them, to face up to the really big problems that would undoubtedly throw up. The alternative was to have them digging and drilling all over the mountain, and who knows what damage they might have done? Showing them in turned the situation round.

As he was being shown towards the entrance to the temple, Tinti turned to the *carabinieri* and told them that he considered them 'the Praetorian guard'. With this high-handed flourish, the prosecutor, three of the *carabinieri* and Oberto went into the temple. Another policeman followed them, filming everything.

An hour later they came out, the prosecutor first. He was a changed man. He put his hand on Oberto's shoulder and said simply, 'We have got to do something to save this temple.'

Everyone was amazed to see the difference in this upright and proud man who had been attacking Damanhur in newspaper articles and on television for over a year. As Coboldo noted, it was not just what he said about saving the temple, but his whole attitude. 'Often a person's behaviour speaks volumes and that was the case here. Bruno Tinti's head was lowered, he had his hand on his chin, he was thoughtful.'

Tinti immediately sequestrated the temple, but placed it in the custody of the Damanhurians, stating that they were the only ones who could use it. This was clever, because it meant that nobody could take action against the temple without his agreement. In Italy, there are no laws to protect buildings erected without planning permission and they would normally be destroyed.

Bruno Tinti also did something else of extreme importance: he did not break the news of the temple's discovery to the press at once, but gave the Damanhurians the choice of whether to talk to the world about it, and when.

It was at this point that Esperide first came to Damanhur. She was working for a large public relations company at the time and was called in to handle the public relations campaign. She and Coboldo had set in motion a massive and well orchestrated media campaign. On 9 October the first press conference was held in Damanhur to announce the existence of the temple. From that day on, for three years, virtually every week there were journalists and television crews at Damanhur. Coboldo said:

> We started an action that became a chain reaction. It was all new for us. We had been used to building the temple in silence and secrecy. Now, from one day to the next, it became the subject for public discussion. It was really strange and difficult.
>
> But the prosecutor had given us a life-line by authorizing us to visit the temple, even though it was under sequestration. Journalists politicians and technicians, architects and engineers were also permitted there. So we were able to show the temple to all sorts of people and ask them to help us find way of saving it.

Bruno Tinti, from being the Damanhurians' greatest foe, had become their greatest friend. In the face of adversity, he gave them a chance, and they gladly took it.

The local ruling body was the Council of Vidracco, which could have easily legalized the temple by finding a way of incorporating it into the building plans of the village, but it was in open opposition to Damanhur and refused to do so. The councillors sent the matter to the Mountain Community Valchiusella, the regional organization made up of the 12 local town councils. Its president promptly called for the temple to be destroyed, and failing this – bearing in mind it might be difficult to destroy a temple set inside a mountain – it should be given to the region and become a tourist attraction.

A Disneyworld temple! The Damanhurians were horrified. The temple was not something to be gawped at by tourists, it was the sacred heart of their community, and without their heart they could not live. This factor had no doubt been the focus of many discussions between politicians and members of the Church. It was all part of the campaign against Damanhur, with Cerutti and his lawyer firmly behind it. Now the real reason for Damanhur had been exposed, they hoped the community would break up and go away. However, this view failed to take into account two important factors: the action that Prosecutor Tinti had taken and the determination of the Damanhurian people.

When the president of the Mountain Community Valchiusella realized that he could not take unilateral action against the temple, he suggested that the two parties should stop talking publicly about it and try to resolve it between themselves. However, the motives that underlay this approach were too obvious – to quietly take possession of the temple and destroy the heart of Damanhur – and the Damanhurians, far from keeping quiet, actually intensified their public relations campaign. They asked journalists from all over the world to write about them, they invited photographers and television crews to take pictures of the temple, they put an appeal out on the Internet, they went all over Italy to collect signatures for a petition to save the temple – and got over 100,000.

The campaign worked. The more people came to Damanhur, the stronger it became. Now visitors were coming from many parts of the world, not tourists coming to ogle, but serious people interested in Damanhur's ideas, interested in the spiritual journey. Damanhur would never be the same again. It was no longer engaged in building a secret temple, but in playing host to the fellow seekers of the world, finding common cause with other individuals and groups on their own spiritual paths.

Italian MPs were among those who visited the temple and many of them felt it was necessary to bring the problem directly to Rome in order to find a solution. In 1995 the temple was declared a work of art by the regional Beaux Arts authority and finally, in 1996, all actions against Damanhur and Oberto Airaudi in relation to the temple were dropped. The Italian government passed an amendment to a national Bill which gave Damanhur the legal basis to save the temple. The community was required to pay the sort of fees it would have been asked to pay when making a legal planning application and was also required to have a whole range of structural tests, seismic readings and land surveys carried out, as outlined in Chapter 1. The temple, however, could remain.

Luigi Berzano has written a comprehensive sociological account of Damanhur, published in *Religiosità del nuovo areopago – credenze e forme relgiose nell'epoca postcolare*, and entitled *Damanhur: un monastero per famiglie nell'età dell'acquario* (Milan, 1994). Monsignor Berzano is Professor of Sociology of Religions in the Faculty of Political Science at the University of Turin. He sees Damanhur as a unique community that places art at the centre of its philosophy. I went to visit him at the university and asked him about some of the antagonism of the Catholic Church, particularly the vociferous attacks made by Cardinal Saldarini and the Bishop of Ivrea, with his implied threat of excommunication, calling all those associated with Damanhur 'no more Christian'. Professor Berzano explained that the Bishop was well known as liberal and open in his outlook. Therefore, his attack on Damanhur seemed even more damning. However, he was open only as far as social aspects were concerned, a champion of the lower classes, marching on the streets with the workers. Maybe spiritually he was something of a reactionary.

I asked Professor Berzano if the Bishop's attack was an attempt to gain political credibility, by taking on board the hostility of the local people against Damanhur. But he felt just the opposite, that the condemnation of the Bishop had fuelled the fears of the locals. He also felt that this had been a mistake, but that his views had now mellowed.

During 1997 the case of Filippo Cerutti, too, was resolved. He accepted a settlement that was less than what the Damanhurians had originally offered him way back in 1991. Now he appears no longer interested in speaking about this episode.

It had been a strange and enigmatic case, and had changed the face of Damanhur. But what Cerutti had sparked off ultimately made Damanhur and its people much stronger. It gave them a challenge to respond to – and they responded with conviction.

This was a classic case of turning negative energy into a positive force.

chapter 7 – oberto airaudi: man of vision

'Oberto says' is a phrase you hear a lot in Damanhur.

Philip Short – BBC2's *Newsnight*

And the rule I gave myself was that I had to invent at least one new thing per day and also read one book per day. For many years now that has been my fixed rule.

Oberto Airaudi

As will have become obvious, Oberto Airaudi wields a huge influence over Damanhur. His presence is everywhere, whether he is there in person or not. Just on a visual level, his paintings are always present, in offices, workplaces and homes. Yet he appears mild-mannered, unassuming, a little shy maybe, though with a wry, intelligent and somewhat mischievous sense of humour. So why should such a reticent individual, who no longer holds an official position in the community, have such a pervasive influence?

The answer is not obvious, but after spending some time in Damanhur, I have become well aware that the people there hold Oberto in the greatest respect. To them he is a spiritual guide, a master – not the sort of master who demands adoration, or even to be followed, in the religious sense of the word, but simply a man who leads by example. He is the reminder that there is the master in all of us, that we all have a potential that can be fulfilled, that we all have a responsibility for our plan-etary home, for the universe we live in.

Through Oberto's influence Damanhur has developed as an artistic community and he himself expresses much of his teaching through his artwork, largely through his paintings, which are vibrant, colourful and expressive. Legend has it that he does four or five before breakfast every day. I don't know how true that is, or even where I picked it up from, but Oberto certainly creates work on an almost daily basis. Esperide explained:

> The paintings are a bit like Selfica, with different kinds of energies. They are able to bring onto our plane of existence energies that otherwise could not interact with us. It depends very much on the titles, which are like meditations. Some are used for intuition and some for dreaming, while others help concentration. People are drawn to titles or pictures. If you like a picture, you very often find that you are very in tune with the title. You tend to be attracted to both.

Of course, the paintings are only one manifestation of Oberto's influence on Damanhur. For it was this unassuming man, who quiet-ly goes about his business, chatting affably to those he meets, who persuaded a few people to start digging a hole in a mountain... Oberto is largely responsible for the whole of Damanhur.

I asked him about the original conception of Damanhur:

> The idea was born when I was 14. I wanted to create a place where a group of people could live in a completely inde-pendent way, using all their time to study, to do research, to create a new society.

I was amazed that Oberto already had such a plan at such an early age. But he told me:

> Yes, that was when I wrote my first book on this topic. I was still at school, but I was training myself in giving conferences

and talks. I studied in a Jesuit school and I was able to convince two of my teachers to leave. That is when I said, 'OK, it works!'

When I was 14, I wrote, for my own use, the first treatise – though 'treatise' is a big word – of all the basic philosophical principles that I would develop in time. Then in the two following years, thanks to the memories coming back, and also to different experiments, I was able to define everything much better.

First of all came the idea of a place where we could do research. After that, for many years I was travelling with other people, trying to define the flowing of the synchronic lines all over the planet.

In June 1996, Oberto and Esperide and a host of other Damanhurians visited England to attend an event organized by the editors of *Kindred Spirit* magazine. Some 200 people came together for a weekend of seminars, workshops and demonstrations on Damanhur. Oberto took part in a question and answer session with the audience, something he had never done before outside Damanhur. During this, he told the story of an old man who had brought him a chest full of books, books with words that would disappear once he had read them. I asked him about this:

When I was 14, I already had all that material. It was to form the basis of my later work. In the beginning, I was using out-of-body journeys, a technique which can be used in this kind of research, to define the synchronic lines. That was a period in which I was doing very many experiments of all kinds. When I was 14, I had 80 people experimenting with me, using hypnosis and many other techniques that we developed. We did a lot of very weird things. At that age, it was easier for me to develop things like levitation or materialization, so I was doing all those kind of things. However, everything had to have a practical application. I never played football, but I trained my friends, using hypnosis. I would make a face appear in front of the goalkeeper so that he would get scared and not stop the ball. I made the first aerostatic ball, made of paper. Because I wanted to fly, I had a bicycle with rockets.

And the rule I gave myself was that I had to invent at least one new thing per day and also read one book per day. For many years now that has been my fixed rule.

And you always had groups of people working with you?

There were many groups, but they were not all working together, they were like many cells, all doing different experiments. There was no unifying name. There were about 35, 36 groups. We would choose a particular topic or a theme and then we would develop research in an independent way in order to compare results.

All this led to the Horus Centre in Turin. At the time the Horus Centre started we were also looking for suitable land, a place where the synchronic lines met, in order to start building Damanhur.

I got married when I was 18. Everything happened very fast. I did not go into the army to do military service, as I already had two children by that time. But really it was so the work could continue unbroken.

This original grouping of 80 or so people, how did they come together? Were they friends from school? Were they older people?

The people who already knew each other were those in the Lanzo valley, in various groups, and about 100 of those moved to Turin. But they had an adolescent approach to the research – they were more interested in the phenomena than the practical application.

Then I started giving talks every evening in which first there was a theoretical part and then a practical part, based on our earlier research. The first important group was selected and people were chosen to help look for the place for us to settle. There were 12 people in this first group. Soon after that, we bought the land that would become Damanhur.

And how old were you, at this point?

Twenty-three. Before the houses were finished, there were people living in caravans at Damanhur. In the beginning a few families lived in Lanzo, in rented apartments that were all close to each other. They started the project, while at Damanhur people started the building.

Between the ages of 14 and 23 is this all you did or did you ever do anything ordinary, like go to work...?

I have always worked. My parents are not wealthy. When I was born, my father had already been retired for a few years. He was born in 1909 and was a partisan in the war, and in civilian life he was in the *carabinieri*. He is still alive. My mother was a teacher. They had a little coffee shop in the Lanzo valley.

First of all, I started selling encyclopaedias, then I used to set up aquariums, with fish of all sorts. I used to operate on the fish, involve them in my experiments! Then I started selling insurance. At that time, I was the youngest insurer in Italy. I had 1,500 per cent growth per year for the first three years and then steady growth of around 300 per cent.

Is this because you used to hypnotize people into buying insurance?

No, but rumour had it that those insured with me never had a car accident. *[Laughter]* And then I employed a group of disabled people in my office, people in wheelchairs and with other disabilities, who could not find jobs. My work was always increasing, but I was making no money. *[More laughter]* But I was coming on very well from this. I had these people looking after my insurance office, keeping the money circulating, and my wife was secretary of the agency. So I could do the job and at the same time carry on with my experiments.

During that time I was already working as a spiritual healer, but I was not asking people to pay me. For seven years I did that for free. Then, when pranatherapy became my main occupation, I gave the insurance agency as a present to someone

I knew, because I did not want to have anything from my previous life. It is part of the unwritten rules.

And we always assumed that you had sold your insurance company to start building the temple...

No, no. That was how it went.

So the temple was a new departure, then?

When we started building the temple I was working in Turin. I had two little children, so I did not have too much money. These are two parallel stories. First, I was working in Turin, as an insurer, and even though I was making a lot of money, I did not have very much, because life was expensive. So I had many economic difficulties, literally. It was bread and mozzarella, milk and bread. That was why I was always so thin! Then I developed an insurance agency outside Turin, becoming the youngest insurance agent in Italy. I did this with the disabled people.

When I started being a pranatherapist and being paid for that, I gave the agency away and I also started running courses. From that moment on, we started buying the land here.

My work was increasing and I developed many centres for pranatherapy all over Italy. Then I began work on all the books and all my other activities – I normally have about 15 things on the go at once – and everything that came with them. I put all that I made, over all those years, into the temple. Up until four years ago, no money was taken out of Damanhur for the temple, because it was something that I had to do myself. I gave myself an objective and even though I needed a very big sum of money for it, I achieved it.

Was Damanhur started before work began on the building of the temple?

At the same time. While people were setting up and establishing the first rules for living together, a very small select group of people went up to the house where the temple is and started building the temple.

How many people?

In the beginning no more than 12, at a time when there were perhaps 40 people at Damanhur. Later, when there were about 100 at Damanhur, no more than 30 worked up there. The others did not even know that the temple existed. They saw us coming home all dirty, covered in dust, and we always told them that we had been working on the terraces, doing agricultural work. Now, in Damanhur, the devotional work is still called *terrazzatura*, which means 'terracing', 'making terraces'. It is a word that does not exist in Italian, a word we made up. This helped us to create all the workshops and the artistic activities linked to them, to create a higher artistic level all over Damanhur. We always tried to give the most gifted people a chance of learning an artistic technique and creating a workshop. The goal was that everybody should contribute something to the development of the temple.

So you bought all of the land there?

Not all of it. We only bought the top part. In order not to kill the trees that are behind it, we built the main building there. Then we bought the lower part. If not, there would not have been enough land.

And at the same time, you bought the mountain? Or just the house on the mountain, to begin with?

The house was bought in the name of a man whose wife had been the first person to die in Damanhur. Then, when work on the temple was already underway, this man left and we had to buy the house, paying much more than it was worth, so that we could go on with the work. Then we had to buy more land, because if not, we would have been building under someone else's land. So, little by little, we bought the whole mountain.

Building constructions within mountains is very difficult. Where did the engineering knowledge come from?

I had a very big head, so I thought I could do it. I also thought that in the Middle Ages they built cathedrals without being engineers or architects. So, if they made such things, why not us?

Then we used books and research papers for the technical information and some we developed from experimentation. Mostly, we learned from the direct experience of getting to know the materials, the land, the rock.

Was there a plan? Did you know exactly what you were going to dig, and where you were going to go, and how big it would be?

Certainly – down to the last centimetre. The first thing that was prepared, in 1978, was some drawings. When the builders started to ask which way to go, I took these sketches out of my pocket and showed them.

How did you get the degree of precision in the building?

It was difficult. In the beginning we had to use a compass to see what direction we were going in. Then we had a tachometer, but that was difficult to use, particularly on the bends, because planes are very difficult. We had a very good friend with us, Orson Bear, who was very good at this work. Unfortunately he died last year in a car crash. He was the only person who knew all the planes of the temple, because for 20 years he was director of all the works.

Didn't people know what they were building inside the mountain?

Not exactly, no. Very often one person did not know what another was doing in another sector of the temple. For many years, one of the most beautiful moments was when new people were brought to the temple, or to new parts of the temple, for the first time. In the large halls they would find all the other people of Damanhur waiting to see their face! Everyone would be very emotional.

So, as the temple was growing, the people who were in Damanhur, or who came to Damanhur but were not involved in the building of the temple, were gradually brought in on the secret?

Exactly. Many people did not know about the temple for years. Some did, but others did not. They were selected. In order to keep it a secret for 16 years, we had to be very careful.

But then you had to increase the numbers of people who were involved in the building of the temple.

Yes, but all the people were, of course, working on the temple outside their normal working hours. Some people were giving more time, but the energy and the pleasure that are given by working in that place are incredible. The maximum number of people who knew about the temple and worked on it was about 75.

When you took people into a new chamber, would it be in a finished state or would it just be the raw rock?

The rock, because it generates great emotion. Other parts would already be finished, though, and the beautiful artwork was always a real inspiration to everybody, making them willing to do more.

Construction was also a very complex process because first of all we had to dig, then we had to break down all the material into powder and then we had to bring it outside and make it disappear. So we had guards and radios. It was all very complicated.

So you broke the rock down into powder?

Yes, when we had to get rid of it. And when it was necessary to cover up the noise of the work – people always worked in silence, but when they were doing work close to the surface, there was always a danger of noise – they recorded on a tape the noise of an electric saw and they played that, very loud, over and over. Or they would actually saw wood, the same piece, over and over. It was like making tooth-picks with electric saws! But it was important to cover all the noise of the compressors, drills and stuff, because at first we used hand hammers and chisels, then it was electric hammers and in the end it was pneumatic hammers.

Even so, it was a huge undertaking with just basic equipment. The original people involved in this with you, what sort of people were they and did they share your vision?

Certainly. Many of them are still here, so you can ask them. There is film you can see of the temple being built and also of the concrete being poured down – 36 hours of concrete being poured into the chamber! There were also people working outside the temple without knowing what was going on inside. They thought they were building a cellar, or a well, or whatever! It was all done in such a way that it was not easy to understand what was going on. Also, when the first house was bought, it needed to be redecorated, so people thought the tracks going up and down the hill were for that. But there was more concrete going in there than there is in two or three villages in the whole valley! There was a huge quantity of concrete.

Was the secrecy very important?

To be sure the idea of the shared secret was a strong bond. But having fun and playing were always a part of building the temple, too. There was always the seriousness of knowing the objective, like getting in touch with the synchronic lines for instance, but on the other hand, there was always this playfulness.

For many Damanhurians, having taken part in this work is like having won a gold medal. Building the temple is one of the few cases where the mythical aspects do not surpass the facts. Often, when you tell the story of an event, the story becomes bigger than the event itself. But in this case it is just the opposite – the people actually did far more than what the myth says.

What I have become abundantly clear about these last days is that your big achievement here, the one that most people in the outside world seem to miss, is that you have actually found a way for people to live together in a way that is more to do with co-operation than competition.

Competition does exist here, and that is also useful, but there are different phases. What is interesting, maybe, is that the results we have achieved now are the consequences of a policy we applied in social science. It is very important – fundamental – to have many different objectives in which people can get involved. From what I have observed of other communities, this is the distinction between those that last and those that disappear. Most of them do disappear after a few years – normally communities don't last a long time. Each one starts out with wonderful ideas, but then the momentum is lost. We tried to do the opposite – to start slowly and then grow as we went along, learning how to change our objectives and our direction whenever it was necessary.

It is a renewal of ideas as well as the growth of a social structure.

Yes, just as we are now building the great stone circuits in the woods – new ideas, new growth.

There are always new ideas at Damanhur and probably most of them originate with Oberto, still reading his book a day and inventing a new thing each day, but then other people pick them up and run with them. By now they have grown accustomed to Oberto's prolific information output, but for us outsiders it is still hard to comprehend – Oberto has written well over 300 books and countless other short stories, articles and theatrical pieces, and he holds seminars at least twice each week. There is no doubting that his ideas are widely circulated.

However, one thing that greatly impressed me, as I began to become more familiar with the Damanhurian way of doing things, was how people are also allowed to develop their own ideas and creative expression. There is a certain degree of experimenting and taking ideas to their ultimate, very much in line with Damanhurian principles, but also a great deal of sharing of ideas. No one seems to hang on jealously to their own discoveries. I asked Oberto about this:

> We worked hard to make tasks rotate from the very beginning, in order to avoid an excess of specialization in many fields. On the one hand, you do need specialization to get very high results, but on the other, you need to have another activity, or more different activities, as well, so that people have a broad outlook, so that they do not over-identify themselves with any one area.
>
> In Italy, up until a few years ago, there was a lot of fear about changes at work. Here at Damanhur, we always got our people used to the idea of change, to the idea that it was a normal thing to change jobs. It does not have to become excessive, but now it is accepted as a normal thing, a normal rhythm, and nobody gets scared by it.

I also asked Oberto about some of the other principles behind Damanhur. I had always been puzzled by references to the Enemy of Mankind. How did this fit into the general scheme of things?

> We identify as the Enemy all that negative potential in Mankind that has not a direct origin from Mankind. In the traditional esoteric teaching, there is the concept of absolute evil which does not originate within humankind, but is something external. This is not to say that we should not take any responsibility for our own bad actions. But we start from the assumption that there is a little part of this evil in every human being. This

part does not belong to the human being, it is an external element and can dominate the human being.

As the Enemy can be identified with an absolutely negative force with a lot of power but very little intelligence, the way to oppose it is to use fantasy, invention and creativity. You can consider the Enemy a rigid and unavoidable opposition that can be contrasted only with elasticity and fantasy. This is to make it very simple.

Something else I had been wondering about was the symbol of the Grail, which appears in a lot of Oberto's paintings:

The Grail is usually seen as a container of all the energies, as an alchemical mixer. According to us, from an esoteric point of view, a Grail is a special force. It can be a subjective but also an objective force and cannot be identified with just one single object, as in the movies, but goes through different objects, just as the soul goes through different bodies.

We have built a part of the temple just to keep, maintain, host and protect the idea of the Grail. So from this point of view the temple can be considered to be the place that is destined to keep the idea of the Grail, this very vast concept, in touch with the Earth and with all of humankind.

As well as the Grail, at Damanhur there are often references to the god Horus, even to the extent that, if you have a meal there, the simple purification rite has got Horus in it. I asked about this, too. Oberto told me:

Horus symbolically represents the new cycle, beyond religions and beyond Christianity, the Christianity as it is normally found today. It is the representation of light, of the sun and all the symbology linked to the awakening of the human being.

There is so much to find out about Damanhur. It is a complex society. I asked Oberto a more personal question. What, for him, had been the best thing that had happened in the history of the community?

Many beautiful things have happened. First of all, having been able to turn, in a way, the faults of people into a positive force has been one of the most important things that we have been able to do. And the second thing, for me, has been being able to build a society that has become more and more detached from me. For we have a long road ahead of us.

I had to ask the other big question: 'What, for you, is the worst thing about Damanhur?' Oberto replied simply:

That people forget they are initiates. Spiritual growth is just like freedom – if you do not keep remembering what it is for, you lose it. Initiation is a process that is used to become something more – to evolve, to grow, to go after the goals for which the human being was created. It is like soup or fused metal – as long as it is kept hot, it can go on being transformed, but when it gets cold it cannot regain the state that it had before.

Given that only 10 per cent of the temple is in place, I wondered about what might be called the 'master plan for Damanhur'. Was the equivalent 10 per cent of that also in place? On another visit to Damanhur, in July 1997, I asked Oberto that very question. 'Less than 10 per cent,' he replied. Then he jumped up. I thought the interview was over, that perhaps I had asked something that had touched a nerve, but he continued, 'I will take you to see the new chamber in the temple, right now. You can continue the interview in the car.'

On the way, Oberto told me something of the latest plans for the temple:

There will be a cupola about one and a half kilometres across and a special electric train that will run from the Labyrinth to it. It will be on three underground floors and will be about 26 metres [86 feet] high. In the central part you will enter a sort of spiral in the walls. And each one of these floors will be around the size of a football pitch. We also want to have there, in an underground space, a library of the largest

Plate 1: Oberto Airaudi, founder of Damanhur

Plate 2: Mosaic of marble and glass around the balcony in the Hall of Mirrors

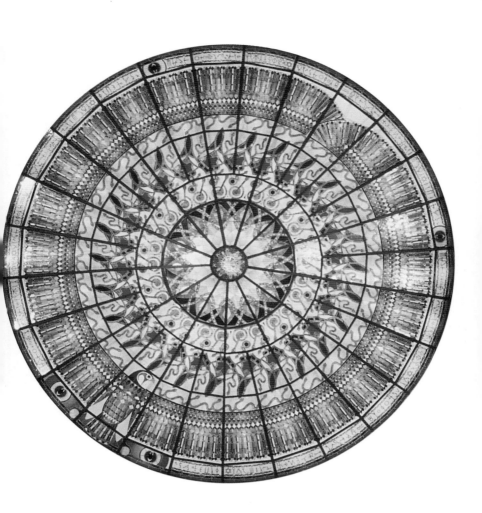

Plate 3: Cupola dome in the Hall of Mirrors

Plate 4: One small section of the Earth Hall wall painting

Plate 5: Spiral circuit used for meditation

Plate 6: The Open Temple, used for ritual and celebration rather than worship

Plate 7: Mountain region of Tentyris Community showing Magilla

Plate 8: Magilla, a large house undergoing extensive renovation, where two nucleo families live

Plate 9: Archive photograph of the Water Hall construction

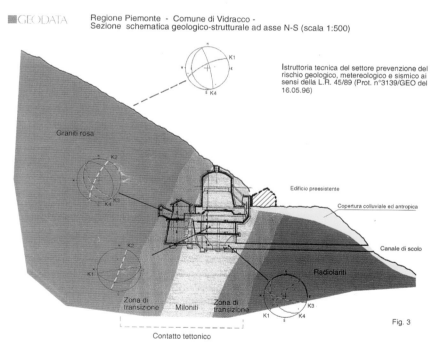

GEODATA

Regione Piemonte - Comune di Vidracco -
Sezione schematica geologico-strutturale ad asse N-S (scala 1:500)

K1
W   E
K4

Istruttoria tecnica del settore prevenzione del rischio geologico, metereologico e sismico ai sensi della L.R. 45/89 (Prot. n°3139/GEO del 16.05.96)

Graniti rosa

K2
K4 K3

Edificio preesistente

Copertura colluviale ed antropica

K2

Canale di scolo

K1

Radiolariti

Zona di transizione   Miloniti   Zona di transizione
K1   K4   K3

Fig. 3

Contatto tettonico

Plate 10: Illustration from Geodata report on the temple showing how it fits exactly into a rare seam of milonite

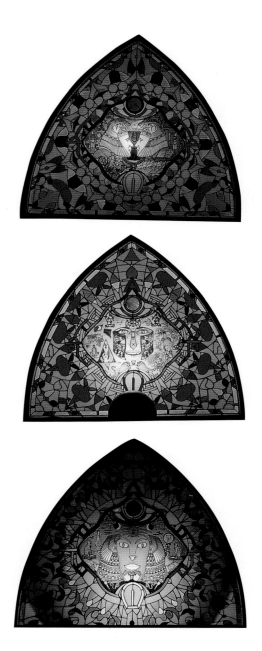

Plate 11: Stained-glass windows in the Labyrinth depicting Horus, Pan and Bastet

Plate 12: The Water Hall – dedicated to the feminine principle

Plate 13: The first corridor seen through a fretworked door

Plate 14: Second corridor with individual terra cotta figures made by Damanhurians

Plate 15: The Hall of Spheres with its chalices and Spheroselfs

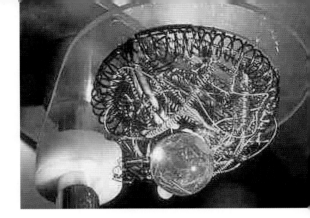

right Plate 16: Selfica in position at the top of a time cabin

below Plate 17: Selfic painting by Oberto Airaudi

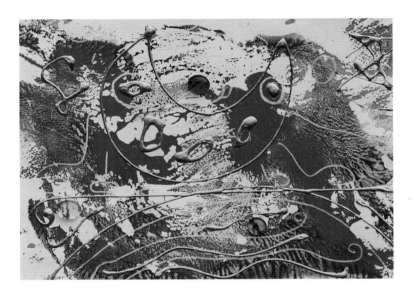

Spatial bridge, supporting the tired moon, so that part of us may rest and gather even more strength than before...

The waters are soft and enveloping, the light, coming from the very close moon, intense and reflecting...

So that mind learns, when its turn comes, to reflect thought and concepts, knowledge, with the aim of possessing them fully...

4–7 November 1996 (256)
with three stones

Plate 18: Weaving on wooden looms at Atelier Damjl

Plate 19: Luxury food produce from Compagnia della Buona Terra

Plate 20: Food production workshop showing Selfic panel (top centre)

overleaf Plate 21: The Moon door in the Earth Hall, situated opposite
the Sun door (on cover)

collection of esoteric books in the world. On top of this there will be all the arts laboratories that create work for the temple and there will be a big space for conferences, for hundreds of people, and a space for concerts. A cable car will go up to the various levels, taking visitors to the conferences, concerts and so on.

There is only one problem at the moment and that is that we still have to buy the land. The owner does not want to sell it to us and we have been trying to buy it for years. Once we do get hold of it, it will take us one and a half to two years to realize our plans. Most of the excavations have already been done.

No wonder, when I asked Oberto whether he had any idea what I should use to represent Damanhur on the cover of this book, he said: 'A photograph where there are pickaxes and buckets.'

Well, dear reader, you will find the picture of pickaxes and buckets on the back cover. It is a symbol of the monumental achievement of the community in the closed valley in the Italian Alps. Oberto Airaudi is indeed a man of vision, a vision which is gradually being realized at Damanhur.

From those lands, one day, much later, a gnome and a man picked up the Philosopher's Stone. From the sometimes reddish stone, a wise man, many millennia later, drew wands of awxiuyk. Mankind does not even know what it is any more. From the wise wood of the trees, which spreads in slow pilgrimage, by strength of seeds and wind, was made the central keel of the first ship, which descended from the rivers towards the sea, guided by the stars. From the leaves of certain plants, the wisdom was drawn, which still now the Oracle writes. And finally, from that living, mysterious soil, other humans and subtle creatures found ground for a new alliance.

The wind – listen carefully – knows how to read the words from the branches and from the herbs. It reads loudly, for those who know how to raise high their human antennae.

Then, the greatest of all creatures of the skies said, 'On this ground paths will rise to reawaken and find again what the Enemy has taken away from the bridge-creatures of the world.'

The second star-creature said, 'Here the forces will rise and the forces will shoot lightning bolts of knowledge amongst them, and those who walk by, one day, will remember.'

And the third star-creature said, 'Here under, here above, here inside, human beings and plants will establish a new alliance. It will be like the one uniting the worlds on the path to the total soul; dialogue will be possible, with respect and agreement amongst forms.'

At the sound of those mighty voices, mistaken for summer thunders, for telluric tremblings, every being with legs fell on their knees, those with two, those with four, those with even more. It was as if all the species had simultaneously knelt, even those tiny forms that don't have ears.

The powerful creature still in the egg also slowly consented. It was not yet its moment, there was not yet the awakening necessary for the great return, with the message of the 'Yes' or 'No'.

Having known all these things, Pan, who was far, came to speak to the new forces of the wood that was to fall under his spell. He still comes, and in the gorges, in the most tangled places, among the rocks and the more ancient trunks, he leaves messages for his star friends, and they listen attentively and sing the common song. Also, the human being who overcomes the subtle tests, and the manifest ones, can reach out and expand and nourish the subtle parts, which by the nature and ancient need are always hungry. Listening, walking a few footsteps, dancing words that make the eyes sparkle, stopping, moving where the spirit pulls from the sleeve of the body, following the splitting path; choosing, meditating the upright stones, approaching the spirals, turning backwards and round again – this is a dance to the rhythm of the wood, where the leaves know how to sing.

There are living stones, small and talking. There are friend-trunks, to hug and merge with, everyone choosing his own wise tree. And the Earth speaks. She adopts a people, as she did thousands of years ago, and in the symbiosis, she is protected by it. The ground is written with small slopes, or steep dips and climbs that make you pant; rocks are waiting for passers-by to touch them. The birds know these things very well. They speak to pilgrims questioning them, but often they do not know how to answer.

The cosmic egg matures. It is nearly ready to hatch, but already for thousands and thousands of years it has been listening and talking to the Earth and to those walking on her. The great book is always open. It is waiting for eyes able to read the secrets from the stars, secrets so ancient that, when they were written, the planet did not even exist.

part three

the game of life

chapter 8 – life as a game

Travellers of the soul, on the roads traced in everybody's heart.

Game of Life group

By 1983 families had settled in Damanhur, courses were being run, seminars mounted and the work on the temple was progressing nicely, in secret, up the hill. The mission was underway. The sun was shining. Things were, well, comfortable. And that, for Oberto Airaudi, was just the problem. The dynamic of Damanhur had lost something of its impetus. So he left.

Damanhur had come into being because of Oberto's vision. The temple had been started at his instigation and was developing under his guidance. Imagine the consternation at his departure. Nevertheless Oberto set out. He travelled all over Italy and out to Sardinia, making contact with new people, largely younger than those he left behind at Damanhur. As they travelled, more joined them, mainly by word of mouth. Some three months later, Oberto returned to Damanhur with a large group of new people. They camped out high in the hills above Lugnacco, establishing a new base at a small mountain refuge that had fallen into disrepair, the building that has now become the Baita. So the second generation of Damanhurians was instituted.

However, matters did not rest there. The established citizens of Damanhur were not altogether happy with the amount of time that Oberto was spending with the newer group. Oberto himself would go and tell the new group this; then he would go and tell the older ones that the newer ones were more vibrant, buzzing with ideas, dynamic and enthusiastic. This spreading of dissension went on for some time and then Oberto made his move. He had been developing the idea that games could be one way in which people could be helped to get along with each other. Now he set up the conditions for a war game – a full-scale battle, with strategy, planning and briefings, but with elements of a game, capturing flags or 'killing' opposition by taking their armbands or handkerchiefs.

When the battle came, it was fought with a fierce determination. The older ones actually pushed a jeep, with the engine off, so as not to attract attention, right to the top of a hill overlooking the camp. Then they turned the headlamps to full beam, played loud music and descended straight into the camp of the newcomers.

The fighting reached a furious pitch and some claimed that it was becoming real. Then Oberto blew a loud whistle and called a halt. He got everyone to sit down and talk about what they had just been through.

The game had been a tremendous learning experience. The community became much stronger as a result and what happened in these weeks would lay part of the foundation of the social structure, for this was how the Game of Life came into being.

A great realization came out of this episode – that play is the best way to learn how to live. Is it not through such simulation that children learn how to become adults? Play allows individuals to experiment with different aspects of personality, offering a means of expression, one of total involvement, affirmation and change. If you hang on to this young spirit, face situations with fantasy and imagination, and do not let difficulties upset you, even when you grow old, you can fully enjoy your existence and live life to the full.

For the Damanhurians, the war game also brought the understanding that through play, everything could be put under discussion. Every obstacle could be overcome through thought, action and good wishes. Joy and imagination were seen as fundamental tools, making it possible to break rigid patterns and personal restrictions. So a group was set up to explore the possibilities of using games to optimize social living, to play the Game of Life.

One of the main tools of the Game of Life is the Journey. Oberto initiated another major one in 1984, this time to seaside places, to make contact with the subtle forces of water and the feminine.

Other journeys have taken Damanhurians all around Europe, with people often being called to go at short notice, thus fostering a helping and deep relationship with others, who have to replace the traveller at work and support their family circle. I met two people who had been on the early journeys, Furetto and Fauno, who told me:

> During journeys, everything is even more deeply shared than in Damanhur. They are camps around the fire, we sing, we play, we sleep under the stars, the complexion changes with the sun and the open air. We learn to be totally present and ready to read all the signs of nature – a stone found on a beach, a dog arriving unexpectedly, the wind trying to cover everything with sand, a rock with strange signs, the crackling of the fire that at times seems to erupt like a volcano – always ready to change route, to dismantle the tents, to leave again, to change the course of thoughts, to build spirals and labyrinths, to launch small boats to illuminate the sea and entrust to it our dreams, thoughts, small offers of flowers and words.
>
> You must know how to make a decision in a hurry, how to set up a tent and build a stone altar. You must be always available, sleep with an eye open and your antennae straight up. You might be responsible for precious objects and magical instruments, or have to resolve koans and study the ancient myths of the history of Mankind. All this involves being happy together, having a lot of fun, helping each other.
>
> Through time, the Journey has walked many different roads, but we are still not accustomed to its magic and its mystery. Travellers of the soul, on the roads traced in everybody's heart, every metre we drove, every beach we touched, every city we crossed is a conquered part of our being.

The next big Game of Life project was known as the Warm Oil project. As well as attracting extensive news coverage throughout the world, this project sparked off a whole new way of thinking about life and about community living. It was so important it was one of the first things Esperide told me about when I first came to Damanhur:

It had a very practical and also a magical aspect to it. The practical was, we bought a derelict mountain hut and we wanted to make the surrounding territory absolutely clean – clean from the physical point of view, but also with regard to the subtle environment. There was a need to find a way how to do it, so the Warm Oil project started.

Warm Oil comes from an ancient myth that we use in Damanhur, which is called 'The Myth of the Sapphire Masks'. In this story, at a certain stage, the heroes find themselves in a cave. They have to leave all their clothes outside to dry, because it is winter and they are all wet. So they hang their clothes in the first part of the cave to dry and then they go inside the cave. When they wake up in the morning their clothes have been stolen and they cannot go out. A little elf appears and gives them the Warm Oil cream, a magical compound keeps the cold out when you put it on your skin. So that makes you self-sufficient, you do not need clothes.

So with this idea, the Warm Oil project started and it was an experiment in total self-sufficiency. It went on for a year. Six people went up to the mountain hut. There was no electricity, no running water and they could only bring clothes that had been made in Damanhur. Also, with this experiment, there was a very big impulse towards craftsmanship, so all the artisans began to develop, as there was a need to make things for the project. So, for example, the people who went there took a loom and started weaving, so they had clothes, but they didn't have buttons, they could only have what they were able to produce. Of course, the number one preoccupation was always how to find food.

One group of people stayed there for the whole year and then almost all the citizens of Damanhur went in shifts, a week or maybe two weeks at a time, to live in this dimension, so that this territory was really colonized, in a way, by everybody, and it was a shared thing. The idea was to relive the different steps of human civilization and development over the course of a year.

In the beginning the group that went there was totally isolated, but after about a month they had already started to produce more than they were consuming, even in terms of clothing, so they were allowed to come to the Sunday market in Damanhur and to bargain, to exchange things. So, little by little, they could have things that they did not produce, but only by trading them for things that they had produced. Otherwise, they would have just said, 'OK, so now we know how to survive.' But this was a new stage. Everything had to be conquered.

In this way they cleaned the territory. There was also quite a big oak wood there, so they cleaned the oak wood. Then they prepared the house. They virtually built it from the remains of the mountain hut. At the end of this year, that became a really important and significant place: the Baita, now one of our most sacred places.

Another project, in 1986, that brought a lot of attention to Damanhur was when, as Coboldo explained,

> We put out to the media that we were looking for a spaceship. We actually did nothing more than write a letter to NASA saying that we had evolved ways of successful social co-existence and that we were willing to offer this expertise to help the space programme. We hoped for positive publicity, but this brought about sensational world-wide press coverage.

'Italian city plans an expedition to be the new world in space', as the *Chicago Tribune* described it. But this project was actually more a way of making the community's presence felt to the world than seeking to leave it behind.

> That was the time that Damanhur started to consider itself as a social experiment and defined itself as that, as a living

laboratory. What the world is not able to get in its scientific lab-oratories, we are able to achieve here, because this is real life. And this went on until about 1989–90. At that time, Damanhur felt that the phases of the experiment was over and that it was a reality. In these years, it was more 'We are a social laboratory, we are a social experiment.'

This was the start of the big media campaign. But it was to underline that we were creating a new form of sociality.

The spaceship project shows Damanhur always open to exper-iment, using new ideas in a spirit of play. It was also important as a way of differentiating Damanhur from cults and sects, because at that time there was a strong campaign by the Italian government against all sects.

The success of this project eventually led to the formation of the People. It became clear for the first time to everybody that they had to feel themselves a group, rather than just people living together because they shared the same ideas. But for that level of relation-ship to be reached, the group had to be different, more intimate, stronger. So this project resulted ultimately in many changes, both in the way people were feeling and in the organization of Damanhur.

There followed a similar exercise when the Damanhurians offered themselves as 'ghostbusters', offering to go out and calm any poltergeist activity. This was the time of the *Ghostbusters* film and once again the project resulted in widespread press coverage but also demonstrated that there was a serious side to ostensibly crazy ideas.

There was also a 'Battle of the Arts' project, where groups had to create particularly spectacular artwork. Only when they had cre-ated something amazing were they allowed out of the game. The winners were the ones who had created the most amazing pieces.

The animal and plant names at Damanhur also grew out of the Game of Life. As already mentioned, as well as testifying to the desire for renewal that each individual feels, acquiring an animal name also means connecting with an animal race, learning to rec-ognize its characteristics and symbolically representing it. Once the name is given, it has to be accepted by all the community, to find a common resonance. There is a story about a man who wanted to take the name Jaguar. He was a martial arts fanatic, very forceful. He obviously fancied himself as a Jaguar. However, there was a quiet lady who also wished to take an animal name. The Damanhurians voted that she be called Jaguar and that the martial arts expert look for a new name. The name Jaguar has done wonders for the woman's confidence. She is now more self-assured and outgoing. Martial arts sulked a bit, but still has no animal name.

A more recent Game of Life project was the Journey into the Woods, which over a three-month period in 1994 mobilized the whole of Damanhur. Groups of citizens were called up unexpectedly to spend a period in the sacred wood. Esperide explained:

> You did not know who else would be part of the group, for how long you would be away, where exactly in the big wood you would camp. You did know the objective well, though: to form a 'group' in the deep sense of the term, opening to the others and throwing away all masks, overcoming likings and antipathies in order to experiment true union, which comes only from real acceptance of oneself and others.
>
> The number of citizens had increased in the two preceding years, bringing deep transformations in the way of thinking and a big increase of the complexity of the Damanhurian society. We felt the need to create new bonds among people, to get to know the new citizens better, to 'tune in' everybody's hearts.

The calm and magic atmosphere of the wood – the outdoor extension of the Temple of Mankind – offered the most suitable of settings. It is a place where it is easy to see what happens inside yourself in relation to the surrounding nature, the ideal place, concrete as well as symbolic, for feeling deeply with nature, with others, with the different sides of yourself.

Without watches, following nature's rhythms, without radio or television, but with the melodies of the songs that always accompanied the common work, the group cooked on an open fire, one that was not be allowed to go out, as it was a symbol of each individual's inner flame, uniting it to that of the others. They built the most incredible wooden houses, using the natural timbers of the wood, rough hewn and fastened with natural materials. Once the alchemy was accomplished, once the group's fire was indeed alight, somewhat unwillingly they redescended into the normal 'world', going back to their homes and their daily activities, while another group took themselves away to the woods. With this collective support, nearly everyone was able to undertake the journey.

What was left at the end of this project were nine truly beautiful wooden houses in various parts of the forest, all individually built, with unique features, and imbued with the incredible group effort that went into the building and the living process.

Like all Game of Life projects, the Journey into the Woods had implications above and beyond the actual project. Ideas and emotions carried over into other aspects of life. As the Game of Life group put it:

> When a sufficient number of citizens had been enriched by the experience in the wood, where they left habits and fears, this great process of communion and inner renewal began to involve the whole of Damanhurian society. The dynamics of play arrived inside the homes, creating catharsis and deeper bonds, or moves to find the ideal friends for the journey, so that the fire could remain lit in everyday life. Since then, to define the new, more deeply united families, we use the term 'Home-Journey'. So, mutual attention, sharing, availability, speed, engagement toward important objectives – which are the fundamental features of any journey – become components of our daily life, constantly improving its quality and creating more and more profound and true human intercourse.

> The Home-Journey is a 'fusion device' connecting the individual to the group to the People of Damanhur. So the objectives of the individual, out of choice, become the goals of the whole community.

> And from the homes, the desire for renewal spread also to the Damanhurian firms, so that solid, harmonic and united teams were created in the working sphere, able to share responsibilities and objectives for the common growth.

Today, the Game of the Life is one of the three bodies of Damanhur, together with the School of Meditation and the social organism.
Its main task is to bring to everyday life that spirit and knowledge the
Journey represents. It helps the People to grow and keep alive
through a continuous and harmonic transformation. That's why the
People, and the paths of growth of the individuals composing it, are
connected to this aspect of Damanhur.

I asked Caimano about the Game of Life. He has overall
responsibility for the direction of the Game of Life group and exam-
ines suggestions that are made for projects. He explained that the
main function of the Game was constant research, continual renewal. There is a purpose behind each project and it ultimately has to
be useful for everybody. The Warm Oil project, for example, was
about being able to utilize resources more effectively. The insights
gained during the games are always brought back and applied to
everyday life.

Caimano told me that there is also the basis of the game within
people. The three bodies of Damanhur live inside people. So the
dynamics of a game can also be understood as putting into play
parts of your own being, in the things you are doing and in the contact with others. During the Journey into the Woods, for example, it
was when all of the people belonging to a particular group put into
play sufficient significant elements of themselves that they could
light the group fire and return from the woods. Thus a group entity
was born.

Joining the Game of Life puts the individual into a synchronic
flow of events which is faster than the usual one. The choice of participating in it requires an openness to change, overcoming personal limits and conditioning. Just as for any experience that Damanhur
proposes, each individual shares their path with a wider group of
players, but the occasions, the speed and the events are unique for
each one.

The main purpose of a games approach, a playful approach,
is to create advanced forms of innovation through collective
action, thus enabling the expression of each person's maximum
creative potential. The results and changes that are brought about
through such effort can become the solid and useful elements of
everyday life.

chapter 9 – quesiti: questions and quests

Mankind as a divine being. Mankind as a spiritual being.

Usignolo Mirica

There are no rules in Damanhur save one – 'No Smoking' – and the signs for that leave you under no doubt whatsoever – 'No Smoking: Not here, in the corridor, in the bedrooms, outside, in the car park, in the gardens, or anywhere on our territory'. You can't get much clearer than that! However, though there are no lists of rules, there is a set of principles that the Damanhurians live by, called *Quesiti*. This interesting word has no direct equivalent in English. It is somewhere between a 'question' and a 'quest', so after much discussion we came up with the term 'Questi'. There are currently seven of these and there is soon to be an eighth. They are active and dynamic concepts that people can use to enrich their lives, and are central to an understanding of almost everything about Damanhur.

In order to learn about these principles and other aspects of Damanhurian philosophy, I was assigned to Usignolo Mirica. She proved an excellent guide. Her first name means 'Nightingale' and this suits her so well. Under her former name of Alessandra Luciano she has written a string of books about aspects of Damanhur and the particular magic of the locality in which it is situated, as well as a romantic novel called *La città sotterranea*. During our regular meetings over several weeks, Usignolo took me on what seemed like a magical journey, as the philosophical and spiritual concepts of Damanhur gradually unfolded before me.

We started off by looking at the relationship between Mankind and God. The Damanhurians view this from a singular standpoint. As Usignolo explained:

In our vision of the relationship between Man and the divine, *Uomo*, Mankind itself, is at the centre of our philosophy – not God, but Man. Man is written with a capital 'M' to indicate a divine being.

Our concept of the Supreme God is as something very distant and inconceivable. We refer to this Supreme Being as the Unmoving Mover. It is the Divine Essence. It is within everything that is within creation and outside creation, everything that is stationary but at the same time moving. The principle is that everything moves, everything emanates, from the One, the One Being. This Being is so big, so vast, it is beyond contact – or, more precisely, it can only be contacted through a series of smaller divinities that act as a link, a bridge, with it. So, for us, it is one thing to talk about God, but another thing to talk about divinities.

Beneath the Unmoving Mover exist very large divinities, which we called 'primeval divinities', and one of these primeval divinities is Mankind. For us, divinities have two levels, two kinds of nature: that which is primeval and self-generated, and that which Man himself creates with his own thought Every people, every race throughout time has created its own divinities. Thus they are all a part of Mankind. They are like intermediaries – Mankind descended into the world of forms

So, according to the Damanhurians, Mankind was a great divinity, a primeval divinity, who came down to Earth as a result of a descent into matter, giving human beings the capacity of thought, free will and the concept of a soul. The ultimate aim of Mankind is to retrace the steps and rediscover the original Divine Being. The two aspects of Mankind are the divine and the material. Man is a bridge being, a link with the Divine. However, a person cannot become enlightened without the help of others, which is why a communal life is so important.

Every human being has a responsibility in the task of retracing the way back to the Divine: to choose evolution or not to choose it. When you do not choose it, then you do not bring forth the divine aspect of Mankind and you are buffeted by events.

The *Quesiti* were devised to help people follow the evolutionary path. They are not rigid commandments, but developing ideas to be applied in as many different ways as possible. Habits, static energies are a manifestation of the negative energy which is the Enemy. Consequently, the *Quesiti* are not dogma, not rules to be doggedly followed.

In fact, it proved no easy task for even Usignolo to get hold of a printed copy of them. They are written up in a book called *The Horusian Way* and I would have thought that everybody would have a copy, but, remember, this is not dogma, this is not rigid regulation. So there is little need of a book with the Questi written down. Better than that, everyone knows them, uses them and finds ways in which they can be applied practically in their lives.

However, a search did eventually uncover a copy of *The Horusian Way*. Insofar as the Questi can be recorded, then, here is a version of them.

DAMANHUR'S QUEST(IONS)

Since the beginning of its growth process, Damanhur has felt the need to trace a path to guide every single individual and the community as a whole toward an harmonic and synergic spiritual evolution. This sort of spiritual *vademecum* is what Damanhurians call *Quesiti* (Questi), principles of behaviour which represent the basic formulas of individual and collective growth.

We can compare the Questi to the different floors of a building: the ground floor supports the first, the second and all the others, and it is impossible to get directly to the top floor without going through the preceding stories. At the moment Damanhur's spiritual building is composed of seven Questi, but as it is a growing reality, our capacity to intensely inhabit all the floors might open up to new levels of spiritual growth.

Questi I

A) Complete and aware action.

B) Purity of intent.

C) To live the synchronic moment to the full.

COMMENTARY ON THE FIRST QUESTI

The Damanhurian approach is through a School of Initiation which has action as its basic foundation. Action means to work responsibly and with purity of intent for the spiritual progress of others, because only by doing this does one have the premise for one's own evolutionary growth. One has, moreover, to live fully the synchronic moment, which means to 'live in the moment': not to be bound, that is, egotistically, to the fruit of the action carried out. To act also means to choose, and to live the moment is continuous choice, instant by instant. The first Questi is the highest expression of free will.

Questi II

A) Coherence and continuity in action.

B) Continuous choice, instant by instant, to give
        substance to Questi I.

C) Respect when giving one's word in faith, whatever the cost.

COMMENTARY ON THE SECOND QUESTI

Spiritual choice, once made, is to be coherently and continuously kept going in time. The lamp that has been lit should not be put out, because 'to be put out', in esoteric terms, means that it may never be lit again.

The second Questi gives substance to the first. There one talks of ACTION, here of COHERENCE AND CONTINUITY in action. To do that one needs to have a deep respect for oneself; only thus will one have the inherent strength to keep one's word, in faith, what-ever the cost.

Questi III
A) Inner transformation
and
C) Rebirth to the sacred
B) Through new logics and a qualitative leap (of course directed consciously by choice).
A–B–C: formation of a new People
and
A–B–C: of a new culture.

COMMENTARY ON THE THIRD QUESTI

It is the Questi of inner transformation and return to the sacred. Humanity must grow, must lift itself from the state of matter in which it has been restricted and rise on high, towards those spaces that once were its own domain, due to its divine position. This requires, above all, that each individual transforms himself and works so that even others might complete that inner alchemical transmutation which leads, through a new culture, to the creation of a People, the primeval cell of the future Reawakened Mankind. And this is the importance of the return to the sacred, to that mystical vision of life which permits one to overcome pride and individual egoism and ensures that the single threads of the mosaic take the rightful place assigned to them in the great Divine Plan.

Questi IV – feminine
A) Aware availability, not egotistical, of oneself.
C) Dignified progress towards perfection and respect for the completion of femininity.
D) To be an element of union.
Woman stabilises.
Woman and man will come together again in the III and VI Questi.

It indicates those premises that are indispensable for overcoming the bound condition of woman. The road passes through awareness of a feminine Self, which manifests in continual giving and thus constant presence. It also deals with the completion of the gifts usually attributed to man's companion, opening up new characteristics which unite gentleness with strength; these conditions, which every woman can rediscover, find a gain in her peers, searching for the completion of her own missing parts, even amongst those that are masculine elements (be it, however, with respect for diversity, expressed in different necessary functions). Woman as weaver and source of friendship (understood as an element of union), able to bring back together in a single thread the 'scattering' of humanity and so put back together the secret symbol of Mankind, shattered into pieces in the distant times of its undeserved defeat.

Questi V

A) Stability and firmness (in ongoing)

B) Harmonious inner revolution.

C) Intelligent discovery and rediscovery of habits, and looking again at them, with the aim of overcoming the conditioning of the three Rivers [1] (creating, therefore, a stable and continual harmonious inner revolution).

The elements of stability and firmness belonging to the masculine should be permanently strengthened through continual inner evolutionary movement. Making use of the intelligence he possesses, Man should know how to eliminate 'conditioned' habits (those 'taken for granted') in order to rediscover (re-choose) as conscious ritual strength, able to give a vital rhythm to his own actions. That means overcoming

---

[1] The conditioning given by culture, education, environment and genetics.

the conditioning required from one's education and one's environment through a voluntary and conscious expression of free will.

Questi VI

A) Inversion of the Fourth and Fifth Questi. The former becomes masculine, the latter feminine.

B) Union generates life.

Rituals

In point B) there are three parts:

1) It is born of silence.

2) It causes everything to grow and mature.

Prayer

Everyone adjusts to the eco-system of the pure I by searching, when working with the preceding Questi.

Definition of point B):

Individual and mutually agreed synthesis.

C) Imagination, Fantasy (in the sense of Art, Life).

D) Generosity-Goodwill.

form – action – formation
   (education)

Form, a created object, is now alive.

The next step will consist in making it real in the Mother Worlds and the Echo Worlds, condensing the essence so that it becomes alchemy, thus to obtain the spirit of life, just as life has been obtained from form.

The living God Atom.

(Generosity, goodwill and altruism are the return spring of this mechanism!)

E) The search for unification within human forces is the measure of things (dimensions) between them.

Spiritual fractals.

It deals with LIFE. Life is well and truly creation, substantiation of 'nothingness', and not simply moving energies from one reservoir to another. It is the 'anti-entropic'[2] principle *par excellence* which shifts the concept of a 'closed system'[3] to a divine level, with the result that there is no degradation of energies during their various transformations. The 'divine spark' which is inside each one of us is part of GOD and therefore can, ritually, create.

Humanity is an aspect of the great divine 'Fractal' and even that which 'substantiates' cannot be other than God's own imprint. To do this it is necessary to mix the various ingredients in just measure: generosity, goodwill, action-form, education, art, imagination and fantasy. Only thus will the divine spark fill the creation of Humanity and give life to matter.[4]

The first Law of Magic:
AS ABOVE, SO BELOW
is the formula of the Sixth Questi.

[2]*Entropy:* The system whereby for every transformation of energy in a closed system there is a degradation of that same energy, that is to say, a diminution of the total energy available in that closed system.

[3]*Closed system:* See above. A system which does not receive energy from external sources.

[4]*Fractal:* From the Latin *fractus*, past participle of *frangere*, to break up. In geometry: an object or phenomenon which has a 'jagged, angular' structure. Examples of fractal objects are: the outline of a snowflake or of a cloud, the jagged shape of a coastline. A characteristic of fractal objects, besides their irregularity, is their 'similarity amongst themselves' if one views them on different levels.

Questi VII

A) Uncertainty – Doubt – Adaptability
Create the True Real, moment by moment
B) Demolition of certainties
To edify every existence in constant mutation. Evolution
The real-form is a bubble of appearance
C) Solidity built instant by instant

In further discussions with Usignolo, I discovered that the Questi are based both on the internal development of individuals and on that of the People of Damanhur as a whole. The first Questi was developed in 1983, when Damanhur first began to see itself as a newly directed spiritual path. It puts the focus on action, on never being static, on living life to the full. It is better to act and make a mistake than to not act for fear of making a mistake. The second requires the continuity of that action you have undertaken – not to leave a job half finished, to always follow through on any decisions that you make. It focuses on constancy and fulfilment, acting every day, choosing to act every day, keeping on practising, keeping up the rhythm.

These principles were brought into being after much experience. Every nuance of every term was considered in relation to how it might be applied to people's lives. Each was concerned with a return to the sacred and each related to each person making their own internal transformation, even as the community itself was transformed around them. Indeed, this was when the concept of a People evolved. The first three Questi all worked towards defining the People as an idea.

While the first three Questi set the Damanhurians off in a positive direction, the fourth caused them to shift their way of thinking quite substantially. This Questi was the one where everyone, men and women, tried to discover the feminine aspects within themselves, to cultivate them in all parts of their lives. There was a long period over which this one developed and it was accompanied by a huge amount of artistic activity. Much of the artwork for the temple was created using the energy transformed by the work on this Questi.

The fifth Questi was concerned with change, transformation, movement; the sixth was specifically related to creation, creativity;

and seventh relates to the idea of ending all certainties such as unquestioned beliefs, finding what is real and certain inside oneself instead, and putting forward the idea of doubt as a means of searching. Usignolo explained:

> This is the phase we are working through now. It involves a lot of work on oneself, inside oneself, looking for autonomous replies that are inside oneself. This work on the development of the Questi has its own logic. It is related to being an individual within a larger entity called the People, where the individual is important, but so is the development of the People. One relates purposefully to the other; they are not contradictory.

I remembered an apocryphal story about Oberto. When a large group of Damanhurians were gathered together one day, he asked everyone to take off their wristwatches and to place them in a basket that he brought around. Everyone did it happily, thinking that Oberto was going to perform an experiment in time travel or some such wonder. When he had collected all the watches, Oberto took the basket round again and asked everyone to take one out without looking. Of course, those who had put in a cheap plastic watch might take out a top quality gold one or vice versa, until those at the end were left with whatever was left. Then the whole exercise was repeated once more. Oberto did this to show that people should not be too attached to possessions and also to unite everyone's individual sense of time, to bring about a communal time. People got to keep the watches they had finally chosen and so even years later someone would see someone else wearing 'their' watch and be reminded of the importance of the People.

There is no fixed number of Questi. As Caimano told me,

> If anyone wants to develop a new path, with a particular purpose to it and sufficient energy for it, and this is recognized by a large enough number of people, then these collective people could create a new way, a new spiritual path. But this is a serious thing. It requires a certain capability.

So the Questi may yet develop further. In fact, those of the Way of the Word are developing an eighth Questi, based on expansion and the road towards truth.

The Quests of Damanhur are central to an understanding of almost everything about the Damanhurians and their socio-spiritual philosophy. In Appendix II at the end of this book you will find a chart, 'On the Threshold', that shows the complex intertwining of the Questi into all other aspects: the primeval Laws of esoteric physics, the spiritual ways, the chakras of the body, chromatherapeutic colours, positive and negative characteristics. This is further evidence as to why, when you ask a question at Damanhur, you do not always get a straight answer. It is not that they are being evasive, but that the complexity of their view of life is not so easily described in cut and dried, black-and-white terms. Subtle shades are important in their big picture.

Our aim is to create free people, human beings with an open mind and a wide perspective.

Stambecco Pesco

I was very impressed with what I saw of the Damanhurian school system. I have spent most of my life in education, as a teacher, as an examinations board visiting examiner and as a community arts organizer. In my years, I have seen many forms of education, many approaches to teaching. At Damanhur, the schools work with small groups of pupils, with an informal approach and a high degree of participation by the young people. They carry out a great deal of project work. I saw a particularly impressive multimedia project where the young people had actually produced a very versatile interactive computer programme based on a story they had written. It was a stunning piece of work. I saw a language class with a great deal of interaction between teacher and pupils, where everyone had a chance to participate and where the level of learning was very high. I saw a mathematics class that was equally impressive. The level of work was as good as any I had experienced in many years of educational work.

Of course, many teachers would say, 'Well, anyone can be a good teacher when you have only six pupils.' That is what it is all about. The people of Damanhur have seen the wisdom of investing in the education of their children. It is not easy. To run an internal independent education programme is very expensive. But the parents of the children, the nucleo households that they live in, the community that they are a part of and the overall Federation of Damanhur all play a part in ensuring that the education programme is delivered.

Stambecco Pesco, the overall head of schools, told me that the school is only one component of education at Damanhur. Beyond are the families and the wider community, which of course, has at its core another school – the School of Mediation. Stambecco believed, however, that in spite of the importance Damanhur places on the bringing up of children, they still have not found the ideal process. People at Damanhur often do more than one job and sometimes not enough time is spent with children, extending their experience in the wider community. So the school does often become the most important aspect of a child's education. In addition to the regular teachers at the school, however, many other people give occasional lessons on specific subjects. And Damanhur has a reservoir of very talented people.

The educational policy starts with a dual premise: first, the state curriculum; and second, the sensitivity and spirituality of the experience at Damanhur. In addition, each child is an individual who needs their own particular education. So the school is the meeting point of these three aspects.

The Damanhurians take particular care to ensure that the young people do not become too used to Damanhurian ways. Their aim is to create people with open minds and a wide perspective. In spite of the wide range of facilities available at Damanhur – computers, music, art and horse-riding, for example – the young people are also encouraged to take part in such activities elsewhere. It is important to have this contact with the outside world. They also take part in the state academic examinations every year.

Stambecco showed me a table of how the overall school structure is organized for the complete education of children at Damanhur:

Six months to five years: childhood school. 8.30 a.m.–5 p.m.
Five years to seven years: primary school. 8.30 a.m.–5 p.m.
Seven years to 13 years: secondary school. 8.30 a.m.–1.20 p.m.
  Afternoon options.
Over 13: to an Italian state school.

In the childhood school and the primary school the students work for longer hours than the state school. But the secondary school only meets in the morning. In the afternoon, the young people can choose to take part in drama, music, the arts, horse-riding or other activities. Also, each class does extra lessons beyond the state curriculum one afternoon a week in such areas as foreign languages and computing.

Sending the young people to state schools at the age of 13 or 14 ensure that they have a broader perspective than just the experience at Damanhur. Every effort is made to allow young people to make up their own mind about Damanhur.

Stambecco is head of all the schools, but with a particular personal reference to the secondary school. I asked him about its curriculum:

> The secondary school operates a standard curriculum that pupils have to pass through in order to pass their examinations, like any state school. But we do more than that – we do arts projects, cultural activities and developmental work. For example, every day begins with 20 minutes of meditation, inner harmonizing, which concentrates the children's attention throughout the day.
>
> The dramatic projects in particular help children to come out of themselves, to change their ways of relating to other young people, to find other characters within themselves.

I mentioned a rehearsal I had seen of a particularly fine comedy version of *Romeo and Juliet*, where the opposing parents fell for each other. That solved all those stupid conflicts! 'The children worked the scenes out themselves,' Stambecco told me.

And music is in a world of its own, with lots of opportunities here. The same with painting and sculpture. The young people can learn how to become very precise in the way they work, but also how to develop an appreciation of things. For example, on Italian television these days, there is much that is of indifferent quality, but we do not think that it is sensible to forbid such things. Rather, it is better to show the young people that there are also beautiful things in life. They are surrounded by artistic things here and we use that.

This approach shows that though there could be a tendency to have one's head in clouds in a place such as Damanhur, Stambecco and his team obviously have their feet placed firmly on the ground. They provide an education that is centred in the real world, making the best of every aspect of it.

There are radical plans for future education in Damanhur's schools. The aim is to have a classroom as big as Europe – children will be taken away in the camper vans on a regular basis for maybe one or two weeks at a time. They will travel to the famous places of history and science, learning about Waterloo in Waterloo, for example, or about particle physics in the underground particle accelerator project at CERN. This is radical thinking indeed and part of Stambecco's dream of an integrated education system for the children of Damanhur.

Just before Christmas, on my second visit, I was invited to a school concert. It was a particularly fabulous event, with highly original com-edy pieces, excellent costumes and sets, and the most enthusiastic participation by the young pupils. It was the one of the happiest, jolliest affairs that I have ever been to. I realize I am using a lot of superlatives here, but Damanhur is a world where superlatives are needed!

THE FREE UNIVERSITY OF DAMANHUR

Libera Università di Damanhur, the Free University of Damanhur, is the face of Damanhur that many people first come into contact with, for it offers a wide range of courses that many people come to Damanhur to take part in. The Free University, of course, is more like the Open University than free of cost. But it does also aim to be free of dogma, free of institutional culturalization.

The idea of free universities is not a new one. They were around in the United States and in Britain during the sixties and seventies. R. D. Laing, amongst others, helped run a free university, offering subjects on the fringes of psychology or radical political thinking.

At Damanhur, open courses were staged as far back as 1978. At that time there were in fact no other activities there. But after this initial period, when centres were opened in Turin, Milan, Bologna, Rome and other places in Italy, not so many courses were run at Damanhur itself and only one person was responsible for organizing them there. They were known at that time simply as 'Damanhur courses' and were concerned with inner research and development. Based on Oberto's teachings, they covered such topics as hypnosis, the paranormal, extra-sensory perception, natural medicine, communicating with plants and harmonization. But by 1987, when Gazzella Mimosa was based in Turin with a group of people, they felt it was important to have a larger organization and to order the courses into broader areas of study. So the Free University came into being.

I talked with Gazzella and Anaconda, who works with her, in the new Free University offices, under the main building at Damanhur. Reviewing the early days, Gazzella told me that at first they offered courses on natural medicines, hypnosis and communication, and the widening of perception. Initially in Turin teachers shared space. One of them was Benedetto Lavagna, a famous healer who used pendulum browsing and so on. He was famous for chromatherapy and had a centre where he often held conferences. It was he who introduced people to Oberto, who was in his early twenties at that time and little known about outside his own circle of friends. So Oberto became known to the general public. His conferences were extraordinary affairs. As Anaconda said:

> What characterized these conferences was that they were very practical. Oberto believed in demystifying things that were considered paranormal. He did a great deal of experimenting and gave magical things a very practical

aspect. He showed extraordinary effects and said that there was nothing special about them – this in a city where magic was all about power and secrecy! But he said that it was just nature at work.

According to Gazzella and Anaconda, Oberto was very into bending keys, using hypnosis, and so on. But he would always demonstrate such effects in a way that went against the tendency of the time, presenting them as natural phenomena that could be investigated, rather than as something to fear or be in awe of. Anaconda said:

> Oberto's courses have always been about what is practical, what can be shown, what you can experiment with. They are courses about the fact of researching, not just stopping at common ideas about things, or being theoretical. Courses that were held at Damanhur were also based on this grounding – communicating with plants, having plants opening doors or plants that watered themselves. This work with plants has developed into more musical research in recent years, but at that time apparently there were many other experiments with them, like connecting plants to door locks, through sensors, so that they would open doors as certain people approached. Oberto no longer shows much enthusiasm for these things that look like miracles, extraordinary things, paranormal effects. They had a purpose then; now it is time for more positive things related to the inner searching of individuals.

After two years, a school for spiritual healing was started. Gazzella explained:

> That was a very important testing ground. Up until then, because spiritual healing is based on such delicate relationships, the knowledge had been reserved for Damanhurians. It was related to the spiritual initiation in Damanhur. It was a sacred investiture. But now, as many things have changed in Damanhur, there has been an opening for a three-year course to prepare external people also. The three years ensure that,

as a minimum guarantee, people have sufficient preparation to be able to establish a therapeutic relationship on a sound spiritual basis.

The courses have always been the main gateway to Damanhur. Most of the people there now first came to hear of the community by passing through the Italian centres first. This gradual getting to know Damanhur is something the Damanhurians would like to preserve. Many people who come into contact with Damanhur courses then go on to the School of Meditation. It is a smooth transition.

So, currently there is the School of Meditation for people in Damanhur and the courses run by the Free University for people from outside. But it is never so clear cut as that. People in Damanhur also do univer-sity courses such as the spiritual healing or the past lives courses. Also, people from outside can join the School of Meditation. So there is to be a review and a restructuring of the system, and a University of Meditation is to be developed. This will consist of several elements:

Ritual studies – the path of meditation
Esoteric psychology
Healing arts
Creative arts

and the teachers will be under the direction of the Way of the Word, whilst the current staff of the Free University, Gazzella, Anaconda and Onitorinco, will have overall administration of the university. To influence and guide this transition, radical new ways of looking at human beings are under consideration.

Anaconda is optimistic, especially in the light of what Oberto has told him about his own hopes for the project:

He says that the aim is for the University of Meditation at Damanhur to become one of the main, if not the main, teaching institutions in the world, offering spiritual courses by the year 2000.

As Anaconda points out, things do move very quickly at Damanhur. When he first came there, in 1989, there was nowhere at all for guests to stay. As soon as a house became free, there would be people ready to move into it. Guests were just not a priority. Now things have turned right round – there is the splendid Rama accommodation block, reserved for visitors and guests, and another guest house at La Mela D'oro.

Anaconda continued:

> One thing that Oberto stresses is that there are many courses ready, many things that have not yet been divulged, many more than he has been able to give so far. Once such courses have been launched, the University of Meditation will take on a much more important role. So we should be ready for anything.

And if you want to come back to my side
I will sing your name across Everywhere
And inside of me.

Grillo Mirto

Damanhurian concerts are elaborate affairs, with many months of preparation and a great deal of collaboration by musicians, singers, dancers and people working on a text. They normally take place within the temple, inside the Hall of Mirrors, where light, colour, sound and movement are all multiplied and amplified, creating a unique spectacle. Just like the visual artwork on the temple, this process of collaboration requires a great deal of preparation. Also like the artwork in the temple, it grows out of a group process, part creative endeavour, part meditation, with a high degree of experimentation and improvisation. A whole team of people is responsible for the production.

Those who make music in the temple are part of the Way of the Word. They use the music as a spiritual path, sometimes improvising, sometimes composing together in both the sacred language and Italian. Lepre Viola told me it is easier to sing in the sacred language, because they have become so familiar with it and have found ways to work with it intuitively.

In the sacred language it is easier, because the word connected to the idea, more related to its meaning. When I compose in the sacred language, I think in the sacred language and these are words that open your mind.

Lepre outlined the method of group composition. First a group prepares with harmonizing or breathing. Then follows an hour of inner harmonizing and a devotional study, 'The Way about Music', may also be used as preparation. Then the group brings their ideas together. Usually one or two people write them down and then they are developed by the group as a whole.

Ritual concerts also take place at the Winter and Summer Solstices and Spring and Autumn Equinoxes. As well as the music, these celebrations involve many rituals. Then again, sometimes, of course, the musicians get together to play just for fun!

I was lucky enough to see several performances of a concert that Lepre and the director Gatto had been preparing for performance in the temple. It was called *Vel Velj* (pronounced 'Vel Velly', *Vel* being the sacred language word for 'love' and *Velj* for 'friendship'), and was based on the titles of Oberto's paintings that relate specifically to love. These titles are meditations, a set of ideas, for example:

- United hands, a promise of love, a game of common and unwritten rules, as unwritten are the looks and the smiles…
  I unite, I call, I emote those thin lines of personal colour, of human scent…At your service, I do not deceive…
- I would like a mature love, made of trust and secret sweetness, where the things done for the one you love are quivering and tender secrets. I would like a very young, adolescent love, full of madness and transport. I want you, my love, who are all these things, whatever your name may be, and your secret names.
- In the mind, an activated circuit of love, it must not make you suffer, but bring the joy of the reciprocal recognition,

of the new light in a world previously grey and without the search for colour, without life intensely invested...

These three pieces, however, are only starting-points. In the same way as Oberto would use a meditation as part of the process of creating a painting, in such a way that the painting and the title are intertwined, become as one, so the singers and musicians take these texts and use them as the basis of their own creative process. The results are often immensely beautiful. The most obvious and striking aspect is the qual-ity of the music. There are exceptional melodies, those that give you a lift when you hear them and stay in your mind after the event. Over the years some 'classic' Daman-hurian songs have emerged. One that was featured in *Vel Velj* is called 'Moonray'. It was greeted with a spontaneous burst of applause almost as soon as it started.

The main theme of *Vel Velj* was love – love in all its expressions, in all its shades, from affection to sensitivity, from passion to friend-ship. There were different movements in the concert: solos, duets and choral pieces. Dance was also a featured part of many of the pieces. The orchestra was made up of guitar, cello, flute, Celtic harp, violin, synthesizer and percussion.

The concert began with an overture of the 'music of the trees', a technique which has been devised and developed at Damanhur where trees and plants are connected to electronic synthesizers by means of special sensors, so that the sensitivity of the trees or plants actually plays the music. Usignolo, the Nightingale, was featured in a duet with a tree on top of the mountain, with the sensor leads being run down into the temple and coupled to the electronics. Most of the six evening performances went really well, but one night there was a thunderstorm outside and the tree was showing signs of great anxiety, which was reflected in a particular wildness in its music. Usignolo found it difficult to sing with her musical part-ner that night.

The concert itself was a delightful experience, an inspiration. Comparing it to many national dance and music groups I encoun-tered when I was involved with a large-scale international arts festi-val, I realized a distinctive Damanhurian style was emerging. The people who took part also enjoyed the performance, probably more so than those of us lucky enough to see it. High creativity, much enjoyment.

Previous temple concerts have been based on esoteric physics, the Damanhurian journeys, the arts, mandalas and dreaming. A gala concert, under the title *Peal* ('Eternal'), collected together some of the favourite music produced at Damanhur and was staged as 'the concert to save the temple' in 1993.

RITUAL OF THE WINTER SOLSTICE

I was also fortunate to experience one of the Solstice rituals at Damanhur at the Winter Solstice in December 1996.

The Solstice and Equinox rituals are quite large affairs that are open to the public, and the ritual of the Winter Solstice actually takes place over the whole of the Solstice day, from daybreak to sunset. It is not continuous in terms of people being there the whole time, but there are elements that carry over from one section to the next – ritual fires that are kept burning all day, for example.

The ritual day itself is a big family event at Damanhur. Everyone is up early in the morning, dressed in their School of Meditation robes of white, red, yellow and blue. The sight of many hundreds of people entering the woods dressed in their brightly coloured robes is quite something. Everyone wears a crown made from twigs and leaves of the forest – oak at the Winter Solstice. However, this is not just a dressing up, family fun day. There is a serious purpose to the ritual, protecting and preparing the spiritual energies for the coming months, and working with the subtle forces to cement the bonds between humans and nature.

When I was there it was a cold but extremely fresh winter's day. The forest looked absolutely fabulous. There were actually about five different rituals throughout the day, from the lighting of the fires at the break of day to the putting of them out at the setting of the sun.

Here is the text of a document prepared for visitors who took part in a course to find out more about the Solstice celebration:

The music of time stresses various rhythms of life, and if it takes the planet a year to accomplish an entire cycle of renewal in a continuous alternation of rebirths and evident death, Mankind is required to go through several seasons, more 'births' inside and outside himself, more inner and obvious separations from his outside world in order to complete an evolutionary segment. On this path, sun, Earth and nature have always been the elements through which Mankind accomplishes the rhythm of life.

Everywhere on the planet, at every fragment of time, Mankind has watched and loved the sun and stars. He has conceived and built the bond with the Earth, he has explored himself through the symbolic relationship with nature.

For thousands of years he has been sharing a territory of the soul with these forces and shapes, as large as the thought that is able to contain it.

For that reason he has felt the need to manifest and perpetrate that bond that we will define of spiritual type, looking yet for the lowest common denominator between his rhythms and those of each force, and finding it in the two Solstice moments.

This ritual expresses, with the witnessing of gods, the Alliance agreement sealed between Mankind and the spirits of nature, a sort of marriage that requires renewal as a time commitment beyond the perishability of the form.

The fire receives these conjugal promises, made through the offering of herbs and oak-leaf crowns, then being sealed.

At this particular time of the year, in which the day seems to be leaving its place to the night being the longest of all, Mankind interrogates the elements around him, reads the signs and, inside the sacred circle which is common to so many ancient cultures, channels the forces of Earth and nature, so that, together in the bond of magic, they will be able to call the sun back to its path, urging it to rise and run again the way of the sky towards the perpetuating of life.

Participating in this ritual means recognizing yourself in the rhythms of the universe, in your own liabilities towards the world. It also means producing an act of presence before the Superior Forces that inspire and protect the planet.

The proper mood to be in is the one of a person who with simplicity approaches the ritual to feel, know and find himself.

SUN AND MOON PEAK PHASES

Sun phases are celebrated by men, moon phases by women.

The alternate placing in the circle (men–women) represents the balance between the opposites.

During the ritual's middle phases, the offer of propitiation to the Divine Forces takes place with the mistletoe purposefully gathered, with the oak-leaves pulled off the initiates' crowns and with the crowns of the previous year.

These offerings are burnt on the sun fire at local noontime and burnt on the moon fire during the peak moon phase.

SETTING OF SUN AND MOON

The fires that are lit at dawn and watched throughout the day are put out at setting times by the male officiators (sun fire) and by the female officiators (moon fire).

So the Winter Solstice Ritual reaches the end.

CONSECRATION OF THE MISTLETOE

Mistletoe represents the fire of the Earth, witnessing among Mankind the presence of the Creator. This plant, sacred to ancient people, is consecrated on the moon fire, and thereafter distributed as a propitiatory element for the entire course of the year.

Other rituals not usually open to the public, though occasionally they may be. This is one of the strange things about Damanhur – sometimes they make decisions on the hoof and then are not sure how to deal with the results. They will sometimes have guests at closed events, for example, but as such a guest, you are often left uncertain as to whether you really should be there or not. It is a strange feeling. But, as in everything else, the Damanhurians try to be accommodating. That is one of their endearing qualities.

I attended a ritual for the purification of the People as a guest. Here are my impressions.

RITUAL OF THE PURIFICATION OF THE PEOPLE

A strong smell of incense wafts from the stairway leading to the Prayer Temple underneath the central buildings of Damanhur. In the outer corridor people are putting on School of Meditation robes and changing their shoes for slippers. I have no slippers, so I slip off my shoes and enter in socks. It reminds me a bit of group therapy.

I am confused when I first enter the temple chamber. A lot of people are sitting around and there is an assemblage of things in the centre of the floor. I am directed by *Re Guida* Orango to follow those who came in before me along the right-hand side of the room.

I move in amongst a tight group of people. There is almost no room to sit down, but I manage it anyway – another similarity with those growth things. Then I'm immediately freaked by anxious persons asking me if I trod on or in the magic circle. With the usual language problems, I'm not sure what they are saying. Am I in the magic circle? Maybe there's some sort of rule that you can't be here unless you know David Berglass, then that strikes me as a silly idea, and I begin to fear I might have done something wrong. But I think I haven't. I'm probably in the clear.

Panic over, I settle down to the atmosphere of the room. Now that I'm actually in here, it's great. The place is dripping with atmosphere. Esperide comes over to ask me if I know what is going on. She tells me the routine. In the centre of the room is a picture of the People of Damanhur. Next to it is a candle, specially made with a number of different coloured People bracelets embedded into the wax, so that as the candle burns down, the bracelets burn also. People will come into the circle, which is opened and closed by means of a magical instrument, and stand for some minutes in front of the picture. There are also the crowns and sceptres of the *Re Guida*, in their boxes, and a couple of other bits of ritual paraphernalia.

A small ensemble in the corner: Gattopardo on guitar, Usignolo on Celtic harp, Cabriolo on flute. Beautiful, smooth, soothing music. A very calm atmosphere. People come to stand in front of the People with great dignity. They are obviously experiencing an intensity of feeling. As the circle is opened, one person steps in, one person steps out. As they cross they both make the sign of *con te* towards the picture. Then the circle is closed again.

This sounds monotonous, but is actually very beautiful. The atmosphere is serene, the music varied, but always relaxing. There are occasional readings from prepared texts.

I am enjoying the occasion and mellowing into it when Esperide comes to tell me that Gazzella, who lives in the house where I am staying, is about to go. She tells me to follow her down the other side of the room, not the way I came in, lest I should tread too near the magic circle again! I want to stay longer, but the spell has been broken now. I am led out of the room, feeling a bit like a naughty schoolboy!

On the way home, Gazzella told me about the ritual. Its purpose was to take away negative influences affecting the whole of the People. Other rituals can be performed to take away negative forces acting against individuals. The bracelets of different colours represented the People, from the humblest pink threads signifying being one of the People to the yellow threads symbolizing the highest stages of the School of Meditation. The burning of the bracelets was an act of purification, a ritual act to benefit the People of Damanhur. I no longer had the sheepish look of the schoolboy, but the joyful grin of someone who had just participated in something of invaluable significance.

One of the most pleasant tasks I had to undertake in preparing the material for this book was to attend a very special gathering when the people of Damanhur came together to celebrate the formation of the People. People simply told stories, stories about

Damanhur, stories about how it had all come about. There were sto-ries from young and old alike, there were stories that made you laugh, stories that made you cry. The hall was packed to capacity and I regard myself as fortunate to have been there. The evening was introduced by the representative of the Way of the Oracle, Sirena:

> At this time the People represents, for us, our mother and our father, but at the same time we are the father and mother of this People.
>
> When people have had phases of preparation to become linked to this People, it is as if the People were born inside each one of us. So we are not only talking about a creature, some-thing formed by all of us, but it is also as if that creature exists inside of each one of us; so that I am People, we are People.
>
> Tonight, we want to think further about it, to think about us, the real People, to heat up the waiting for the baptizing, so that we can all go together, moving in the same direction. We will retrace the main steps that brought us to the formation of the People.
>
> If we are here, it is because we wish to be here. We use our will to come to listen to this. It is as if we are representing a branch that we are, that I am, that we all are, that will be part of that bonfire that at the right moment will be lit. This is an important preparatory step. We are preparing the bonfire. The fire is not lit yet, but it will be at the right moment.
>
> So it is the creature that we all are that is going to receive this baptism, and through this ritual passage we will be recog-nized and presented to the major forces. You know about the Triad, you know about the forces that compose the Triad [see Chapter 15]. As a People we are making one more step, at last to be recognized as a people, as an important creature, with its own place in the magical design towards the awakening.
>
> This evening allows the older people of Damanhur to think about the past again, and the younger people to understand the lines that Damanhur has traced through time, since its beginning. There has been another moment, a preparatory moment, a ritual moment, the burning of the negative energy that these people have accumulated, as a People, so that we

can be presented pure and purified at this event. This was the ritual purification of the People, last Sunday evening. This is a rite that is repeated every Solstice, but in this case it had more precise parts, allowing us to reach the level of purification that we needed and also to have a major awareness of ourselves as a People.

From the history we will hear tonight, we will also see those elements that characterize the People, the characteristics that give the People elements of civilization, of distinction.

There followed two hours of fascinating stories: the journeys, the start of the building of the temple, the first Damanhurian marriage, the early battle games, the birth of the People. The atmosphere in that hall was one I have rarely experienced – it was a truly joyous gathering which will long remain in my mind. Though if I do start to forget, well, I have a video of it.

THE MYTH OF THE ARROW OF COMPLEXITY

It was time out of joint. They were gathered together in a place of refuge. It could have been the Café at the End of the Universe. Or the Four Seconds Bar. Only it wasn't. Chaos knew exactly where they were, knew exactly what to do.

'Being able to separate planes is something absolutely great,' he said. 'To accomplish it you need not only magical knowledge and the means of doing it, but also a huge serge of emotion and a high expression of free will.'

So, day by day, through the things they had said, they drove themselves towards this huge expectation and emotional charge. They made themselves emotionally high and talked much about Illumination. Chaos said, 'In order to save this planet, our great planet, we must perform a huge action.'

A group of them stayed together, in that place, for days and days. And then they were ready. They wanted to do something to save the planet. Not just because tomorrow it was going to be destroyed. It was not just the catastrophe. But they talked about opening the paths of the mind, and the heart, and the soul. And they talked about the way to give up your life, for a project of this kind.

'After all,' said Chaos, 'it is the easiest thing to do. In fact, if we look at it now, it would have been much easier.'

And the gods laughed.

'Because it is continuity of action that kills you much more.'

Gales of laughter from the gods.

'But,' they said, 'but how, but how? How shall this be done? This creation of the new plane, how shall it be done, and how shall it be opened to the spirit?'

And as they spoke emotions grew and grew and grew.

They had with them an old medieval crossbow. They were at the place of the pyramid. One had to offer to be killed and another had to offer to kill.

Charged emotions, heightened spirits. They all agreed what was to be said, that one had gone crazy and killed the other. Someone left, saying they were all crazy. 'It is all too dangerous, bye-bye.'

Tension grew amongst those who stayed. They later said, 'It was worth doing it for the result, but the pain at the time was unbearable.'

There was a woman amongst them who offered herself to be killed. Another offered to kill. A third agreed to be the one blamed for everything. Of course, the woman who offered to kill was the one trembling most with fear. She asked to walk outside first. She returned. She took the crossbow, loaded the dart-arrow into the shaft, raised the bow and set the sights on the heart of her friend. Then she asked of the others, 'Would you do this if you were in my place?'

Everybody said, 'Yes, without fail.'

So she renewed her aim and started to squeeze the trigger when everything stopped, frozen in a moment of time.

The Arrow of Complexity. The act of will, the woman's decision to shoot, had been expressed 100 per cent. On the subtle level, the shooting had happened. So the action of dividing the planes has started. On the subtle plane, it did happen, because they had all been absolutely convinced that she was going to do it.

Free will, transformed to divine force, had made the separation happen.

And on the other plane, the plane they left behind, the woman really killed her friend and the military took away the third, who went to prison. All that happened, but it happened on the plane that they had left, the one that is on the brink of catastrophe.

part four

adventures in time

---

*It is not difficult to realize what a man is, it is the preparation
for his realization that is long and difficult.*

Usigolo Mirica

Whilst I had been finding out about the *Quesiti*, the set of principles on which Damanhur is built, I had been surprised to find out that Mankind was a divinity, and a primeval divinity at that. I had also heard that the Damanhurians had a pretty fascinating theory of personality. To discover more, I set off in search of Gattopardo Tek, who has something of a reputation for his grasp of esoteric physics, and who stands on the stage next to Oberto at the Thursday evening gatherings, where up to 300 of the community engage in theoretical discussions, and makes the necessary drawings or diagrams.

We met on a sunny day in early September, shaded by a tree still in blossom but beginning to shed its petals. Gattopardo began by telling me about the nine primeval divinities.

Mankind is a divinity, one of nine primeval divinities. The other primeval divinities are not part of us and it would be difficult, at this point in time, for us to understand what they are or to give them a name. They may relate to the nine primeval forces in some way.

The primeval divinity Mankind has been given the task of conquering the world of forms. The other primeval divinities are observers, they do not intervene. They do, however, benefit from the results.

It is as if the divinity that is Mankind has a mission to carry out. It has to conquer the world of forms, as we know it. It has to make matter divine. 'Matter' is the universal forms inside the speed of light. But our world is not composed only of the world of forms within the speed of light, but also contains lots of other worlds that exist beyond the speed of light, but are still within our universe. We are not speaking here of other possible universes. Within our universe the human being is concerned with form within the speed of light. In other strata of existence, beyond the speed of light, we understand that other primeval divinities intervene there.

We know that there are eight other divinities, because, just like Mankind, they emanate from something superior. And Man, as a primeval divinity, has a lot of knowledge from beyond the world of forms that he would not have just within the world of forms, unless he were to become one with the primeval divinity, that is, Enlightened. But the path of knowledge must be gradual, therefore it does sometimes throw up some contradictions and ambiguities. There are things beyond the human being that are part of the Great Divinity, without having to speak of the Great Mover, the Absolute, the Unmoving Mover. We do have a series of collaborations with other beings from beyond the world of forms.

I was beginning to grasp enough about Damanhur to know that the Damanhurians were not polytheistic worshippers of multifarious gods. They had a belief in a Great Divinity, something beyond comprehension that we could only begin to have occasional insights into, but which emanated throughout everything. In this respect, there would be little conflict with the Catholic Church, Judaism or most other religions. However, where the Damanhurians do differ is that they believe that divinity is not only outside, but also inside every human being and they refute the very notion of religion, because they maintain that by the time a belief has become a religion, it is so strangled by dogma that it has lost most of its divine characteristics, is sanitized, dead and defunct. Furthermore, they believe that it is this tendency towards religiosity that has stopped much of the spiritual development of Mankind, by taking away the active, the vital, the crisp, the creative.

The concept of Mankind as one of nine original primeval divinities is one that requires a shift in consciousness. I found it better, eventually, to put all previous concepts out of my mind, to just try to listen to what these people were saying. For a long time, what I already knew, or what I thought I knew, was getting in the way. When I learned to listen, I began to see a clarity in the Damanhurian vision that is quite remarkable.

One of the series of myths that is important at Damanhur is a creation myth that concerns the idea of Man as a divinity. It goes something like this:

Many aeons ago, the primeval divinity known as Mankind was like a huge mirror. During an epic battle with the Enemy, the forces of darkness, the mirror of Mankind shattered into millions, trillions, zillions of pieces. The bigger pieces became lesser divinities, the smaller pieces became human beings, and the tiniest pieces animals, vegetables and plants. Since that time, it has been the essential purpose of humans to attempt to draw back together and reassemble this shattered unity.

This image takes on an even greater potency when you think about it standing in the Hall of Mirrors inside the Temple of Mankind, I can tell you.

The fragments of mirror might be better thought of as 'divine sparks', those little bits of godliness (or the nearest thing we are going to get to godliness) that came through and lodged themselves in each of us, as well as all that is around us.

In the Damanhurian cosmology, the realm of the Absolute is called 'the Real' and the 'divine sparks', the flying shards of broken mirror, pass backwards and forwards, from form to Real, as life begins and ends in its perpetual cycles *(see Figure 4)*. The Real is the realm beyond all known worlds, from where all divine forces emanate. More than the concept of heaven, as the place where God lives, this is the place where Life lives. We can know little of the Real, for it is way beyond our comprehension. But the little spark within each of us is our fragile link with this unimaginable realm.

The world we live in, the world of forms, is separated from the Real by another plane of existence, known as the Threshold. Divine sparks pass over the Threshold on their way backwards and forwards to the world of forms.

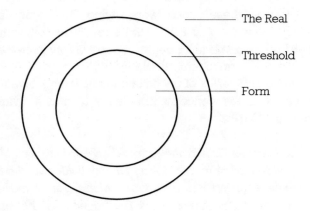

Figure 4: The Real

Gattopardo summed it up beautifully for me one day:

It is quite a fantastic, marvellous thing to realize how a soul is born. It derives from the first of interstellar matter. Imagine, say, a stone travelling throughout the galaxies. It does not contain a soul, but through a series of continuous transformations, physical and chemical, it reaches a particular critical point, beyond which it has to develop a kind of perceptive capability, primeval intelligence, *complexity*.

Complexity, because of its nature, does not 'stay' in the physical world, but 'enters' into the Threshold. On the Threshold any form is expressed as a 'node of intelligence'.

Now, let's imagine that through the Threshold an Attractor passes. Think of this as a diamond-shaped piece of pure intelligence, which comes from the Real. It captures the little node of intelligence which the stone represents. And to increase its experiences in the world of forms, it takes it into another stone, more complex, which also will be capable of expressing a more complex level of perception. This result is then returned to the Threshold by the Attractor.

Another Attractor comes and captures this knot of intelligence. It takes it into a form that is no longer a mineral, but may be something that is single-celled and alive. This node of intelligence will continue moving, at high speed, between the world of forms and the Threshold, taking part in ever more complex forms of life – a cell, an amoeba, a protozoa. As it develops further, into a plant, a tree, into more and more complex forms of the vegetable world, its experience in the world of forms becomes longer.

Finally, that first spark of awareness grows until it can be associated to a form that is equally complex, from a biological point of view, that is to say, the human being. At the moment at which it arrives at this complexity, the knot of intelligence is also capable of hosting a small piece of the divine. That's why we consider the human being as a 'bridge form', because it is innately capable of carrying out the form of a bridge between the world of forms and the spiritual dimension. When the divinity detaches itself and introduces itself into the knot, that becomes a personality. In the human soul, then, the Attractor assembles different personalities into a form that is sufficiently complex.

So, each human being has a soul composed of a 'piece' of the Real, the Attractor, which leaves the Real to enter the world of forms and make experience through the life of a human being. Before linking to a newborn baby, it collects, on the Threshold, several different 'personalities' *(the circles in the 'Attractor' figure overleaf)*, each 'lit' by the divine spark.

This diagram might be thought of as the 'anatomy' of a human soul. When speaking of 'the soul', there is more to it than each

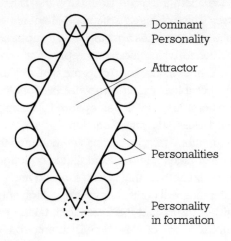

Figure 5: The Attractor

human being having a soul. The physical body has its own anatomy and we have medical practice to keep it healthy. Our aura and other subtle bodies also have their own structure, their own complexity, and require an equivalent understanding, a similar care, to maintain their health. Fundamental to understanding the soul is to recognize the anatomy as the Attractor and its collected personalities.

These 'personalities' are individuals, real individuals, separate individuals. They are lives that have been lived. They are gathered together according to the criteria of compatibility. When the baby is born, it will start to have its own experiences and to develop a new personality, defined as the 'personality in formation'. The whole structure is what Damanhurians call the 'soul' – which interestingly enough, in Italian, is translated as *anima*, with all the echoes of our place in the animal world, of Jungian psychology and the fact that it is a feminine noun.

The various personalities, of which there are a minimum of five, no maximum, alternate in guiding the body according to a complex dynamic, which has much to do with the unconscious and the utilization of memory and the evolution of every part.

However, of these personalities, we each have a dominant one, shown on the diagram as a dotted circle at the top of the diamond. This manifests itself more strongly than the others. The aim of our life is to integrate all our different personalities through love and the opportu-nity to express ourselves creatively, so that the new personality in formation can comprehend all the complexity of the others and be whole.

As Esperide explained:

If things were wonderful, which they very often are not, the personalities would constantly rotate. The dominant personality, if we were perfectly integrated human beings, would let the other ones go around and take their turn. What would be really ideal would be if they did not take their turn by accident, but when you called them. Say this one is a very good piano player and the personality in formation also becomes a concert pianist. Say that day he has a big concert and another personality comes up. He can still play the piano, because the personality has a talent, but he is not as good as he would have been had his piano-player personality been dominant that day. So, the ideal is to integrate all of them and once you have integrated them, to be able to tap into the resources of whichever personality you need at that moment.

Of course, it does not always happen like that. If one of the personalities sticks in the dominant position, it creates conflicts within, and so people get sick. They may be sick in the body, for each personality is normally superimposed on or linked to an organ, as the Chinese said, and, as modern science is discovering now, each organ also has its own nervous system, or they may be sick in the mind. When the rotation is severely blocked, people go crazy. They become totally unstable. This is because not all of their personalities have the possibility of expression. The personalities are not only trying to have their influence, but also to increase their complexity. All need to evolve.

The reason why at Damanhur we put so much stress on doing many different things is because we want to give all the personal-ities the chance to rotate.

Once the physical body dies, the Attractor returns to the Real and the personalities are dispersed, together with the new personality formed out of the life of the individual, on the Threshold. Then a new Attractor enters the Threshold and collects together various personalities to live another life. However, it is not necessarily the same personalities. Some of them might have stuck together because they proved compatible in the last life and had made good progress, but some might not. It is not the case that the soul, the *anima*, stays the same. Once the personalities have been dispersed in the Threshold, a completely new process begins. Luckily, personalities that have managed to co-ordinate themselves will often remain attached and present themselves together in the next soul. If this were always possible, the evolutionary path would be much faster, as no time would be lost in this process repeating itself over and over.

Sardina, who teaches in the school at Damanhur and who lives at Magilla, where I had spent many happy weeks, told me a very interesting story. You will recall that Magilla is an old house, currently being renovated. Sardina told me of the early days when more than 20 people were living there without electricity or running water, all living their lives and building their home at the same time. She recalled the dark nights spent reading and preparing her lessons by the light of a candle, surviving the storms and the rigours of winter. On top of all that, she was pregnant. When her daughter was born, by candlelight, Sardina believes that the personality formed by her aunt, who had recently died, was reincarnated as one of the personalities that now makes up her daughter. Verification came when traits of the aunt became recognized in the child, and when she would often choose objects that had belonged to the aunt when shown a range of objects. Sardina is certain that the work done at Damanhur helped to make this happen.

Most recognized theories of reincarnation say that the soul is a piece of God which carries out experiences in the world of forms. Life after life it accumulates experiences, until it reaches that critical point where it no longer has any need to return to the world of forms. Its experience is complete and it returns to the divine. This is Enlightenment, the leaving of the cycle of reincarnation. Damanhur's theory helps explain how this experience is acquired. Gattopardo explained:

When all these personalities complete the experience in our human form, the bridge form, that is equal to Enlightenment. Once you become Enlightened, when you die, the personalities fuse into the Attractor and it no longer takes them to the Threshold, but straight on back into the Real. This is so we can carry the result of the universe to God. We have always done it. Inside us is the entirety of the experiences of the universe, because we have not just lived lots of lives in different incarnations, but our soul also contains the whole of the world, both animal and vegetable. Having this level of awareness means that we participate simultaneously in the whole of the universe. This is wonderful.

This concept is different from that of metapsychosis, because that says that, according to the level of evolution, an individual being can be incarnated into a stone, an animal, or a man. But that concept we do not agree with, because personalities can be part only of a human being, of Mankind, as it contains the divine spark. We have to realize that there is always a parallel between spiritual complexity and physical complexity. On this planet, the body Man uses evolved from the monkey species; on another planet, Man's form will be different. What is important is that the form, any form, reaches the physical and chemical complexity suitable for playing host to a group of personalities.

Esperide told me how the personalities worked from the point of view of an individual:

You have two personalities at a time in the brain, always – right side of the brain, one personality, left side of the brain, another personality. They are also always switching. This is very important. It is the control system and also the mechanism that gives us the possibility of choosing.

We always have two parts of ourselves, who we have to confront. All these different personalities live the experience that the body is living, but at different degrees. Consider all of them sitting in the same car. One is the driver, who makes most of the decisions, but the others are still there, looking out of the windows, chattering, screaming, telling the driver a better way to go. They still live the experience. This is also important when we talk about memory, because according to the personality looking out of your eyes, you get different memories. Or the same episode can come back with different emotional or other memories linked to it. If you had an accident, say, and at that moment in time, the dominant personality was sleeping, it would not be so bad. But if there were a lot of emotion linked to that episode at that time, then you would relive it with a lot of emotion. So you can imagine the implication this has, linked to the healing of mental programmes, emotions, and so on. Because it is not so simple. We are not just one. One of the reasons we consider pranatherapy to be an excellent medicine is because it has to do with all the various personalities.

There are many techniques for recognizing your personalities. We have done a lot of work on this at Damanhur. The first thing is to bring into consciousness the fact that you have them. With me, it made me much happier. I did not find out how many I had, but there were some that I could see very clearly. But also, it made me feel that life was easier. Because at times I had felt so much conflict, I always thought that there was something wrong with me. And ever since I was a child I had at least two or three personalities. I kept them conversing constantly. I could always hear them and at times I thought I was crazy.

One exercise that we did was, at different times during the day, looking in the mirror and trying to find out who was there. Who is this, looking through my eyes? Or, again at different times of the day, just stopping and trying to see who was there.

Some personalities shift during the day, others come out once a year, others do this and that. They all have their own rhythms. But during the day, we change them constantly. My personality of the early morning is never very good. Just don't talk to me at eight o'clock in the morning!

I had recently been at a Damanhurian nucleo meeting and suddenly I realized it operated just like the personalities. At the

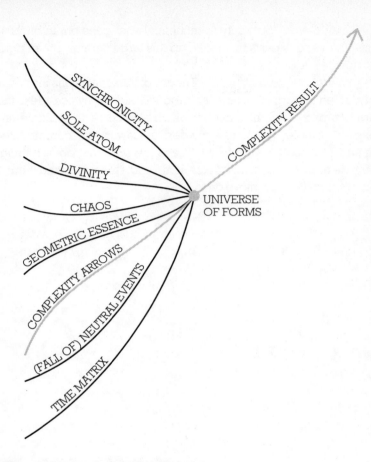

Figure 6: Derivate Laws: The Armistice

meeting the one directing the proceedings often handed control to other members of the group. That way, they are all part of the process, they all belong.

More than that, the whole of Damanhur is influenced by this structure. Oberto Airaudi is held in very high regard, but as an inspiration and guide, as a master even, but not the sort of megalomaniac dictator, with an iron grip over everything that happens, that some journalists and other cursory observers have suggested. He cannot be, otherwise the community would have fallen apart long ago, just as a person's soul malfunctions when one personality takes too strong a grip. Damanhur works because everyone gets their say, their opportunity to influence what goes on, in order to give the various parts that make up this large community an equilibrium, a stable soul.

This whole thing about the Theory of Personalities is inextricably linked to Damanhurian ideas about Esoteric Physics, ideas that are complex in themselves but which also serve to illustrate and explain complexity, where eight derivate laws are accommodated at an Armistice (*see Figure 6*). These are laws that govern things outside of time and form. It takes some effort to understand them, a task that we will now move on to.

chapter 13 – esoteric physics

Esoteric physics is within that sphere we more generally call magic. That is to say, the sum of the total sciences of Mankind: the spiritual, the ethical and the technical.

Gattopardo Tek

Learning about Mankind as a divinity, the divine spark and the soul as a collection of personalities had taken me on quite a journey. But I had learned a lot about what makes us tick, 'us' being the personalities within each one of us. It all adds particular resonance to the people of Damanhur's claim that they built the temple as a metaphor for digging into themselves. It is the Temple of Mankind – and it was built there specifically because of the synchronic lines. These lines seem to be a very important feature of the work at Damanhur. I had always associated synchronicity with things happening in time, things happening by coincidence, but without discoverable causal effect. Does not synchronicity mean 'coming together in time'? Again, like everything else at Damanhur, it is not so simple. It took another meeting with Gattopardo to unravel that one:

Synchronicity is a law of our universe, that is, choosing events inside time in order to carry them within our time flow. And these events are chosen to satisfy complexity.

The synchronic lines put our universe in contact with the entirety of the universe, both from the physical point of view and the subtle point of view. They are roads where thought and information flow. They are roads along which life flows and souls pass in order to reincarnate. Influencing the synchronic lines means you can influence the type of thought that flows out and thus influence events. By influencing the type of thought, you can actually call in the type of events that you want, events that happen in a synchronic manner, beyond apparent cause and effect.

Damanhur, for instance, is situated on a synchronic knot, so that we can influence what happens through the circulation of these lines. In fact, it is written into our constitution that every Damanhurian must behave well because our thoughts are easily reflected through these lines. It is important to know how to utilize, how to extract the energy of the knot, and how to employ it.

There are several of these knots – at Stonehenge, in Tibet, and corresponding to some of the great political and historical places throughout time.

In fact, synchronicity is the first law of esoteric physics.

According to the Damanhurians, there are eight Laws of esoteric physics. I spent some time working on getting a grasp of them. Thanks should go to the many patient hours spent by Esperide Ananas and Gattopardo Tek in getting me even to this limited point of understanding.

Before we go any further, dear reader, some advice. Empty your mind of any laws of physics you may have already learned. We are dealing here not with laws to explain and work within the physical world, but with the Laws that bring our world, our universe, into existence, Laws that originate in the realm of the Real.

It is the meeting of the Laws, and the potential that is in the meeting, that creates our universe, the universe of forms. At this meeting, the Laws are all equal and so it is said that they have an

'Armistice'. In the Real, or even on the Threshold, the Laws do not have an Armistice. They are pure there. They do not meet. So, when you are on the Threshold, what you experience is either one Law or another, according to the emotions you have. When the Laws meet with different compositions, different percentages of each one, they create different universes, but we are not concerned about those. The characteristic of our universe is that these eight primeval Laws meet at an equal potential.

All the laws of our physical world, such as the law of gravity, are derived from that original meeting of the primeval Laws, the Laws that exist outside our universe but have a potential use within our universe.

Oberto recounted the first meeting of the Laws as an allegorical story:

> Let's imagine that these eight Laws all go to a bar and meet there. This is what we would consider the beginning of the universe. From now on, when we refer to that moment, we can call it the 'Four Seconds Bar', as four seconds is the time it takes for a human being to have a perception, on a conscious level. Of course, on a subconscious level it takes much less time. But to bring something to consciousness takes four seconds. So when we talk about an instant, by definition, we are talking about four seconds in our time. Therefore, the Four Seconds Bar.

> So the eight Laws meet. Let's see what they do. Just to make things easier to understand, let's imagine that Synchronicity is the first to arrive. Synchronicity has to be first, because that is what makes the event possible. Without it, nothing happens. So Synchronicity creates the opportunity for all the other Laws to meet.

Whilst I was at Damanhur on my latest visit, they were attempting to redefine their idea about synchronicity. Thursday evenings were devoted to it. After spending four weeks discussing the subject in great depth, only small changes had been made to the original definition, but people seemed happy with things. Sometimes at Damanhur, the very fact of raising awareness about an issue or a concept brings a potency to thought and a meaning to the actions associated with it. Incidentally, at Damanhur you really can go to the Four Seconds Bar – they named their on-site café after it.

■   ■   ■

Back at the bar, the second Law to arrive is the Sole Atom. This is the basic atom, an infinitesimally small particle which constantly emanates and thereby manifests forms. The Sole Atom should not be thought of as a physical atom, rather an atom of potentiality, for it is before time, before matter. It is the matrix for everything, a Law, a function, the vehicle through which all the Laws reproduce themselves in all the forms.

Imagine that the universe has a constant need to conserve energies, to use them sparingly. Therefore the Sole Atom does not create all of a form, but does the minimum necessary for the form to finish itself by itself.

Each form, in order to fit in our universe, must contain within itself the Armistice, that particular relationship of Laws which permits it to stay within the universe of forms. Imagine a form split into mass and energy. The line that cuts through is the symmetry of form. Inside this line all the Laws flow. Every line has the same diameter because, on account of the Armistice, all the Laws come together with perfect equilibrium. So, within every form, the Armistice reproduces itself.

The Sole Atom itself contains within itself all the forms of the Armistice. It could be imagined as the locomotive of a long train, leading at infinite velocity all the lines of all the forms. It could be thought of as being like a television set, where there is one dot, but it very rapidly scans all over all the lines from top to bottom of the screen, before you or I can blink our eyes, and makes a picture.

Let us also imagine that the different Laws flow at different velocities. It is the different combinations of these Laws that differentiates one form from another. The only Law that flows at the same speed through all forms is the Sole Atom, because it is at infinite speed and it carries all the different Laws within itself. It is outside time and distance does not exist.

Every form is noted by its own frequency, which is called the rhythm-number. So the way to intervene in forms is through the Laws. This is what the magician and the alchemist do.

Like the other Laws we are talking about here, the Law of the Sole Atom exists as a primeval Law, representing the possibility of manifesting the universe. But as a derivate Law, it becomes the creator of forms. Certainly, it is an energy, if you wish. But more than anything, it is a *function*. So, if those physicists experimenting with the particle accelerator at CERN, just over the Swiss border, were to spin their particles round from now to Kingdom come, they would never discover it, because it is not a physical particle, not form. The Laws are outside form.

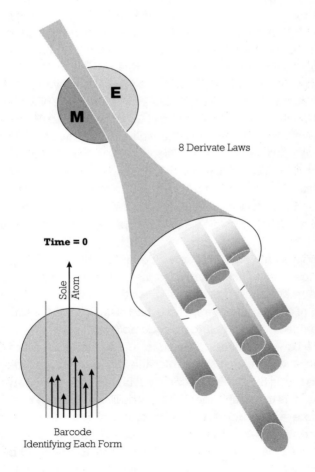

Figure 7: The Sole Atom

So, back at the Four Second Bar, we have Synchronicity creating the meeting, then the Sole Atom arriving and starting to create the universe of forms. There are still just the two of them there, but already the universe is being formed. Then Divinity arrives. In this case, it is the primeval Divinity, Mankind. 'Okay, I am bringing into this form a divine spark, so this matter has the potential for growth. And pour me a glass of red wine.'

In every form, even in the tape recorder I am transcribing this from, there is a little bit of divine spark, of free will, of the shattered mirror. The Law of Divinity is present in all forms. Some express this in complex ways – plants, animals, the bridge form of Man, for example – whereas in others it is a potential only – the microphone of my tape recorder, for instance.

This reminds me of something that my friend Ken Campbell says, that you can develop a machine that can beat you at chess, but does it know that it has won? Does it have the sense of winning?

Nevertheless the microphone has the potential to become alive. Whilst I was staying in Damanhur there was an exhibition of magical instruments. These are considered living forms, gifted with intelligence and free will. It is the same with the Selfica, which are part of the life-force system that sustains Damanhur *(see Chapter 14)*. However, we are talking about a different sort of life here than that of a living, active being. Our concept of life is very limited.

■   ■   ■

And then into the bar comes Geometric Essence. 'Hey', it says, 'let's create relationships amongst them.'

Geometric Essence is what gives the possibility of measuring things, of comparing them, of creating structures in the universe. It is what makes any structure reproducible.

The Law of Geometric Essence, let us imagine, is like a map, a territory, the measure within which the Sole Atom moves, where the various forms find their positioning. It is a spatial map of form. If the Sole Atom is the pencil, then Geometric Essence is the ruler.

There a map for every form of every form and Geometric Essence is present in every form, because it is a Law. Naturally, because solids are more easily measurable, there would be more present within a solid form than within a gas, for example, and it would have a different flow. These aspects of form are part of a particular alchemical knowledge not spoken of in thousands of years.

So that is the Law of Geometric Essence, the geometric matrix, the spatial map of form.

■   ■   ■

And now into the bar strolls Time Matrix. Now that the forms are created, now that they have spatial relationships, it is time for Time to be created. Time is a way of relating forms to each other. If we do not leave in relation to the same time, we will never meet.

The Law of Time Matrix is one law for everything, form and beyond form, but also each of the other Laws has its own Time Matrix in order for it to relate to Time, because this is a universe made of Time.

The Law of the Time Matrix deals with this very complex aspect of the Laws. Form has three fundamental parameters: rhythm-number, colour and time. Rhythm-number is a frequency, the DNA of form, if you will, colour is the direction given to form by the divinities that control the time territories and Time is an actual quality of form.

Three-dimensional space is not enough to understand where a form is. It is necessary to indicate *when* this form is. Every substance will have been created at a different time. So no two things are the same. The time of form indicates its participation in the time flow and measures its capacity to evolve in the direction of complexity, to transform itself.

However, we should consider that all forms in the universe must be in equilibrium. Therefore, if we imagine that the universe as a division of a single mass, the total of the mass must always add up to one. If we have only two forms in the universe and I increase the mass of one form, I have to decrease it on the other. Equilibrium must always be constant.

This is true for all the worlds of the universe. So you can have compensations between one world and another. In magic there is a principle that says, similar corresponds to similar, like responds to like. All the forms in the universe are linked to each other, because the universe must be in equilibrium. Therefore, transformation inside a form produces a compensatory effect in the rest of the universe. It does not happen in a uniform manner, but like responds to like. One form is like another not because they are alike, but because they have the same time, a time that is alike – not the same, but similar. So that forms that have the same speed of evolution respond one to the other.

The Time Matrix, as a Law, measures all the times of all the forms. This is why it is called 'temporal', in order to create the compensations, moment by moment – though Gattopardo would insist that this is really, really simplifying it.

Some of us need it to be simple.

■   ■   ■

After this, the five Laws gathered at the bar are joined by the Fall of Events, aka the Fall of Neutral Events. This brings the opportunity for new events and also the chance to put into operation everything the others have been planning. Things get much livelier in the Four Seconds Bar from now on. The piano player strikes up and there is a much happier mood.

What are events? They are forms. My tape recorder is an event, my microphone is an event. The energy that flows within the microphone is an event. The pen on my desk is an event. The paper is an event. The ink that transfers from pen to paper is an event. My computer is an event. But don't think that an event is simply anything made or done. As Gattopardo said to me, 'Let's go slowly. It is very complicated.' He was about to launch into another of his great discourses. 'For a stone, the event is the stone…'

At that very moment, my chair collapsed.

'For this chair, the event is the chair, or any transformation that can happen to that chair. That was a real Fall of Events!'

So, for the chair, the event was the chair, but also the transformation of the chair, the break, the collapse. However, for a sentient form, one that can perceive, that can exercise free will the event is not only the form, but also the fall, and also the action. For me, to lift the pen is an event. The event is not only the form the pen, but also the history, the action, the choice that I express.

Let us imagine that the Law of the Fall of Events wants to represent a series of possible events which fall, or happen, within the flow of time. Time is a container of forms. For us it is also a container of the events of history. An event can either be used or not used, by our free will. At this moment I can do many things. But I do those that I choose. Thus there exist both events that happen, or are 'saturated', and events that do not, or are 'non-saturated'.

The Fall of Events is not something that is uniformly distributed. Different planes are considered saturated when they have many events that are able to express a lot of complexity. The Fall of Events becomes very intense along synchronic lines, for example.

When it enters into our universe, an event is first coloured by the Divinity, which directs the event in order to protect the eco-system, and then coloured by many other minor divinities and subtle beings right until it arrives at Man, who, in expressing his free will, can then saturate it. In the end it becomes form.

As we increase complexity, the significance of events changes. In the more complex forms, leading right up to the divinities, who are so complex they no longer have need of form to manifest themselves, events do not have to do with a form, but to do with a direction.

■   ■   ■

But the swing doors of the bar fly open and Chaos is standing there. Chaos is like the stranger from out of town. This Law has not been explored very well yet, but, according to Esperide, it is the one to concentrate on.

Chaos here is not to be confused with confusion. It is more to do with forces that do not have a direction yet. When we are talking about Chaos from a scientific point of view, we are talking about the primordial soup. From a religious or philosophical point of view, it is the time before God separated the elements, separated the Earth from the Heavens and gave an order to things. Esoterically, Chaos is the Law which allows for transformation, which permits the system to collapse, to put itself in a state of disorder, in order to achieve a higher state of order.

This relates to being able to question one's own state in order to encourage an evolution. All forms are evolving. The universe itself is not fixed. The Laws themselves may change. There are not necessarily eight of them. This is why, at the Damanhurian esoteric school, nothing can be based on dogma. The truths that we find inside ourselves are always partial truths, not absolute ones.

Mathematicians have discovered that what seems to be chaos often turns out to be a very high level of formation, so complex that it had appeared chaotic. Fractal theory is one example. In fact, at this level chaos and order have come together.

■   ■   ■

'Make room for the big one.' The voice boomed outside the Four Seconds Bar and everyone got ready to greet their old friend. Big in size and big in personality, in came Complexity.

The Law of Complexity, sometimes known as the Arrow of Complexity, is the only Law that comes out of our universe as a product. Imagine that there are many, many different universes. Each universe produces something that nourishes another universe. These are all physical universes, but by 'physical' something different is meant from the multiverse or parallel universe theory of the physicists. Still there are many, many different universes in the universe of forms. And our universe has to produce complexity. This is in fact its whole purpose.

And how does our universe create complexity? By having more information in less matter. Once, for instance, we had huge computers to do quite simple calculations and we now have microchips that can handle millions of calculations. Could it be that computers are spiritual things, that technological advancement comes about because of complexity?

Two things not to be confused, however, are complexity and what we call 'progress'. In many ways, the age in which we live is much less complex than the Middle Ages. Then, Esperide explained to me, there was much more knowledge and there were people who were able to use a wider range of senses, the sense of dream, for example, and the ability to manipulate other forces. She said that we have over 40 senses, yet we use only five of them, and those very badly. Some places on Atlantis apparently also had a complexity that was at least equal to ours, if not higher.

When we talk of complexity, though, you must not think that everywhere is the same. It is like a leopard, with dots here and there. You can have a place where complexity is low, then you have a citadel, or an oasis, like an old university, or like Damanhur, where complexity is higher, and which as a consequence works for the whole of the world.

Complexity increases in leaps and bounds which are known as 'Levels of Justice'. An example would be the evolutionary leap of cells organizing themselves and developing thought. Esperide told me that it was only when forms on Earth had developed far enough that the divine human form chose to inhabit them. The physical bodies had then reached a point where they had all the organs that were needed.

Another leap forward came when the humans were able to transcend their mere survival needs and start creating something that was not just for their immediate satisfaction, art for example.

So where is this complexity taking us, as human beings? It could lead us to become totally spiritual and leave the universe. Then we would not need bodily support any more. 'But,' Esperide told me, 'we have a limited time in which to grow. We have to go on, conquering new Levels of Justice. If we do not do that in the right time, bye-bye. We have failed.'

I was rather taken aback by this, but Gattopardo explained that at Damanhur they are working desperately towards a new Level of Justice. If it is reached, something major will happen. Everything will be affected, not just the spiritual. The physical will have to change in order to support it. New organs will develop in the body, new connections. It might be that we will be able to communicate telepathically, or develop teleportation, or something else we cannot even imagine.

But it will be something that will be crucial to the future of the universe.

Studying Selfs, they have their own mathematics, their own logic.

Cicogna Giunco

Selfica is an ancient science based on the most basic form in our universe: the spiral. It was known by the Egyptians, the Celts and the Arabs, who used it up until the eighth century BC, and has been developed at Damanhur for over 20 years. It is the practical use of spirals and metals to concentrate and direct vital energies. The practical objects that are developed from this science are called Selfs. They are frequently constructed out of gold and silver, because these are the best conductors, but copper and brass are also used.

It was at a Sunday market on my very first visit to Damanhur that I first encountered a Self. There were many of them in a shop, on open sale. My friend Ken Campbell was intrigued. He had just been interviewing the great philosophers Marvin Minsky, Derek Parfit and Richard Dawkins for a programme on British television, a Channel 4 series on the brain, and they had all told him about the almost impossibility of finding the Self, of discovering just what it is.

And here was somebody making them, selling them! There were wristband Selfs to counter negative energies or to improve the immune system. There were Selfs with little bottles on them in which were 'alchemical liquids' that would work on problems with the organs in the torso or sort out sleep patterns and dreams. There were Selfs in their own little velvet bags, Selfs to combat painful menstruation, Selfs to improve the memory. My other friend (or this trip, that is, I do have more than two friends), John Joyce, bought one of these and I can say for sure that he has stopped forgetting things. John is an actor, so he needs to remember his lines, and he does seem to have been getting more parts recently.

But how are the Selfs different from all those other 'cure-all' objects that you get at every New Age festival or exhibiticn? I needed to find out more about the claims made for them. Cicogna Giunco has worked on the development of Selfica for many years as well as being responsible for the Way of the Monks at Ogni Dove. I began by asking her, 'What exactly is a Self?'

Selfs are subtle beings. They have an existence. They have different forms because they have different functions. The simple ones, those that use metals, copper mostly, rather than alchemical liquids, range in function from amplifying the aura of a person to increasing the sensibility and perceptions, from regulating the immune system to helping the memory, or, for houses or motor vehicles, balancing the environment.

For every turn or winding on a spiral form, there is an increase in the speed at which energy flows along it. Angles, on the other hand, divert the energy. It makes a difference whether you use copper and brass or gold and silver.

The person working with the materials has an important influence. I can do this work because I am following the Way of the Monks. For example, when working with copper thread, as I work with it, as I pull it out, as I form it into shape, I can actually charge it with a subtle energy. It is about creating the suitable conditions to create such exchanges and transfer of energies. We prepare and work on both the raw material and the body form. You have to think that when a child is born, first the body is formed and then the soul enters. It is the same with the Selfica. When the Selfic body is ready, the subtle creature from other dimensions arrives and enters it.

Alchemical liquids take the Selfs to another level. The liquids are prepared in a suitable environment and through the accumulation of specific energies and times. Metal already exists, and you make it alive during the process of putting energy into it, whereas with alchemical liquid, life comes with formation. We use a distillation process, an alchemical process. But it also requires people who know what they are doing, who understand how to participate in the alchemical process, as it does not just happen by itself.

The liquid amplifies the work of the Selfs. But it is not true to say the more liquid, the more powerful the Self. It depends on how the Selfic body is formed. Selfs that use alchemical liquid have functions within themselves, for example the ability to dream, to activate other Selfs in time.

So, incredible as it sounds, Selfs are alive. They are intelligent creatures that co-operate with you, that work with you for specific purposes, and they are pre-programmed to carry out certain functions.

Contemporary physics has not yet taken on board the kind of energies on which Selfica is based. As recently as 1992 the French physicist Jacques Benveniste was ostracized by the orthodox scientific community for claiming his research showed that water can be a carrier, a recorder, of chemical qualities. Whilst minds are closed to such basic concepts, there is little hope that they will accept the idea of subtle energies having a practical application in people's lives.

The Damanhurians have looked closely at the work of Wilhelm Reich and George de la Warr. Reich used a similar idea of bringing two metals into a relationship with each other in such a way that they were able to act as a kind of battery and accumulator of 'orgone energy', a biological and atmospheric life energy. However, the American authorities found it necessary to burn his books and to throw the elderly Reich into prison, where he died. This was not even in the Middle Ages, this was in the 1950s.

The late George de la Warr, a radionics pioneer, also did work on mysterious radiation that appeared to act outside time and space according to that law which Carl Gustav Jung had termed 'synchronicity'. He conducted experiments in his laboratories in Oxford and in a 1967 report, *Using Sound Waves to Probe Matter*, wrote:

> ...a basic idea in radionics is that each individual, organism, or material radiates and absorbs energy, via an energy field peculiar unto itself. The more complex the material, the more complex the waveform. Living things like humans emit a very complex wave spectrum of which parts are associated with the various organs and systems of the body.

Radionics uses electronic equipment, with a human 'operator', to detect the particular radiation under consideration.

De la Warr's reputation, like that of Reich, has grown since his death and his work has gained considerable credence amongst more open-minded scientists. But the wider scientific community is still largely dismissive of such ideas. That is why the work being done at Damanhur is of such importance. It is developing outside the negative constraints and closed-mind mentality inherent in orthodox practices.

Once the knowledge of the Selfs had been realized and put to practical use, the Damanhurian way of taking everything to the end of the line was invoked. Giant Selfica were developed for the Temple of Mankind, very powerful Selfs known as 'Spheroselfs' and composed of complicated metal structures, intertwining spiral forms combined with spheres containing alchemical liquids. These are extremely complex constructions, very beautiful to look at and apparently capable of charging up other objects and structures. Such Spheroselfs are used for example to charge up the pentacles that the Damanhurians use for ritual functions or to charge the large spiral circuits that people walk along in order to meditate and make contact with vital energies. However, in the Temple of Mankind, Selfs are incorporated into the very fabric of the place. Each of the rooms was developed to host certain Selfs and their specific energies. They serve to direct energy and to ensure that it is at the right level according to the functions of the various chambers and parts of the temple.

The whole of the Temple of Mankind is a living, active being, full of vital energy that is a result of the interaction between the Selfs, the construction and artwork, and the interaction of those using it. It is now claimed that the temple is itself the largest Selfic structure in the world. It is said to contain some 300 tons of circuits and connections hidden inside its walls and floors, as well as the Selfic qualities that were transferred to the very building materials during the construction process *(see Chapter 1)*.

Damanhur's research groups have continued to study and refine the general principles of the Selfica, creating ever more complex structures. There are now Crystalselfs, built of metal and crystals, which are used as memory tanks, and miniature Selfs, specially prepared using inks and paints, which form attractive jewellery that keeps the wearer in touch with vital energies.

There are also the large spheres which feature in many of the chambers of the temple, but particularly in the Hall of Spheres. These are spherical glass balls, mostly about the size of a football, some slightly larger, with markings over the surface of the glass and liquid inside, often of differing colours. Again, they have a strong aesthetic appeal and if they did nothing else but decorate the temple, they would be fulfilling a useful function. But I suspected there was more to it than that, so I went to consult Giunco. She told me:

> Spheres also have different functions, according to the liquid that each one contains. Some are for inspiration, some for meditation and concentration. The spheres are connected to the synchronic lines, and through them, to the Earth, to the planet itself, and even to other universes.
>
> The whole area around the Hall of Spheres is used for research because the spheres allow us to be in contact with other parts of the planet through dream and inspiration. In the workshop there, particular energies can be brought into play. In the time cabins are the most complex Selfs we have at the moment, ones with the power to transfer and transform energy.

These time cabins have many functions and much experimental work has been carried out in them – experiments in the transfer of particular characteristics from one person to another, experiments in time travel, experiments in healing. This work is ongoing and I have little doubt that in the not too distant future great developments for the general good of Mankind will emerge from this research. Early results have certainly given such an indication and the people engaged in the work, on all levels, remain positive and optimistic. This is always a good sign.

The finality is to link all the divinities in one.

Sirena Ninfea

Damanhur is now in touch with a wide number of other spiritual, ecological and community-oriented groups from around the world, for example the people who originally developed the *Biosphere II* project in Oracle, Arizona. *Biosphere II* was a monumental and ambitious project, just like Damanhur. It was an attempt to build an enclosed living replica of the planet Earth, with modelled versions of desert and ocean, savannah and rainforest, to see how the structure could sustain a wide range of life-forms for an experimental period. Eight scientists, who became known as the Biospherians, stayed inside the sealed structure for two years. John Allen, who was responsible for developing the project, and two of the Biospherians who had been at the forefront of it came to Damanhur and shared some of their ideas.

As John Allen and Oberto Airaudi talked, they realized that their respective communities had many similarities. They had both had to face hostile political opposition that relied on a heavy-handed approach and legal proceedings. John Allen said that he thanked the United States Government every day for providing them with $1,000,000 worth of legal education. Oberto knew what he meant. Fighting to save the temple had turned Damanhurians into experts in many different fields. He and John felt like foundling brothers. In both cases the oppression they had heaped on them had brought them strength. On top of that, there is no doubt that some of their shared ideas will come to fruition. For example, there will probably be bio-sphere projects at Damanhur in the future, heavily influenced by what John Allen and his team achieved in the Arizona desert.

Strong links have also been established with the followers of Io-Ana, a community in France. They felt such powerful spiritual links to Damanhur that they bought a property nearby in order to maintain a regular cross-fertilization of ideas between the two communities. Similarly, links are maintained with a spiritual community in Holland, as well as the ongoing Val di Chy project, which will possibly bring a wide range of people with similar ideas into the valley.

Obviously, not every group that comes into contact with Damanhur finds a spiritual resonance with the community. Some groups, and individuals, often ask why there is such an abundant amount of work carried out at Damanhur on rituals, rites and other forms of spiritual research, often implying that energy is being wasted that could be put to good use carrying out environmental and ecological projects. Others have shown some concern about the seeming emphasis on magic and esoteric or alchemical experiments. Some people have even sent back Selfs that they have bought on the open market or through mail order, claiming that they have been responsible for making them ill or that they have had a strange effect on them.

However, as far as the Damanhurians are concerned, they feel that far from being misplaced, their energy is being put into a very important project in the field of spiritual research. I had often heard reference to something called 'the Triad' on my visits to Damanhur, though it had never really been explained to me. It seems that one needs to be able to change gear in order to comprehend it and this comes through familiarity with the other processes of Damanhur. Finally, towards the end of one of my visits, a meeting was set up for me to talk to Usignolo about the Triad project.

Usignolo began by telling me that the Triad is a complex and stimulating work, an advanced form of ritual alchemical operation, established in 1986, but started way before that, with Damanhur's founders, in 1975, and with the travellers of the Game of the Life. It is a series of theurgic magical rituals carried out by those of the Way of the Oracle. The aim was to recall, one by one, by means of rituals, all the divinities of Mankind throughout history and ask if they would be willing to co-operate with each other for the future salvation of Mankind. Most accepted; only a few declined. Those that did accept were brought into a theurgic magical alliance.

I wanted to know more about these divinities. Usignolo explained that the Damanhurians had undertaken wide-ranging historical re-search and, on the basis of this, invoked many almost forgotten deities.

Each one of these divinities, in its own territory, is a carrier of thought forms towards those men and women who think about the deity. They are all carriers of evolutionary force towards these people. In that way they have helped Mankind to evolve.

Some of the ancient divinities, on the other hand, that might once have appeared bad to us, because in the past they would have required sacrifices, those types of divinity have been modified and corrected so that they no longer harm anyone. They help Mankind in his fight against the Enemy.

This work took many years. It was a long process because these divinities were contacted one by one and there were thousands of them. They were invoked and a relationship was established with them. Then they were purified of their negative aspects. They were unified and condensed, in that some of the minor deities were fused with the larger ones into one greater deity. There were 'weddings' between divinities to create new divine forces that are favourable and positive for Mankind. For us, the unification of all these divinities has been the first step in recreating that ancient divinity that is Mankind.

The divinities that were contacted came from many different times and traditions, including the Native American, Egyptian and Atlantean. The project was called the Triad because the divinities were unified to the extent that there are now three main groups: Horus, the feminine and the Earth. All of the different divinities fall within the province of one of these three. The names relate to specific functions, reservoirs of energy, rather than the individual gods themselves. So Horus is not the Egyptian god, but a great energy tank that can be contacted using that name, that frequency. The same is true for the other two forces.

Usignolo recalled:

Horus was awakened right at the beginning, in 1976 or 1977. Then, from 1983 to 1986, we contacted all those deities related to the feminine aspect, those linked to water, the sea. We would go, for example, to seaside places and make contact with goddesses and deities there. This was also when we developed the Fourth Questi and when there was a great resurgence of our own feminine aspect. The female divinity of the Triad has many names, but she is known mainly as Bastet.

Then, from 1987 to 1990, we worked on the invocation of all the god-forms associated with the Earth, under the heading of Pan, but the idea of Pan, not the specific divinity.

Horus, Bastet and Pan.

Once we had awakened the main divinities we went on to contact all the lesser divinities and link them to one of the three greater divinities.

Finding out about the Triad was very important for me, because it opened many doors and it made me understand much more about Damanhur. The project is reflected throughout the artwork in the temple and in the circuits on the hillside. I am now convinced that it is one of the main reasons why Damanhur exists.

If the many spiritual energies from around the world and throughout the ages can be unified, as Usignolo put it,

Damanhur will have validated and participated in the union of the parts of the fundamental mirror of this space-time. This implies unifying the systems, extrapolating the fundamental divine laws for an extraordinary human–gods relationship such as has not existed for at least 20,000 years.

The Great Forces were divided. Now is the time of unification, the recomposition of the lost, confused parts of the great gods. The magic spaces so 'reprogrammed' can modify the incidence of the rain of neutral events, so that they cannot be oriented by the Enemy any more, but from the unity-Mankind. Damanhur is involved in changing the structure of time itself, leaving a new sign to the world, a renewed time line, a hope of beauty and peace.

In this way the arrivals and departure of souls in the great circuit of the synchronic lines among inhabited worlds can be restored. What has kept Mankind imprisoned for thousands of years will then be broken and the Earth will reopen to the assembly of distributed lives.

The strengthening of the Triad gives Damanhur a new and larger possibility for growth and action. Connection and contact with such forces is a motive for practical endeavour and inner spiritual growth.

Sirena Ninfea is responsible for the Way of the Oracle and also for the ongoing development work on project Triad. If I was to consolidate my understanding of this concept, I would need to speak with her.

I asked Sirena to explain a little more about the eventual unification of the three Triad forces. I wondered if this had anything to do with reassembling the fragmented mirror?

The finality is to link all the divinities in one. You must think of it as a crystal with many faces. The crystal will be the awakening of Mankind, but it will have many faces. These will also be the divinities, purified and unified. The crystal will be a mirror, but a new mirror, not the same as the ancient one.

Horus is a key to opening the possibilities of Mankind. It is the biggest piece of this crystal. But our esoteric way is not the only one and our goals may change. Once one level is reached, others open out ahead. In five years, six years, our goals will be different. There will be other stages that we will have to reach.

Not all the divinities that exist on this planet are part of this project. However, the work is evolving. Over time, other divinities will be linked and brought into the project.

The completion of the Triad will allow a new Level of Justice. You remember what a Level of Justice is – when the level of complexity grows so much that it creates a stable system able to maintain itself and changes totally what was there before. It is like having the cells of a brain, then thoughts coming into the brain. Such harmonizing is a level of complexity.

All the people of this world will keep on adoring and praying to the divinities of their traditions, but these divinities will now be purified energies. They will be cleared of all the negative aspects. So we will have worked for the evolution of those people.

The work on the Triad is nearing completion. Many thousands of divinities have been contacted, purified and cleansed of negative influences, and brought together in the three broad areas of harmonization. The next stage is the unification of the Triad forces and this is a process that will occupy the Damanhurians over the coming years. The aim will partly be achieved by the formation of magical alliances. This is a long and complex work.

In making contact with a particular divinity, through meditation, rites and rituals, Damanhurians work with the essence of that divinity, before it has been contaminated by dogma and religiosity. Some deities are almost irrevocably bogged down in a plethora of religious dogma, whereas others have not become so hidebound. However, as already mentioned, it is the essence of the deity that is contacted and linked. For example, Gaia is linked to the female forces. By 'linked' is implied 'contained', 'different energies brought together like different circles, one inside the other'. In the end, there is a huge reservoir containing all the energies. The energy of Gaia is within the larger Bastet reservoir. She is a function of the larger body, but does not lose her 'Earth' qualities. Similarly, deities become associated with and contained within the collective reservoirs of Horus and Pan, bringing particular qualities to enrich and energize them. Another way to look at it is to imagine weaving forces together to create a new fabric.

Those of the Way of the Oracle are particularly prepared with special knowledge to perform rituals at the highest theurgic level. They often use special magical instruments. For example, during a Solstice ritual I saw a special tracer being used to close a circle after all the celebrants had entered. When people learn how to make energies work for them, they know what they need in order to better access and facilitate such energies.

The rituals are intriguing to witness, with rhythmical music, the use of fire and other natural elements, magical instruments and the participants in their coloured robes. It could all easily be seen as sinister and cultish, of course, but that would totally miss the remarkable good humour and strong sense of community that is always evident on such occasions. In these latter respects the rituals are much like village fêtes or those harvest festivals that were common events in the north of England when I was young. However, there is a serious purpose behind them and that is why people always participate with some degree of dedication.

And I did mention to Sirena that whereas many people wore white, red or yellow robes she was the only one to wear a blue robe. Surely this did not mean that she was the High Priestess? 'Certainly not,' she said, 'it simply means that I am the only one to have reached this level at this moment in time. In future there will be many people who reach the blue level and then there will be a green level, and so it will progress.

'But not black?' I asked.

'No. Not black, there will never be a black level.'

beyond the dream

On my most recent visit to Damanhur, Anaconda of the Free University gave me a bag full of videos of all sorts of spiritual thinkers. One of them was of the great man of myth Joseph Campbell, talking about the transcendent. 'What's the meaning of the universe?' he asks. 'What's the meaning of a flea?' We humans have engaged in doing so many things to achieve outer value, we have tended to lose something of the inner value, the rapture that is associated with being alive.

Often people attempt to talk about God. God is a thought. God is a name. God is an idea. But in reality it is something that transcends all thinking. The ultimate mystery of being is beyond all categories of thought.

Campbell points out that the very best things cannot really be talked about, because they transcend thought. Next best are those thoughts that so often get misunderstood, because they refer to that which cannot be thought about, so one gets stuck with the thoughts. Third best is that which we talk about.

Myth Campbell identifies as the field of reference to that which is transcendent. He recalls, when first seeing the Michelangelo 'Creation' on the ceiling of the Sistine Chapel, feeling that this idea of

God as a bearded old man with prickly temperament was a strange materialistic way of thinking about the transcendent. He contrasts this with first seeing the Mask of the Eternal in a cave on the island in Bombay harbour. The face looking directly at him there *was* the face of God, the transcendent, a perfect metaphor for the experience of eternity. And it was a three-faced sculpture, being flanked by two profile faces, one male, one female.

Everything in the field of time is dual, past and future, male and female, light and dark, dead and alive, being and non-being, is and isn't, right and wrong, good and evil. The central face of the Mask of Eternity is a representation of the transcendent, the middle way. This is the path of transcendence. The particular religious influences on our culture have tended to give us a perspective skewed towards the right and the good and against the wrong and the evil, but that is a path that takes us away from the transcendent.

The people of Damanhur have locked firmly into the centre path. They have built their elaborately beautiful temple inside a mountain that is itself a metaphor for the spiritual search within themselves. However, the people who have undertaken this great work have also developed a way of life that reflects and supports their achievements in the mountain. They have developed a social system that is democratic, flexible and fair. They have evolved a spirituality based on an extensive research programme, bringing together strands of spiritual thinking that correspond closely with Joseph Campbell's idea of the transcendent.

People with open minds accept Damanhur for what it is – qualities, warts and all. No one is encouraged to go there in order to find Paradise, but people are encouraged to go if they have a genuine desire to help create it. Paradise is only built when hands and limbs are used as wisely as hearts and minds. Unfortunately, there are too few open minds. Many onlookers imbue Damanhur with their own skewed views and prejudices. The citizens of Damanhur have become very patient with regard to such things.

It is easy and obvious to see 'cult' or 'sect' whenever a group of people gather together on a journey of self-discovery, and I suppose that the many stories of notorious cults appearing in the global news media have created ready responses of fear or cynicism. Branch Davidians at Waco, Aum Supreme Truth planting sarin nerve gas on the Tokyo underground, the Heaven's Gate and Solar Temple mass suicides, Moonies and loonies – there is no shortage of material to be sceptical about. And Damanhur certainly is a group of people, albeit over 700 of them, with funny ideas, who sometimes wear coloured robes and participate in rituals, and who rename themselves after animals and plants. Some superficial observers, therefore, tend to assume 'cult'.

On the subject of cults, I interviewed Massimo Introvigne, director of the Centre for Studies on New Religions (CESNUR) in Turin. According to Introvigne, there is no such thing as a cult. He is very critical of the anti-cult movement and some of the ensuing hysteria that such organizations have generally fuelled. He sees Damanhur as unique, being a community in the 'ancient tradition' rather than fitting into the idea of 'new religious movements' as other sociologists have suggested, especially given that Damanhurians would vigorously reject both the terms 'religious' and 'movement'.

In fact Introvigne sees Damanhur as being in a 'magical' tradition, as outlined in his article for the main academic journal for such studies, *Communal Societies*, which he entitled, 'Damanhur: A Magical Community in Italy'. Written in 1996, this is probably one of the best overall sociological studies undertaken, along with the study by Luigi Berzano referred to in Chapter 7. Introvigne and I discussed the terms 'cult' and 'sect' and he agreed that they were such corrupted words that they had no use in academic study. Yet the popular media persists in the use of such words and, ironically, some governments formulate laws to deal with groups described in this way.

So what is a cult? The original meaning related to a system or community of religious worship, especially one focusing on a single deity. In this respect *all* the world's major religions are cults. However, 'cult' has come to mean an obsessive devotion to a person, principle or ideal, usually with some implied weird or sinister intent, and is used in a derogatory way. Similarly, 'sect' has come to mean an extreme, intolerant and exclusive group. In such respects, any sensible and balanced review of Damanhur, such as I have hoped to present in this book, makes it clear that it is neither cult nor sect.

For sure Damanhur has an underlying belief system, but it is only a belief system in the sense that contemporary science is a belief system, though stressing that there is no such thing as absolute truth.

Citizens of Damanhur do not have a closed set of beliefs foisted onto them, but are actively engaged in developing, experimenting with and finding practical applications for that which they do believe in.

The work carried out on the temple brings satisfactions beyond belief, for such work cultivates deep spiritual understanding in those taking part. That is why the temple is so important – it is a profound symbol of a spiritual journey, as well as a reservoir of collected energies. When the first few people started digging into the mountain, they could hardly have believed that they would create anything so large, so beautiful. However, the temple is evidence that their dedication has pushed them beyond their beliefs. It is a constant reminder of the Damanhurians' developing principles: action, change, growth. Damanhur is there because people have dreamed and then found ways to realize those dreams.

Beyond the dream is a purpose. Damanhur has had to survive many threats. There have been times when the community has appeared fragile and vulnerable. Yet it has invariably managed to turn negatives into positives. The Temple of Mankind is fundamental to such energy transformations. In truth, the Enemy of Mankind is the epitome of such negativity. It comes in many guises, but potentially lurks within all of us. It is for this very reason that all this work at Damanhur has been undertaken: to save us from ourselves. Beyond the dream lies hope.

So the mind learns, when its turn comes, to reflect thought and concepts, knowledge, with the aim of possessing them fully...

afterword

As I have tried to stress througout, life at Damanhur is based on a first principle of constant change. As this book is about to go to press, Lepre Viola has just been elected Regina Guida, with fellow Re Guida Orango Riso re-elected. Lepre is not the first woman elected to this position, there have been several before, but her election is significant at this point in time because Damanhur is undergoing great changes, is growing, becoming more complex. Now, there is a need to have a female point of view more than ever before. Lepre feels that people at Damanhur need to understand this moment, to move very fast, exploring the many different possibilities, opening up, whilst focusing the goals. There might only be one chance to get the future set on the right course. Now is the time to jump and grab that chance.

She recalled that Oberto had recently talked of the need to grow inside. Each person at Damanhur needing to grow in order that the community as a whole might grow. Thoughts needing to be elevated.

Every year, each organization produces a Letter of Intent, containing their hopes and ambitions for the coming year. So the heads of communities would produce one, those responsible for the spiritual ways would produce one, as would the offices of internal, affairs, foreign affairs, the Welcome Office, the Free University and so on. As spiritual leaders of the People and as heads of the Federation, the Letter of Intent produced by the Guides is obviously of some significance. Lepre had only been in post for 10 days when I spoke to her, so I assumed she would not yet have produced a Letter of Intent, but I was wrong. She and Orango had already developed their ideas together. Their goal for the coming year is 'being Damanhur', towards the 'Metamorphosis of the People'. The process of metamorphosis is an interesting one, where one thing changes into another both gradually and suddenly. It is a long process, but the actual moment of transformation is a sudden one, like a caterpillar turning into a butterfly. The caterpillar becomes a lava and gradually develops, but in an instant the butterfly is born.

Change in one area means change in another. Caimano, who was *Re Guida*, is now the person with overall responsibility for the very important Game of Life aspects of Damanhur. Previously this had been a shared responsibility of four people, they will now work with Caimano as part of a team. The Game of Life is often the instigating process whereby major changes take place. Lepre sees the coming year with hope and optimism. It is a time when 'change' might become the key factor in a new reality, a new era in Damanhur's development.

Meanwhile, building work continues unabated in the temple. On 17 October 1997 I got news of 'la grande gettata', the big throw, the final assault on the new chamber. For a continuous 30 hours a large team of workers completed the final excavations, constructed the wooden shuttering need to accept the structural concrete and poured in the vast amounts of cement required.

The way such building work happens makes it hard to remember that the Temple of Mankind has been built by the citizens of Damanhur, not by gangs of professional builders working to precise architectural instructions. Sure there are some skills amongst the people, but many of those working on the construction have little experience outside of this work.

However, in November 1997 I interviewed Elena Rabbi, a geophysicist at Geodata, the large Turin firm of consulting engineers who were called in to survey the structural aspects of the temple.

As part of the final legal rights for the preservation of the temple, the Damanhurians were required to provide conclusive evidence that the structure in the mountain was safe, secure and free from any ecological dysfunction. Geodata were given the brief to carry out this examination.

Elena Rabbi explained to me how amazed the structural engineers were at the quality of the construction. They carried out a whole range of stress tests and seismic readings, but could not fault the structure in any way. They could not believe that here was a structure built by this group of, well, just ordinary people.

Even more amazing was the geological survey. The Damanhurians have made much of the place where the temple was situated, that it was specially chosen for its special energy qualities, that it was situated on a unique synchronic knot. Elena Rabbi herself had carried out the geophysical survey. She had identified that the temple was situated directly above the place where the large African and European tectonic plates met and crossed each other. At this place, over the millennia, violent collisions of rocky promontories have produced those upheavals of land surface resulting in the Alpine mountain range. However, what is most amazing is that a rare mineral rich in energies, known as milonite, or mylonite in its anglicised version, is found precisely in this place. So precisely, in fact that the temple fits exactly into the narrow 16 metre (150 feet) seam of this rich mineral (see plate 7). Mylonite is formed from the molten rock resulting from excessive friction and high pressure. It therefore records an abundance of energy. Elena Rabbi and her team had discovered this scientifically, the Damanhurians had discovered it through their synchronic investigations, but quite independently. They did not even know what mylonite was.

The citizens of Damanhur must wait now for the legal permissions to proceed onto the next 90 per cent of the construction work, secure in the knowledge that their work to date has been given official approval.

And Camorano sleeps more soundly in his bed these days.

When Damanhurians greet each other they say 'Con Te' to one person or 'Con Voi' to a group. it means 'With you' and is normally accompanied by a hands together gesture. It is also used as a departing good wish. So, together with my hands, I bid you all 'Con Voi'.

POSTSCRIPT –
THE MEDIA OBSESSION WITH CULTS

Rumours should not be mistaken for facts,
or for confirmed and reliable information.

Massimo Introvigne

This cult thing just won't go away. Cults are rife – if newspapers are to be believed. It seems that there may be cultish dangers lurking everywhere and we need to be warned of them. As I said in the Introduction, my own interest in Damanhur was aroused by the BBC Newsnight programme, where a journalist without a story was trying to find something akin to the Oklahoma bombers and militia cults in the Damanhurians. At the time I could find no connection between the beautiful artworks and constructions that I was seeing on my TV set and what I was being told about cults. My subsequent experience of many visits to Damanhur, and lengthy stays there, has done far more than confirm my positive initial impressions. However, the press flies in and then flies out, more often than not with a fixed agenda. In Chapter 6, I examined such agendas, as enacted by the Italian press. It now appears, several years on, the British press is treading similar trails.

Since this book was published there have been a number of articles in British newspapers about Damanhur and more often than not this word 'cult' has been up front. A Sunday Times correspondent spent a very short period of time at Damanhur and then wrote an article implying that the community (deemed a 'sect' in his version) was currently under investigation for a number of wrongdoings by prosecuting authorities – entirely untrue. Another journalist visited Damanhur with the best of intentions, spending much more time there and submitting an excellent article to *The European*. However, by the time it was published in that paper, sub-editors had excised every reference to the word 'community' and replaced them with the word 'cult', altering some of the reportage to make it square with this newly-defined image. The author of this article is much respected as a journalist and was understandably upset by the way her work had been altered. A well-known writer and broadcaster submitted a well-researched article to the *Mail on Sunday*, only to find that his work was also cut and sub-edited to change meanings and emphasis. Meanwhile, in the *Sunday Telegraph*, the arts editor did at least point out that they preferred to be called a 'community', underneath a headline that called them a 'cult'.

But what is it, this media interest in the word 'cult'? The word itself has a range of dictionary definitions. My big *Oxford* lists those pertaining to worship, to systems of religion as expressed in ritual, to devotion or homage to a person or thing. By the time it has been filtered into the *Oxford Concise*, the emphasis is less on the worship and more on the popular, particularly the sort of popular fashion followed by a section of society.

These media articles are obviously not trying to make the point that Damanhur has the sort of popular following ascribed to the likes of Elvis Presley or Manchester United; one accepted contemporary usage of the word 'cult'. No, in the wake of Waco, the Solar Temple and Heaven's Gate suicides, or the Scientology and Moonies investigations, the implication is more akin to a 'cult' with the word 'sinister' implied. In other words, a group of people we should be warned about, a group of people we should take care to avoid, lest they come in the night and steal our children from us.

Sometimes the cynicism with which this 'cult' business is presented is breathtaking. I will never forget Jeremy Paxman's introduction to the aforementioned *Newsnight* piece, where he referred to the fact that there are cults that are dangerous and those that are benign. The difficulty comes, he stated with something of a glint in his eye, in distinguishing one from the other. It could easily be deduced from this, reading between the lines, that the report filed on Damanhur in no way matched the main point of discussion: that of cults resorting to terrorism, like the Oklahoma bombers, and whether we have any of these in Britain or Europe? If being entirely honest, Paxman could have easily added that this report has been made and filed, so we may as well show it you, otherwise we might be accused of wasting BBC resources. However, by not telling us this, but using the benign suggestion instead, the implication appears to be given that there might just be something sinister lurking inside Damanhur, so be careful.

In September I spoke at the CESNUR conference in Turin. Some 200 professors and researchers with an interest in new social, spiritual and religious movements came from all over the world to investigate such matters as cults, sects and genuine spiritual pursuits. We showed them a video of Damanhur, took them on a visit there and discussed the particular social and spiritual aspirations of the Damanhurian people. I raised the topic of the media obsession with Damanhur as a 'cult' and there was strong agreement that the use of this word has no academic basis, that it is largely a media invention, under the misguided intention of making articles appear more spicy. It would certainly be true to say that any journalist who shows an interest in Damanhur and who does not have some hidden agenda is a rare creature indeed.

Massimo Introvigne, the director of CESNUR, demonstrated that the words 'cult' and 'sect' are often used by journalists to categorize movements and therefore to denigrate and belittle genuine spiritual explorations. Typical of this was the *Sunday Times* treatment of the story relating to a report recently published by the Italian Ministry of Internal Affairs which looked at all relatively new religious and spiritual movements, including Damanhur. Despite the fact that the report concluded that 'in Italy today no religious or magical movements as such is accused of any criminal activity of any kind', the *Sunday Times* correspondent filed a report under the headline 'Italians probe rich Alpine sect' and stated that Damanhur was currently 'under investigation for arson, aggravated fraud and exploiting its members'. Now, the report is a very lengthy document and in one small section it does say that the only things on file about Damanhur during its 23 years of existence are the reports of two unsubstantiated accusations (like the Filippo Cerutti affair discussed in Chapter 6 – see page 132). However, when a media agenda is so oriented, it seems the conclusion of a report, ie that there are no current investigations, can be ignored and the devil found in the detail.

Whilst this media obsession continues, Damanhur gets on with more important things. There have been, as might be expected, many social changes since the book was first published a year ago. Such changes are too numerous to detail here. However, it is important to say that the new fledging regions are flourishing and building for the future. The open temple has been renovated and undergone some reconstruction, an outdoor amphitheatre is being built, so that dance, theatre and drama can be more readily featured, and the Temple of Mankind now has a new entrance.

Probably the most important development has been in the project Val di Chy, which has now taken a step nearer reality. In future it will be known as the Valley of the Ki, to give emphasis to the vital life force evident there. Also, the first truly international nucleo has been formed, comprising an English couple, a German woman, a Dutch woman, a woman half-Thai and half-Italian, an American man, two Italians and two children. The main focus of attention for this family will be to welcome people wishing to come and try out projects at Damanhur, to look after visitors with ideas, and to act as a catalyst between the community and interested groups in the world outside. The hope is that, as the Millennium approaches, many people will discover the magical valley where Damanhur is situated, and that they will be helped to facilitate access to the vital energies and natural forces of the planet at this important meeting point of synchronic lines.

In a world where much natural creativity and innovation is being stifled by industrial and commercial demands, the valley where Damanhur and the Temple of Mankind have been built offers a unique possibility for study and meditation, to reawaken and re-energize latent potential and dormant creativity. If an individual or a group has an idea that might work, it might be better to work alongside those potentials already realized at Damanhur. That is what the project in the Valley of the Ki is all about. It is an ambitious project and now the intentional group is in place, a dedicated collective of ambassadors who might just help the rest of us realize our own dreams.

Happy New Millennium.

Jeff Merrifield
Great Totham
October 1998

FURTHER READING

There is a limited amount of material in English about Damanhur, mostly in magazines. Here are some recent books and articles that are perhaps worth digging out:

Airaudi, Oberto (translated by Esperide Ananas and Ileana Troni); Tales from Damanhur; a collection of short stories and theatre pieces, with introductions by Ken Campbell and Jeff Merrifield; 1997, Damanhur Editrice, Via Pramarzo 3, 1-10080 Baldissero Canavese (TO), Italy.

Beaumont, Richard, and Yates, Patricia: City of Light; Kindred Spirit, Volume 3, Number 8, Autumn 1995; Totnes, Devon, UK.

Beaumont, Richard, and Yates, Patricia: Magical History Tours; Kindred Spirit, Volume 3, Number 9, Winter 1995/96; Totnes, Devon, UK.

Campbell, Ken; Violin Time - or the Lady from Montsegur; script of solo theatre show performed at Royal National Theatre in September 1996; Methuen Drama, London, UK.

Fanshawe, Simon; Secrets of the Magic Mountain; Night & Day, the Mail on Sunday Review; 20 July 1997, London, UK.

Introvigne, Massimo: Damanhur - a magical community in Italy; Communal Studies - magazine of the Communal Studies Association, Volume 16, 1996; Juniata College, Huntingdon, Pennsylvania, USA.

Merrifield, Jeff; Into the Water Hall - a journey into the Temple of Mankind; Spirit Magazine, Number 7, September 1997; London, UK.

Merrifield, Jeff; Damanhur celebrates the People; Part One – Quest Magazine, Volume 1, Issue 4, September 1997; Part Two – Quest Magazine, Volume 1, Issue 5, October 1997; Chester, UK.

Further Updated information will also be found on the following Internet website: http://www.meryfela.demon.co.uk

Appendix I
Constitution of the Nation of Damanhur

A CHARTER FOR THE PEOPLE

Foreword

The Constitution of Damanhur consists of 21 Articles, representing the continuity of the principles and the goals of our Community Nation. The Federal laws and the rules of the communities are the common denominator of civilized coexistence, but the Constitutional Charter is the main path along which the experience of Damanhur unfolds, be that inner, individual or collective.

The Constitution is intended to be the central and stable pivot around which revolve the reforms and revisions of the Application sections. Nevertheless, it has gone through several phases of adjustment, whenever new discoveries enabled the population to come closer to achieving Damanhur's ideals.

In 1980, the first corpus of rules of Damanhur was established, out of which, in September 1981, the first Constitution was born. This first version was then widely revised in June 1984, and in October 1986 the constitutional principles were separated from the laws. In February 1987, in June 1989 and in December 1992, both aspects of the corpus of rules, the constitutional principles and the separate laws were modified.

These latter changes marked an important step, a transition, that people lived through with great maturity, demonstrating how Damanhurians could manage to increase their comprehension of those principles that had always inspired them. All this, without losing their vitality and the capability of exploring new horizons of living together.

An evolving society requires a constant change of paradigm, and the above steps marked the passage to a more spiritual vision. The elected Guides became *Re Guida* (King Guides)[1] and their power was increased, eventually coming to superintend the three bodies that make up the Nation: *School of Meditation*, *Game of Life* and the *Community*. This development was the prelude to Article 22 being rescinded by Oberto Airaudi;[2] this repeal being later approved by the newly-born High Chamber.

The political and spiritual transformation which triggered these changes was concluded in February 1996, when the rules become Federal laws, under the direct administration of the *Re Guida*, whose number, at that time, was decreased from three to two. This evolutionary process is one of the foundations of the spiritual growth of Damanhur, according to the Horusian School of Thought,[3] in the GIGI patterns[4] leading to TECHNARCATE.[5]

Every new law mirrors a new spiritual and social scenario. This version of the Constitution and Federal Laws reflect the image of a wider and more complex society, which consequently needs a proper 'user's manual'. Our aspiration is to be able one day to repeal all laws in favour of a consolidated tradition, re-discovered and shared ethics.

Damanhur today is no more a mere social experiment; it has consolidated its principles and is moving towards the realization of an utopian vision. It is the place where all its citizens – in part artists and in part engineers – keep on experimenting, striving for the colonization of a noble dream called *Future*.

1. The use of the word in respect of the King Guides indicates a spiritual nobility. It is not at all related to the autocratic nature of monarchy.

2. Article 22 related to a right of veto that Oberto Airaudi once held, during the fledgling and early developmental stages of Damanhur.

3. The Horusian School of Thought evolves according to Damanhur's spiritual growth. These meditations and thoughts have formed the basis of study and continuing development of the *School of Meditation*, Damanhur's own esoteric school and one of the three major bodies of the Nation.

4. I asked Oberto about the GIGI patterns. He replied:

GIGI is a name that grew out of playing with the name of our dog at Aval. GIGI patterns are patterns that grew out of a game. In this game, which involved an initiation in which all sorts of tricks were played on people, it was much easier to work together, without conflict. So it established patterns that were helpful in regulating and developing a community. In *The Horusian Way*, you can see a drawing of the GIGI patterns. Each had different steps leading to an ideal political and spiritual situation:

POLITICO-SPIRITUAL GIGI SCHEME

Spiritual government 3 TECHNARCATE	VI phase

Spiritual government 2
     King and Queen Guides
     Connection with the Damanhur Divinity
	V phase

Spiritual government 1
     Monk Guides
     Ruling administrators
     To give a direction to self-determination
	IV phase

Historical passing
     Bureaucratization
     Automanagement
     Integrated self-determination
	III phase

Democratic governments	II phase
Military form of government	I phase
Leader	Original group

5. Oberto explained Technarcate by saying:

Technarcate is the step beyond where we are living at the moment. I cannot tell you more than that, for this is part of our secret tradition. To be very general, not using proper terms, I could say that it is something that can bring about the best form of political leadership for us, a little bit like that of Atlantis, where there was a much wider political and spiritual leadership than we can contemplate now.

Introductory Statement

The Damanhurian School of Thought has three different bodies – Meditation, the Game of Life and Community. They represent the tradition of ritual, the dynamic aspect and the social realization of such teachings.

The Community takes its inspiration from the principle of solidarity. The Communities together form the Nation of Damanhur. The People takes its inspiration from the teachings of Oberto Airaudi, the founder of the School of Horusian Thought, and commits itself to respect and observe all the Rules of the present Charter.

The creation of a Tradition, a culture, a history and a common ethic, has given birth to the People. The act of belonging to the Nation and to the People takes place on different levels, corresponding to the choice and commitment of the individual.

The Twenty-One Principles

- Those belonging to the People are brothers and sisters who live together, helping one another constantly, by means of reciprocal trust, respect, clarity, acceptance and solidarity.
- Each member of the People takes a commitment to spread positive and harmonious thoughts. Being aware how extremely wide in effect each action of thought is, being multiplied and reflected all over the world through the Synchronic Lines, each person is responsible for their own actions, socially and spiritually.
- Through community life, the Population pursues the formation of autonomous individuals, whose reciprocal relations

are regulated by Knowledge and Conscience. The whole People is moving towards the achievement of a complete self-sufficiency.

- The fundamental rules of life are common sense and thinking well of others.
- Work is understood as a gift of oneself to others and constant prayer, through which everyone takes part, according to their own capabilities, in the material and spiritual progress of the Nation. Every job is valuable and is as dignified as all the others, and when possible tasks are rotated.
- Those who take on roles of social responsibility should carry out their own tasks in a spirit of service to the People, without looking for personal advantages or serving the private interests of others. Only those belonging to the People may be elected or nominated for positions of social responsibility.
- Every Citizen lives in communion with the natural environment and the subtle forces living in it. Spirituality and global ecology should inspire all relationships with the Earth and with animals, avoiding all forms of pollution and waste.
- The body is to be fed harmoniously, kept clean, respected and looked after. The Citizens of the community do not smoke, do not take drugs, nor do they abuse alcohol or pharmaceuticals. They put into practice Rules for suitable living, for harmonious physical, mental and spiritual development. The People expects each individual to be capable of self-control, of alchemical transformation of personal energies and to show maturity of choice.
- The Nation promotes and supports research both in science and art; it fosters and encourages continual experimentation of both physical and non-physical, so long as it is expressed in a harmonious form. All Citizens are expected to constantly improve their own education and to widen and deepen their own knowledge in the field of study, art, work and leisure activities.
- The People is an evolving entity resulting from the organic sum of all the single individuals, groups and organizations of the Nation; it holds and synthesizes all the experiences,

thoughts and feelings expressed by Damanhur and is part of its com-munal cultural, ethical and spiritual wealth. The People is and remains a single body, even when independent communities are created with territorial autonomy. Persons in a single Community should not exceed a number varying between 200 and 220 individuals.

- Every Citizen has a personal space in which to live. The dwellings are assigned according to the needs of the community and those living there are expected to look after the tidiness, the cleaning and ensure the dwelling has a harmonious appearance.

- Citizens undertake to contribute with their own resources with their own work and in every other way to the economic upkeep of the whole Nation, which provides support for the various needs of its members, by means of its communal funds. All those who leave the People, for whatever reason, cannot put forward any claim of a financial nature and have no right to be reimbursed by the People.

- Those Citizens who amongst themselves wish to take on a relationship as a couple should make a public announcement to their fellow Citizens. The couple, by means of a public ceremony, commits itself to realize a union that is solid and useful to the community. The People chooses to programme the birth of children.

- Small children, received into the People, are loved, looked after and educated by every Citizen, who is expected to set them an example by following the communal guidelines on the care of children. Those under the age of consent live within the community, which takes on the responsibility, according to birth programme, of their upkeep, their well-being and their education.

- Whoever wishes to belong to the Population must put forward a written request listing the reasons. If the applicant possesses the basic qualities to become a Citizen, the person will be admitted for a probationary period, during which he/she agrees how to participate in Community life and will have to observe the present Charter and other Community Rules. The request for admission will be accepted only after the applicant has demonstrated a knowledge of the principles and the cultural heritage of the People. This is called 'Concession of Citizenship'.

- The person will cease to belong to the Population by withdrawing or by exclusion, in serious cases of misconduct which make it incompatible to continue the relationship. The exclusion must be preceded by a disciplinary procedure, allowing the person in question a right to a defence.
- The highest authority of the School of Thought and of the People is represented by the Guides. They assure a constant adherence to the ideal aims and spiritual goals in every expression of community life, superintending the three Bodies. They direct and co-ordinate all choices related to matters over and above those of specific community interest. They are periodically elected by the members of the School of Meditation according to the Rules laid down within the School. The unanimous opinion of the Guides is binding for any individual, group or organization of the People. In serious cases of need or emergency they may adopt any kind of measure or procedure.
- Within the sphere of the People, any formation of two or more Citizens who have a socially useful function may be given recognition. The Group is a new entity which, being formed from the interaction between different and complementary individuals, develops a wider ability for confrontation and the development of new ideas, in relation to its aims.
- The functions regarding control of the observance of the Regulations are carried out by the College of Justice. Every Citizen has to respect its decisions. The College of Justice may suspend or annul the illegal documents issued by other bodies, it instructs and defines disciplinary procedures, it takes decisions on any and every ground for complaint amongst those belonging to the People.
- Every community has its own territory, its own People and autonomy within the ways and the limits established by the Federal Laws. The provisions relating to the organization, administration and functioning of the Community, and the

co-ordination of its activities, are adopted by the local Government, periodically elected. The Government and its prospective delegates may even put forward, in a limited number of cases, sanctions against the Citizens, by the means and manner provided for in the Federal Laws. The Community may set up bodies and put forward any Rules that it regards necessary to function more effectively, having regard to the Tradition of the People and the over-riding interests of the Nation.

The executive rules of the present Charter must not contain measures that are contrary to it. The discipline of all the matters relating to the whole Population is carried out by means of Laws which must be observed by all the Citizens. Any revision of Rules contained in this Charter is to be approved by those who belong to the School of Meditation, according to Rules decided within it. In every case where the interpretation of the existing Rules is questioned, the resolution is put forward by the Guides, expressed according to the principles of the Tradition, after having consulted the College of Justice.

Appendix II
On The Threshold

ON THE THRESHOLD

Primeval Laws	Questi	Positive
SYNCHRONICITY Reservoir of events	1st Action	Completeness
SOLE ATOM Potential of creation of universe	2nd Constancy	Happiness
DIVINITY	3rd Rebirth to the sacred cultural civilization	Love
GEOMETRIC ESSENCE On order	4th Feminine availability, improving towards perfection, completion of femininity, union	Sweetness, order
TIME MATRIX Conserving and directioning element	5th Masculine, stability, firmness, interior revolution, movement	Distributed joy
FALL OF EVENTS	6th Inversion of , 4th and 5th Questi, spiritual factors, creation	Beauty, art, shared life
CHAOS Mixing of dimensions	7th Uncertainty, doubt	Certainty, sureness, safety, comprehension
COMPLEXITY	8th Expansion, road towards truth *(under development, via the Way of the Word)*	Curiosity, will to kncw, being

Negative	Ways	Chakras	Colours
Continuous incompleteness	Way of the Art and Work	4th Heart	Orange
Unhappiness	Way of Esoteric Couples	3rd Sex organs	Green
Hardness, loss, detachment	Way of the Monks	7th Top of the head	White
Disorder	Way of the Knights	2nd Base of spine	Brick red
Distributed pain, suffering	Way of the Oracle	8th Mobile	Silver
Ugliness, loneliness	Way of Integrated Arts and Technologies	6th Third eye	Indigo
Fear, terror	Way of the Warm Oil (part of the Way of Integrated Arts and Technologies)	1st Belly button, solar plexus	Yellow, gold
Eternal reduction	Way of the Word	5th Throat	Azure blue

Index